NEGLECTED GENIUS

Neglected Genius

The Diaries of Benjamin Robert Haydon, 1808–1846

EDITED BY JOHN JOLLIFFE

faber and faber

For Victoria

This edition first published in 2012
by Faber and Faber Ltd
Bloomsbury House, 74–77 Great Russell Street
London WC1B 3DA

Printed by Books on Demand GmbH, Norderstedt

All rights reserved
© John Jolliffe, 1990

The right of John Jolliffe to be identified as editor of this work
has been asserted in accordance with Section 77 of the
Copyright, Designs and Patents Act 1988

This book is sold subject to the condition that it shall not, by way of
trade or otherwise, be lent, resold, hired out or otherwise circulated
without the publisher's prior consent in any form of binding or cover other than
that in which it is published and without a similar condition including this
condition being imposed on the subsequent purchaser

A CIP record for this book is available from the British Library

ISBN 978–0–571–29477–0

Contents

Introduction		vii
ONE:	1808–1817	1
TWO:	1818–1825	54
THREE:	1826–1831	104
FOUR:	1832–1837	136
FIVE:	1838–1842	178
SIX:	1843–1846	211
Epilogue		232
Paintings Begun by Haydon		235
Events in the Life of Haydon		247
List of Illustrations and Acknowledgements		253
Index		255

The higher a man is gifted by nature, the less willing he is always to acknowledge any obligation to any other being, however just or decent.

> Benjamin Haydon, February 27, 1824

There is something burly and bold in this resolute genius which will attack only enormous subjects, which will deal with nothing but the epic . . . and so instead of laughing at Haydon, which you and I were just about to do, let us check our jocularity, and give him credit for his great earnestness of purpose.

> Thackeray, *Fraser's Magazine,* June 1845

Introduction

Benjamin Robert Haydon was born in Plymouth in 1786, and died by his own hand in 1846. He was the son of a bookseller, whose mother was born Mary Baskerville, and was descended (according to Haydon) from the great printer to Cambridge University. He also liked to say that his father came from the family of Haydon of Cadhay, 'one of the oldest families in Devon'. No evidence survives to support either claim, but in his autobiography Haydon gives a convincing impression of his father, many of whose traits of character he plainly inherited. In the words of George Paston, the author of *B. R. Haydon and his friends*, Haydon senior was 'a veritable John Bull, who believed England was the only great country in the world, swore that Napoleon won all his battles by bribery, refused to believe that there was a poet, painter, sailor, soldier or statesman outside England, and would have knocked down any man who dared to differ from him'. His son was 'alternately petted and scolded, allowed to take his own way and then punished for taking it'. He certainly 'never learnt self-control in boyhood'.

In 1804 he made his way to London, and his own *Autobiography* gives a wonderfully vivid account of his first steps there, though how much it is embroidered is impossible to say. From that time on, his father refused to give him any financial support in his struggle to become an artist. His furious enthusiasm for his art caused him to work such long hours, often no doubt in bad light, that his eyesight certainly suffered, though this may not have been the cause of his shortcomings as a painter. However, he soon made a number of friends, some of them, like Keats, Hazlitt and Wordsworth, already on their way to great fame. He was also taken up by patrons who included Sir George Beaumont and Lord Mulgrave, though he very soon fell into the regular habit of biting the hand that fed him, and biting it hard. But three quotations from his letters soon after that time indicate that it was not only as a solitary diarist but also as a communicator to others that his gifts were so remarkable. In 1817 he was recommending the consolations of religion to Keats:

I am always in trouble, and wants, and distresses; here (i.e. in prayer) *I have found a refuge*. From my soul I declare to you I never applied for help or for consolation, or for strength, but I found it. I always rose up from my knees with a refreshed fury, an iron-clenched firmness, a crystal piety of feeling that sent me streaming on with a repulsive power against the troubles of life.

And eighteen months later:

The 'agonie ennuyeuse' you talk of, be assured, is nothing but the intense searching of a glorious spirit, and the disappointment it feels at its first contact with the muddy world. But it will go off, and by-and-by you will shine through it with fresh lightsomeness.

At an early stage he made the unfortunate decision to concentrate almost entirely on large pictures devoted to historic and religious themes, at a time when any sort of regular demand for them was quite in eclipse. But Haydon felt he had no choice: 'Nothing moves me but the heroic or the sacred.' This involved setting his face against what was certainly the most probable road to success, that is to say painting portraits or alternatively what Gainsborough called 'sweet landskips'. In 1815, when he took Canova to see a fellow artist, James Northcote, he wrote to Wordsworth as follows:

I took him, by his own desire, to see a painter who once painted some fine things but who, from love of money, deserted his post, and has sunk into a portrait-painter. I could not help watching his miserable mortification, as he brought forth his wretched affairs. At last, and with a face of painful despair – an air of withered littleness – he said, 'We must all paint portraits here, Sir' . . . I feel convinced the pang that cut him was a punishment he will not forget.

In a brief introduction, there is no need to summarise the rest of the career that unfolds in the Journals themselves. But for a rounded view, perhaps no one has given a more perceptive sketch of Haydon than Aldous Huxley in *A Crown of Olive*. Until he descends to sneering at Haydon's religious faith, without which he would surely have foundered many years before he did, Huxley sees him very fairly, though with all the advantages of hindsight, and through twentieth century eyes. He compares Haydon's own self-portrait with the study of him by Georgiana Zornlin in the National Portrait Gallery (see p. 161), which Huxley says 'might be a portrait of Mussolini: flashing eyes, square strong jaw, wide mouth with full, floridly sculptured lips'. Whereas the self-portrait shows 'a very large yet delicately modelled aquiline nose, and a less formidably protuberant chin. It is as though Mussolini had been strangely blended with Cardinal Newman.' He adds that Haydon 'was endowed with a sharp and comprehensive intelligence; an excellent judgement (except where his own productions were concerned); a daemonic vitality: the proverbial "infinite capacity for taking pains"; a mystical sense of inspiration, and a boundless belief in his own powers . . . a gift of expression, even a literary style. Never was anyone more clearly cut out to be an author . . . As a romantic novelist what might he not have achieved?' Sir Harold Acton has said that he finds Haydon a more exciting writer than Ruskin, and his Journal was described quite simply by Max Beerbohm, in a letter to Siegfried Sassoon, as the best he had ever read. Of course, had he written it as a novel, the reader would have been spared his besetting faults, chief of which, anyway as far as writing is concerned, is an obsession with the rightness of his own views and the automatic, malevolent wrongness of anyone who disagreed with them. On the other hand, what we should have missed in his vivid descriptions of real life! The sharpness of his eye, especially in his youth, is very striking. For example, in the Grand Trianon at Versailles, in 1814, after Napoleon's departure, 'the fire place had a look of recent use; the tongs and poker were black'. While he clung with a passionate force to the general strength of feeling of the Romantics, he utterly rejected their anarchy, and anything tending towards it, especially with regard to the wild selfishness and disloyalty of Shelley, Hazlitt and the Hunts, and their general claims to be free from the restrictions and obligations by which lesser mortals are bound.

Of his other contemporaries, his close friend and correspondent Mary Mitford, whose own sketches and plays enjoyed great success, wrote to Elizabeth Barrett (later Browning) that 'those animal high spirits are a gift from Heaven and frequently pass for genius, or rather make talent pass for genius – silver-gilded'. And six years after his death she wrote that 'he was a most brilliant talker – racy, bold, original, vigorous; and his early pictures were full of promise; but a vanity, that amounted to self-idolatry, and a terrible carelessness unjustifiable in many matters, degraded his mind and even impaired his talent in art . . . Anything so rapid, so brilliant, so vigorous as his talk, I have never known'. The other qualities that shine through the Journals are an overwhelming devotion to art for its own sake, a passionate resentment at what he saw as its neglect, and a readiness to suffer the utmost extremes of hardship in order to live up to his own lofty standards; though against that has to be set his willingness to inflict perpetual troubles on his infinitely unfortunate wife, whose endurance and loyalty were almost superhuman. Next was his quite exceptional resilience, and his endless capacity for recharging his batteries, after no matter how many rebuffs and rejections, largely under direct divine inspiration, as he bears witness many times. Only a month before taking his own life, when oppressed by overwhelming financial problems, he could write in his journal, 'When I paint I feel as if Nectar was floating in the interstices of the brain,' that brain which was sadly so soon to become fatally unhinged. The fact that his highly intelligent friends – including Sir Walter Scott as well as Elizabeth Barrett and Mary Mitford – remained devoted to him, though fully aware of his failings, is the strongest possible proof of his qualities. Huxley is therefore not altogether right in saying that 'the magic dwindled as he grew old and tired and querulous and hysterical with repeated failure'. Rather, it was 'the agony of ungratified ambition' (Journal, 20 January 1842) that was to lead to his miserable end.

His real tragedy, in a practical sense, was his failure to realise that the world simply does not owe anyone a living on his or her idiosyncratic terms. It is very sad for painters whose merits are not recognised until after their death, and even sadder if they are not recognised even then; but painting, like anything else, is subject to the laws of supply and demand. If you are unwilling ever to pay the faintest attention to what your contemporaries want, what right have you to complain – especially in terms as violent as Haydon's – when they fail to buy your work? Not even the greatest artists have a God-given right to please themselves exclusively, and also to be paid for doing so. Rather like Hilaire Belloc a century later, Haydon thought he could attack people, and bore them by riding his own hobby-horse into the ground, and at the same time prosper in the world, simply because of the exalted and exalting nature of his aims. Both were aware of this intermittently, but not deeply enough to find the cure which in reality lay in their own hands. (By a coincidence, Belloc's English grandfather, the Birmingham solicitor Joseph Parkes, acted as a trustee in June 1832 for the public subscription to a mediocre painting by Haydon connected with the passage of the Reform Bill.) What Haydon needed was to have lived in the Middle Ages, and to have painted historical pictures as described in a book that he read in the same year 1832, Joseph Strutt's *The Chronicle of England*. 'Historical delineations,' he wrote in his journal, 'are frequent in ancient manuscripts, beside which they had larger pictures representing passages in History and the actions of great men, to preserve the memory of Valour and other Virtues.' This is what Haydon wanted to do, for example in the case of the Duke of Wellington, and on a larger scale in the frescoes in the Houses of Parliament when they were rebuilt after their destruction by fire.

Yet when one looks at most of his pictures, it is not difficult to see why he was rejected. The sad fact is that his powers of execution did not begin to match up to his aspirations, especially in his oil paintings. All the same, no less an artist than G. F. Watts stated that 'his expression of anatomy and general perception of form are the best by far that can be found in the English school; and I feel even a direction towards something that is only to be found in Phidias', (the greatest sculptor of ancient Greece). But for all that, Haydon's *Alexander and Bucephalus* hangs to this day at the top of the back stairs at Petworth, and even as generous a patron as Lord Egremont did not give Haydon more than two commissions. Indeed, Haydon's accounts in his Journals of his visits to Petworth are of far greater interest than his picture that hangs there. *Punch, or May Day*, was acquired by the Tate Gallery, but is kept in store. *The Mock Election*, which struck Queen Victoria and Lord Melbourne as being 'clever, but the colouring not English', was based on the artist's own observation while in a debtors' jail. Admittedly it now hangs in Buckingham Palace, but in a humble position in the Equerries' Room, and not where it might be admired on state occasions. Huxley is surely right in saying that on canvas 'his lines are heavy, hard, uncertain and insensitive'. His composition is often clumsy, and his colours crude and inharmonious. Yet his drawings in the Royal Albert Memorial Museum in Exeter, some of which are reproduced here, bear out Watts's judgement, and a volume devoted to them would be a very worthwhile project. For the purposes of this edition, his major works are on too large a scale to be worth reproducing, even the curious group of Newton, Voltaire, Wordsworth and Keats which he included in the crowd in *Christ's Entry into Jerusalem.*

Nevertheless, although he doomed himself to failure in the world, there remains something irresistibly arresting – inspiring even – about his sheer fervour. 'Call me not hence,' he says in one of the many prayers which he records in the Journals, 'until I have accomplished the great object of my being, till I have entirely reformed the taste of my country . . . till the Arts of England are on a level with her Philosophy, her heroism, and her Poetry, and her greatness is complete.' And on a more mundane level, when he showed his picture of Solomon to his wine merchant and asked him 'whether I ought after such an effort to be without a glass of wine, which my medical man had recommended, "Certainly not," said he, "I'll send you a dozen."'

Malcolm Elwin, in his edition of extracts from the *Autobiography and Journals* (Macdonald, 1950) aptly observes that 'All the busy interest and susceptibility to impressions of Pepys is here.' But apart from their sheer natural verve, the Journals often have an extra particular interest through their author's conversations both with his patrons and with the sitters in his large picture of the Reform Bill banquet which still hangs at Lord Grey's old home at Howick. There are, it is true, occasions when what he records as facts are flatly contradicted in other more reliable sources; but besides Lord Grey and his son-in-law Lord Durham, many of the other protagonists spring to life in these pages, including Melbourne, Lansdowne, Althorp, and Lord John Russell. So too does Sir Robert Peel, who only knew Haydon towards the end of his life, and perhaps for that reason thought so well of him that he gave his son a position in the Public Record Office and his widow a pension. However it is not the politicians but the writers, poets and other artists to whom we must look for a first-hand confirmation of Haydon's gifts. Three years before his death he reminded Wordsworth in a letter how in his younger days 'Walter Scott, Charles Lamb, Hazlitt, David Wilkie and Keats attended my summons and honoured my table'. As well as honouring his table, Keats, Wordsworth, Leigh Hunt, Lamb and Elizabeth Barrett all celebrated him in sonnets.*

*The sonnet which Haydon received from John Keats on 19 November 1816 links him with Wordsworth as two of the leading lights of what the poet looked on as a brave new world about to dawn. It is only fitting to print it here, with a few details of the circumstances:

> Great Spirits now on earth are sojourning,
> He of the cloud, the cataract, the lake,
> Who on Helvellyn's summit, wide awake,
> Catches its freshness from the Archangel's wing:
> He of the rose, the violet, the spring,
> The social smile, the chain for freedom's sake:

The selections from the Journals which follow are only a small fraction of the total. The only complete text is in the five volumes edited with meticulous care by Willard Bissell Pope, who acquired the original manuscript from M. Buxton Foreman, published it at the Harvard University Press in 1969, and died in 1988. Any reader who has an appetite for more should refer to this splendid complete edition, and it is a great pity that lack of space has prevented the inclusion here of many of its interesting and enlightening footnotes. The two volumes of *Correspondence and Table Talk* edited by the diarist's son Frederick Wordsworth Haydon in 1876 consist of anecdotes of varying interest, mostly concerning other people, and not revealing Haydon's own extraordinary character to anything like the same degree as the Journals themselves; but they also contain some revealing and absorbing letters to and from Keats, Wordsworth, Miss Mitford, the Duke of Wellington and Lord Melbourne. Best of all the descriptive books on Haydon is *The Life and Death of Benjamin Haydon* by Eric George (Oxford University Press, second edition 1967), in which the author is extremely successful in his 'attempt to exhibit a vast ambition, and to show the tragedy for a man of brilliant gifts, who for a time seemed to his contemporaries almost to justify his enormous pretensions, but who lost the race'. The Journals themselves may be more vivid and immediate, but for an objective but still sympathetic view of Haydon, Mr George is excellent.

Also of interest is *B. R. Haydon and his Friends* by George Paston, in fact

---

> And lo! whose steadfastness would never take
> A meaner sound than Rafaelle's whispering.
> And other spirits there are standing apart,
> Upon the forehead of the age to come;
> These, these will give the world another heart
> And other pulses. Hear ye not the hum
> Of mighty workings?
> Listen awhile, ye nations, and be dumb.

Haydon replied that he would like to send the sonnet on to Wordsworth. Keats, who was aged twenty and had not yet published anything, though his sonnet on Chapman's Homer was to be published the following month, anwered that 'the idea of your sending it to Wordsworth puts me out of breath', and Haydon duly sent it off with a charming letter of recommendation. Three months later Keats addressed a second sonnet to Haydon as principal champion and enthusiast for the Elgin Marbles, containing the lines

> Forgive me that I have not eagle's wings,
> That what I want I know not where to seek.

Haydon wrote back as follows:

I love you like my own brother. Beware, for God's sake, of the delusions and sophistications that are ripping up the talents and morality of our friend (i.e. Leigh Hunt). He will go out of the world the victim of his own weakness and dupe of his own self-delusions, with the contempt of his enemies and the sorrow of his friends, and the cause he undertook injured by his own neglect of character. . . . God bless you, my dear Keats, Do not despair. Collect incident, study character, read Shakespeare, and trust in Providence, and you *will* do, you must.

a pseudonym for Emily Morse Symonds (James Nisbet, 1905) and *The Autobiography of B. R. Haydon*, skilfully edited in 1927 by Alexander Penrose, a Fellow of King's College, Cambridge, who declared that 'he has left to posterity one of the most fascinating and spontaneous examples of autobiographical self-analysis that exists in any language.' It is however true to say that most of the materials in the autobiography derive from the Journals (which were not available to Penrose) and are presented afresh either to put them in more general focus or simply to show their author in a better light. Before reaching his conclusion, Penrose's feelings towards his subject had gone through a series of stages which may also be followed by other readers. First, a strong attraction to the courage, the intensity and the sheer resilience of Haydon's character, and the Pepys-like qualities observed by Mr Elwin. Next, a loss of patience with the egomania, the wilful and shameful neglect of ordinary obligations to family, friends and creditors, and the growing habit of magnifying the power – and malevolence – of his opponents; and finally, a true sympathy with him in his exhausted dejection (possibly worsened by a disease of the brain) when the crowds poured in to gape at Tom Thumb in the Egyptian Hall, and totally ignored the last despairing exhibition of his paintings next door. A letter that he wrote to Miss Mitford in 1828, eighteen years before his tragic death, strikes a note of warning: 'I like to see a fellow who has not committed murder die like a gentleman! There is something self-willed and grand about that defiance of an unknown HEREAFTER. Don't you think that Cato was more of a hero than Napoleon by putting an end to himself? I suspect I do.'

Nobody could write as good a book on Haydon as those he wrote himself; but the last word may be left to H. H. Asquith, who wrote of Haydon that 'his Autobiography though less well known, is not less remarkable than the Confessions of St Augustine ... he discloses to us his own personality with a freedom not unworthy of Rousseau, though one will look in vain to Rousseau or any of his imitators for Haydon's simplicity and sincerity'.

His violent self-righteousness may have frustrated most of his aims, but his sheer vitality and his quite exceptional powers of observation and description make him an irresistible subject. By means of many omissions one can spare the reader the *longueurs* and the occasional tedious passage, and string together a series of jewels of the English language that have never been available in a convenient form, with the result that they have been quite undeservedly neglected. A few scholars may say they know all they want to know about Haydon, but there are grounds for hoping that many general readers will find a glorious new experience open to them.

ONE

1808–1817

1808

July 23. I left Town for Dover [on] the mail and arrived there the next morning. I walked about in Town and about evening wandered away to Shakespeare's clift; here perhaps, I said, Shakespeare has stood, here Lear defied the Storm, there, as I looked towards the Castle, Cordelia died; how many Kings of England have embarked from Dover to France? For the first time in my life I saw the white cliffs of England, beating back the murmuring surge, and as the Sun shot a last gleam athwart the ocean, I caught a glitter of the distant coast of France – how I felt. There, I thought, is France, the proud enemy of England.

I staid on the clift of Shakespeare till twilight was far advanced, and as I moved down towards Town, and turned round to take a last look for that night of the clift that towered in the Sky and was almost lost in the *embruno* tint of twilight, how grand it would be, it flashed into my mind, if there [were at] the top a Colossal Statue of Britannia, with her Lion at her feet, surveying France with a lofty air.

I recollect once I happened to say a great colossal Statue of Neptune at the Admiralty, one foot on one side & one foot on the other, holding in one hand the telegraph, towering in the air so as to be visible for miles, would [be] an ornament worthy of such a city. 'You had better,' said a collector of Dutch Pictures, with a sneer, 'propose it to Parliament.' 'That I would,' said I, 'were there the least chance of success.' It's a melancholy thing for those whose whole ambition is the advance of the National taste – to see all the faculties of men, squeezed into an inside of a tasteless dutch Room, with a woman clouting a child – all the delight English men feel is in cocking their nose close to the Picture, and let its intellectual qualities be what they may, condemn or praise in proportion to its mechanical excellence. They talk of Raphael & the Cartoons, but they merely talk – for God knows they feel e'en little enough. Wherever I dine, wherever I go, a string of technical phrases that are for ever on the tongue, without effort or reflection, are perpetually uttered – how that floor is imitated, what a colour that turnip is, how delightful is that cabbage, look at that herring – wonderful – what could you expect from infants if you talked to them about art – but that they would be enchanted at the imitation of their doll, or their bells. People might be forgiven – but Noblemen, refined, educated, classical Noblemen, the ministers of the Country, the government of England, instead of standing at an awful distance, and surveying with dread great works, instead of being ambitious of having their Souls elevated, and their minds expanded, instead of this, to see them rush, with their heads jammed as if in a wedge, clap up their glasses before a Picture, and uttering exclamations of ravishment and rapture, at a smutty crock, or a brass candlestick. What do they admire in it? The character or the mind? No, the dutch part, the touching, the knifes, the pewter plates, and tin saucepans – this is all they comprehend – this is what they look for, and this is what they see —

God, I wish for the spectre of Michael Angelo to frown them into grandeur, but even his spectre, and a vision of the Capella Sistina at his heels, would stand a poor chance, with such an opponent as Jan Mieris, at the Table of an English Noble Connoiseur.

Good God, is this the end of Art, is this the use of Painting? Mere mechanic deception; can Painters really excite a Man to Heroism, or urge a Man to Repentance, or excite a Man to virtue? No, certainly, not in such minds it never can; Pictures with such properties would pass unheeded by. O God, why was I not born to be known to Pericles or Lorenzo di Medici? O God, how would I acknowledge in Gratitude thy kindness, could I but find such Patrons, such Protectors, could I but find some one of rank who would relish grand fancies and promote grand art – In thee I trust still – Amen —

September 20. Began my Picture once again [The Assassination of Dentatus]. Wilkie Breakfasted with me on his return from Lord Lansdowne, a portrait of whose Lady he has brought home, which is truly exquisite. I had no idea of his being capable of so much, it gives me real pleasure. God Bless our exertions, and let Death only put an end to our improvement.

October 16. Let me not reflect how sillily I passed this precious day, no Greek or reading in the Bible till the evening, and then I fell asleep and did not wake till one o'clock.

October 17. I felt in the evening an inclination to see Macbeth, I went, but whether it was that their performing in the Opera house gave the figures less effect, I fancied Mrs Siddons acted with very little spirit in the scene where she comes out when Macbeth is in Duncan's chamber she says, 'That which had them drunk, hath made Me bold,' &c., she ought to have been in a blaze. I, who had been accustomed to read Macbeth at home, at the Dead of night, when every thing was so silent that my hair stood up, grew quite enraged & disgusted and left the house before the third act – No Academy – negative day.

December 3. Improved the hand and arm of my Hero, put in the head but took it out again. O God grant I may do it right at last.

December 4. Breakfasted with Wilkie; at church Sidney Smith preached – he took his stand for Xtiantity on St Paul's conversion – if his vision & conversion were the effects of a heated brain or fanaticism, it was the first time that madness gave a new direction to a man's feelings. I have never heard a more eloquent man. Spent the evening in writing my ideas about art, at Mr Hoare's request, who is publishing in the encyclopedia [Encyclopaedia Britannica, 4th edition, published in Edinburgh in 1810].

December 5. As I walked along Fleet Street, I felt hungry and went into Peele's coffee house to have some soup, it was such an idle thing in the middle of the day, that I shrunk in, blushing, fearful to look up for fear of meeting the eyes of Michel Angelo's spectre, crying, 'Haydon, Haydon, you Idle rascal, is this the way to eminence?' – in spite of such reflections in I went.

December 7. People say to me, you can't be expected in your second Picture to paint like Titian, & draw like Michel Angelo but I do expect it, and I will try – and if I take liberties with Nature, and make her bend to my own purposes, consider you should not venture to do what Michel Angelo might, but I will venture, I'll dare anything to accomplish my Purpose.

December 8. After a night of continual interruption and reflections literally excrutiating about my Hero, I arose quite in a fever of anxiety, and set about it. I hope I have it all right to go upon, but I cannot tell till tomorrow. O God grant it may be so. Sat up till one, writing some Ideas about the art for Mr Hoare as I promised him; it is not my business to write, old men should write and give the world the result of their experience.

December 10. Went on with my head; improved it; there must be no delicacy of feeling & refined sentiment in the head of a man bred up in Camps in the stern heroic feelings of a Roman. Arranged the Rocks rightly.

On the helmet of one of my figures I have put some light, airy ostrich feathers, which give a more ponderous look to my Hero —

December 12. Called on Fuzeli, staied three hours, talking of the Art, Italy, Michel Angelo, Homer, Virgil, Horace, enough to make a man mad. When Fuzeli dies, where shall I meet 'his like again'? I do not know any body I feel a greater affection or reverence for.

December 15. Seguier called, liked my head much; thinks it will do, so do I in some measure, with a few alterations. Improved the position of my dying figure.

What are painters doing who from neglecting Nature have degenerated into Manner? A man of real Genius will not suffer Nature to put him out, he will make Nature bend to him, he will force her into his service.

December 20. Altered the leg and thigh of my Dying Figure. After every victory and every exertion of Buonaparte [Madrid fell to Napoleon on Dec. 3, 1808] the people of this country console themselves with finding fresh difficulties that must be insurmountable. What man of Genius thinks of difficulties? To indolent asses they may be difficulties, but to Buonaparte only stimulants. Nothing is difficult; it is we that are indolent.

1809

January 23. It has been the fashion to talk of the Greeks as beings above us, all attempts to reach whom were absurd, and a very proper way of talking, if we were contented with looking and not exerting, but how far did ever useless rhapsody advance human intellect? How far Winckleman or any other learned rhapsodist conduced to the improvement of modern art, impudently attempting [to] ridicule our ever possessing the faculty of refinement, because our London atmosphere happened [to] be smoky and our days rather dark. Painting requires more protection & encouragement than Poetry, Philosophy, History, Law, or Music. An Artist must be employed, or there must be a prospect of a Protector.

January 29. At Church. All last week I spent days & nights in excrutiating anxiety about Sir John Moore and our brave army in Spain. Thank God he beat the French; it's pretty clear now that our Soldiers are as great as our Sailors. What would I have given to have been in the Battle of Corruna, and to have finished my Picture afterwards. O God, grant I may astonish mankind as a great Painter and then die in battle, and let me not die undistinguished. I fear it will be impossible for me to die in Battle – how can it be brought about I don't see, but I live in hopes as these are strange times.

Feby. has ended. I neglected to go on with my Journal. My Picture is advanced, & I hope improved. Drury Lane Theatre burnt down. I ran down and got up on Somerset House leads. Nothing could exceed the sublime Horror of the Scene. I saw the whole South front, 450 feet, fall in at once; it sounded like a distant crash of ten thousand rocks. When the explosion of gun powder burst out, a column of fire expanded upwards at least a mile and then vanished.

March 1. Every thing the Greeks did must have been on a clear principle, which could be pointed out to all, of distinguishing characters.

In the finest Greek works, the art and principles are compleatly concealed by being united with a feeling for the simplicity & beauty & Nature.

Before Lord Elgin brought those heavenly productions into England, it was always a matter of caution to young Painters to beware of mixing the principles of Sculpture with Painting, to beware of making your figures like the Antique. Nothing could be more disgusting than to see young men square out their forms with all the Pedantry of knowledge, but now copy precisely any figure from the Temple of Theseus, and it will have all the probability & simplicity of inartificial nature and be adapted exactly for Painting, tho executed with as much art. There is nothing like Stone, nothing like regulated system apparent, all art lies hid.

March 5. Raphael and Michel Angelo had less difficulties to combat, in giving satisfaction than they that are born in the present age. Their works were alone the criterion, and the People's taste was as progressive as their improvement, but now the eyes of connoiseurs are so debauched by the works of Rubens and the Venetians, that form will not satisfy alone, without all that soft voluptuousness of pencil, which is the result and not the beginning of labour.

April 24. Passed the day in reading Shakespeare. Had a beautiful conception of Romeo leaving Juliet. Made a sketch. Also Lady Macbeth besmearing the faces of the pages with blood in dim half tint, while in the back ground Duncan murdered, stretched over the bed, and the door open. Macbeth seen leaning against the banisters.

Romeo & Juliet. In the garden the trees limpid and glistening with the dewy grey tone of morn; day just broke and shooting against the vault of Heaven, the moon fading at the approach of light, the morning star.

In a balcony Juliet & Romeo; Juliet hanging on his neck, telling him it's not yet near day; her hair carelessly diffused about her heavenly neck. Romeo, a fine erect, heroic limbed youth, pressing her gently to his bosom, pointing to the east, unable to tell her what is really the truth, that day is beginning to break.

How odd that such opposite conceptions should come into my head, almost at the same instant, as Lady Macbeth, smearing blood, and Romeo leaving Juliet. I cannot acct. for it.

April 28. Lord Cochrane has had the order of Knighthood conferred on him. I could not read the ceremony without feeling an envy of his glory. Painters never can expect such honours. How I should have been delighted to [have] been in that battle with him. I like the idea of fire, shot, shells, dying groans, tremendous explosions, enthusiastic huzzas, dying efforts, blazing fires, and all the horrors, terrors, fury, rage, & smoke of a thundering battle.

May 13. How success or a prospect of success operates on men's minds. Two months since I dined at Lord M[ulgrave]'s with Sir G[eorge] B[eaumont] & W[ilkie]. L. M. & Sir G. B. were delighted with my picture. There was then every prospect of it being hung in a good situation in the Royal Academy and attracting public approbation. All their conversation was on the beauties of my Picture, on my perseverance, how fine this was or how fine that. I finished my Picture, sent it to the Exhibition, where by the rascality of Mr West it was hung so that nobody could see it. Of course every body pitied me, said it was a shame. Lord M. behaved to me like a noble fellow and expressed his feelings with indignation. Wilkie's Pictures were hung where they deserved, and still excited as much applause as ever, which they deserved also. I dined again at Lord Mulgrave's and with some company. Two months since, when I shewed an inclination to speak, every body turned towards me and listened with attention and smiles, but now my observations were drowned in clamour.

May 14. I began to study in London in lodgings in the Strand, 342, May 20th, 1804, and studied night [and] day, till I brought a weakness in my eyes, which obstructed me for 6 weeks. In January, 1805, I first entered the Academy. March, went into Devonshire, where I obtained bones from a Surgeon of Plymouth and drew nothing else for three months; returned to the Academy in July; met Wilkie there first time. Studied incessantly, sitting up many nights, shattered myself so much obliged to leave off. Went into Devonshire for the recovery of health. Began to paint after two years' application to Anatomy & Drawing, May, 1806. Commenced my first picture, October 1st, and finished it March 31st, 1807. Went into Devonshire for 6 months. Studied heads from Nature. Came to town. My dear Mother died at Salt Hill. January 1st, 1808, commenced my second Picture, Dentatus.

Journal of a jaunt into Devonshire in company with Wilkie. Wilkie and I left London on 22 June for Portsmouth, with a letter of recommendation to Sir Roger Curtis, the Port Admiral, from Gen'l Phipps (Lord Mulgrave's Brother) telling him if an opportunity occurred to send us on board a man of war for Plymouth.

We set sail to see the Caledonia, 120 Guns, then at Spithead. There is in our Navy a sublime, terrible simplicity; nothing admitted but what is absolutely useful. The cannon, the decks, & the Sailors wear the appearance of a stern vigour, constituted to resist the elements. Every thing inspired one with awe & admiration. I felt as if I could have stood like a rock on such a deck and braved the fiercest battle. There was nothing elegant or tasteful that would excite indolent, luxurious delight; every thing was rough, terrible, & firm, that roused the fiercer passions. There was a grandeur in the sight of 350 Sail at anchor at Spithead. We rowed about amongst them & returned to Portsmouth.

After waiting three days we became quite hopeless, and calling on Sir

Roger to take leave, we obtained two places in the packet-boat. Just as we were on the point of embarquing, Sir Roger came puffing in to desire us to delay our present plan as he could get us something better than the packet. He would recall the officer who was under weigh by signal, which he did immediately, & introduced him to us. We were soon on board, and soon again under weigh. The transport we convoyed shortly followed us, and we dwelt with delight as we floated by the shores of the Isle of Wight. We passed through the Russian fleet. The sailors stared at us. How unlike English Sailors they appeared, their lips covered with nasty, sandy coloured mustachios, some in hairy caps, some in green jackets. When they laughed it was like the grins of Jackalls or Apes. Their ships appeared strongly built ships.

All that day we were at Sea. Wilkie became very ill, obliged to keep his bed. I was slightly so for ten minutes and soon recovered. I found the Master an intelligent fellow and the Commander a compleat seaman.

I relished their salt beef and biscuit, and never felt more vigorous and strong. As the Sun was setting we shortened sail. Poor Wilkie still continued totally unable to stand up. I pitied him lying on his back with his nose close to the deck, pale, hollow cheeks, blue, quivering lips, gummy, red blinking eyes, and unshaved.

The next morning [we saw] the Mew-Stone at the entrance of Plymouth Sound, and by three that afternoon we anchored. The poor Sailors all were on the tip-toe to get on shore. One wanted to see his Mother, and another had a bad hand, nor did they cease to importune their Commander till he thundered out 'Silence.' We landed at the Pier and soon reached home, where we were frankly received by my Father.

I felt the want of my dear Mother; her bed, room, every place reminded me of her.

Nothing refined, I found, would do at a country table. Every thing must be broad & farcical to have any effect.

The People in Devonshire treated us handsomely, but in all their parties there was something wanting. From being all known to each other, brutality & ignorance are pardoned, and he that forgives it in his own house, expects the same indulgence in another's. The consequence is a regard for the comforts of another is neglected, and every man thinks only of himself. They are hospitable but unpolished.

We bathed, and Wilkie learnt to swim at a place called Two Coves, near Plymouth, a delicious luxurious bathing place.

We left Plymouth the very day five weeks [after] we came out of London, and came to Exeter that night, after travelling the most delightful road in England, the Totnes Road to Exeter.

We visited the beauties of the Country, saw the tremendous Cheddar Rocks and Cavern. There was something terrific in their appearance, a wild, ferocious, sullen tone with a burst of light in the sky behind, which shewed their projections sharply – a place fit for Banditti.

We left Wells at Six next morning and breakfasted at Bath. I hate Bath. There is a stupid sameness notwithstanding the beauties of its Buildings. There was a confirmation at the Abbey Church, and as I looked on and saw the venerable Bishop lay his hand on the heads of two sweet beautiful girls, I fancied I saw the Almighty and their Saviour, contemplating the scene, with sublime, heavenly complacency, while quoirs of cherubims and Angels uttered a swell or strain of breathing, dulcet, undulating symphony. O God, could I always feel so, who would be happier?

We left Bath again the next day and entered dear London after being abroad six weeks [August 3], much renovated in health.

September 21. When Lord Elgin examined the Parthenon and saw several of the figures lying about, that had fallen from the building, it occurred to him that many might be buried. He therefore bought the House of the Man that lived under the portico, pulled it down, and excavated the whole to the solid rock, and found a fragment of the breast of the Jupiter, & of the Minerva – he then thought he might be equally successful, at the other end, where several figures were wanting, he procured the House of the man that lived there also and dug down here as well, but found nothing – the Man then to whom the House belonged, told him he could have saved him all that trouble, for the figures that [had] fallen from this part of the temple, he had ground down himself into lime, as it made such excellent mortar to build his house with, and that the greatest part of the citidal had been built with mortar procured in the same manner – with such an example before him of barbarity, he thought himself fully justified in securing those that remained, for in all probability, were they to fall, they would share the same fate, – to this energetic resolution England is indebted for these exquisite productions.

Lord Elgin has done more for English Art [than] was ever done by an individual in any Country; he deserves indeed well of his Countrymen, and [instead] of affectedly lamenting, as some do, that he stripped Athens of what remained, we should rather lament he was not there to strip it sooner.

These facts I heard Lord Elgin deliver to Mr West, Nollekens, and myself yesterday, Sep. 22nd, 1809, at his musaeum for the first time – it was after the company were all gone, and we remained behind. It was excessively interesting to hear him say 'that I picked up myself at Eleusis,' &c &c, 'This I found outside the Acropolis,' &c &c &c.

December 9. I went to Covent Garden to night. The Duke of Gloucester made his appearance in his private Box, and was instantly greeted by repeated cheers, a good private character has always its weight with the People. They sung God save the King, in his Presence, and again gave him three cheers when he retired.

December 12. What do the Rooms of the English Nobility exhibit but inefficient sources of imbecil intellects? What books do you see on the tables? Do you see Homer, Milton, or Johnson? No, these are [too] powerful for their enervated faculties; they take more delight in studying court intrigue [than] in being roused to Heroic action by a passage of Homer.

1810

January 4. It is now three years since I first became acquainted with Sir George B[eaumon]t. I was at first fascinated by his affability, his smiles, his flattery, his advice expressed and uttered with all the warmth of sincerity and regard. He called on me, liked my Picture, about a day or two afterwards he again called, and expressed a wish to have a sketch, when I had concluded my Joseph and Mary; tho' approving it he advised me not to exhibit it; this first excited a doubt in my mind of his sincerity; from this moment I examined his character with wary suspicion. Sir G. B[eaumon]t is a man who wishes to have the reputation of bringing forward Genius without much expence, if a young man promises any thing, he immediately procures a slight sketch for a trifle; if this youth succeeds he has something to shew, to prove he first employed him, he first had acuteness to discover his talents – if on the contrary he fails, the sketch passes into oblivion, he denies all knowledge or recollection of him. Such a man of rank is a dangerous character, for when the feeling is not regulated by principle of him who has power, what misery can he not produce?*

April 21. I yesterday, 20th, Good Friday, for the first time since my birth, received the sacrament. I had put it off from year to year, and I was determined to delay no longer (I thank thee God I did not delay it). Tho burdened with Sin yesterday I ventured to approach the Altar; about two days before I had reflected on every thing with deep meditation – and conviction flashed on my mind at intervals – I never before felt the grandeur of the scheme of Christianity; when I considered this, when I thought on the impossibility of the whole plan of the law and the Gospel, being mere human invention – a plan of such comprehension, such grandeur, I dared not doubt, I felt as it were urged on to receive. I eat the bread in awe, and drank the wine with firmness, and prayed with fervor it might be effectual to my redemption & reformation – as I returned home, the fancy of having drank wine & eat bread as our Saviour himself did 1800 years ago, and commanded us to do in remembrance of him, made me start – I have indeed done it, I thought, I am now a Christian – I shall

---

*Sir Walter Scott, on the other hand, called Beaumont 'the most sensible and pleasing man I ever knew'. For an unbiased account, see *Collector of Genius – A Life of Sir George Beaumont* by Felicity Owen and David Blayney Brown (Yale University Press, 1988).

Study for *Macbeth*

begin tomorrow a new existence. Christ Jesus have mercy on me, inspire me, purify me. I have now entered the road thou hast directed those who wish to find thee; may I keep firmly in it without stumbling and without deviation – O God, protect me and bless me, thou Great good, incomprehensible Being – for Jesus Christ Sake. Amen.

April 22. After Sir G. and his Lady called, and seemed totally to forget that I had ever been painting a Picture for them [Macbeth], by their never hinting any thing about it – I shewed the correspondence to everybody who wished it – and People soon began to talk how shockingly I had been used. I swore to all I would finish the Picture to the utmost of my power, and then publish the whole to the world —

I went on quietly for nearly a month and Sir George, who used to call every day, let me proceed with as much indifference as if he never knew me – to my surprise about a month after he last called – I received a card requesting me to dine with him; after some hesitation, I determined to go, supposing that some proposition was to be made me about his Picture.

On my entering the room, Sir George arose in evident agitation to receive me, while Lady B. instantly drew me off to the Window and kept me from observing him, which I did in a most determined manner – Sir G.'s attention to me was marked – my opinion was asked, about every thing – and we shortly retired to dinner – here his attention to me was quite rediculous. Lady B. on one side and he on the other – however I was not thrown off my guard. I began to suspect he had heard of my intentions about publishing his letters – and had invited me to flatter or intimidate me out of it.

After dinner in the course of conversation, Barry was mentioned – 'talking of Barry', says Sir George, 'I recollect something that Sir Joshua told me of him – that he once published something in the papers which he had entrusted him with in confidence – now you know,' says he (while his face and lips grew pale as he spoke it, and his eyes and head were turned straight forward, without appearing to look at any thing), 'now you know, nothing could be so shocking, to publish letters or any thing of that sort, nothing can be [so] shocking' – ah, ah, the whole at once beamed on my fancy. I appeared totally indifferent and agreed nothing was so shocking. The conversation took another turn, and I turned round and looked calmly at Sir George, who appeared ruffled, notwithstanding his forced smile and apparent gaiety – his character was now at stake before the world, he knew I had dived into his soul, and that I had it in my power to expose him.

All the evening I was singled out by Lady B. 'Don't you think so, Mr Haydon, have you had time to read this or that, Mr Haydon?' 'Do sit,' said Sir George – 'how d'ye get on with Macbeth?' – !!! ha, ha, he now condescended to mention Macbeth. Bless my heart, he has not then quite forgot that he engaged me to paint a Picture at which I had worked 5 Months and began it three times – it is very odd, surely, that he be so lucky as to recollect Macbeth now and to be unfortunate as to have entirely forgotten it when he arrived in Town – but some people have these convenient memories —

These were my reflections before I spoke, and I then told him that I was proceeding and hoped to get it finished – when we rose to take leave – 'Good night,' said they, 'Mr Haydon,' and bowed to all the rest —

July 11. In passing Piccadilly I observed in some horses galloping the various positions of their limbs – what was the position of the fore legs when the hind legs were in such a position, &c – it is astonishing how truly you get at their motions by thus scrutinizing; I made some sketches, after I arrived home, and they seemed to spring and had all the variety I could possibly wish – and such a look of Nature and activity!

I spent five hours with Fuzeli Sunday last spouting Homer, Virgil, Dante & Milton. I flatter myself I can adopt so much of Fuzeli's fire & pungency as I find necessary for my own purposes, without suffering him to lead me astray, by his enthusiasm. I thank God I always had from the first moment I commenced studying a judgement of my own, a desired plan which I felt an internal conviction of was the only right one.

Enveloped as it were with these principles, I trusted myself fearlessly with all men. 'Beware of Fuzeli' was the advice for all, but as this caution was necessary only to those who having no object of their own, were at the mercy of unsettled whim, I never felt it operate on me an instant. I have now known Fuzeli five years – and consider his Friendship on the above principle a very, very great acquisition – no man has like Fuzeli the power of directing your fancies to a point – if you mention to him any conception, any subject, he sees instantly its defects and always (perhaps a little overstepping the modesty of Nature) points out its capabilities. Tho' he may do this rather furiously – it is in the right road – tho' too far. Fuzeli is such a man as does not appear in two centuries – and that they'll think when he is dead.

August 5. I this day again received the Sacrament, and from my Soul I thank God I did so; I felt afterwards a veil of purity & cleanness of heart spread as it were over my mind. The great scheme of my life is to be a great Painter, and to let the means by which I struggle to obtain this end be so virtuous at the same time to make me worthy when I die of obtaining eternal reward also hereafter – I will, if God permit me, receive the Sacrament monthly. No means are so effectual to me as constant employment, and constant Religion.

My scheme of life, what I always arranged since I first came to Town, is what from my frailty and indolence I have never been able strictly to adhere to – (To rise at five, pray sincerely, to be in my painting room by Six, set my palette &c and begin at Seven, paint till nine – breakfast, begin again at Ten – paint till five, with a quarter of an hour's intermission for some slight refreshment at two – at five dine – at Six make studies, for the next day, or if you are in no want of preparation, consider what you have been doing, or proceed with it – at eight clean palette & brushes and then walk – and [at] nine take tea, read, retire to bed shortly after ten; from ten to five is Seven hours rest, which will fit you for the next day's labour.) This it is impossible to do regularly – business must be done, accidents will happen, difficulties will occur, which it will be impossible for human nature to prevent or provide for – but when you are settled with respect to your intentions, what delight is it to put one's hand on one's heart by ten at night and be able to review a day of such employment & effort – and with vigourous alacrity does one spring, the morning following, from one's couch; again to struggle for eminence and fame. This is indeed a happiness, and how often has he occasion to lament his human imperfections who has once relished the delight of this stimulus.

September 9. I walked to see Wilkie yesterday to Hampstead; as I returned about four o'clock the Sun was on the decline – and all the valley as I looked from Primrose Hill wore the appearance of happiness & Peace. Ladies glittering in white, with their aerial drapery floating to the gentle breeze, children playing in the middle of the fields, and all the meadows were dotted with cows, grazing with their long shadows streamed across the grass engoldened by the setting Sun. Here was a mower intent on his pursuit, with his white shirt and brown arms illumined in brilliancy; there another, resting one hand on his Scythe, and with the other wetting it with tinkling music – some people were lying, others standing – all animate & inanimate nature seemed to enjoy and contribute to this delicious scene, while behind stood the capital of the World, with its hundred spires – and St Paul's in the midst towering in the silent air with splendid magnificence.

What a change would Buonaparte make in such a scene of liberty and peace – could he but once set his withering foot on this dear land. The state of the rest of the World came into my mind as I stood abstracted, and every other country that my fancy pictured, I thought I saw a dingy lowering cloud hanging over it – a beam of light burst through the cloud that enveloped Spain, but it appeared dripping with blood – England alone laid open her peaceful meadows, lit up by gaiety & innocence.

1811

January 16. Painted vigourously not more than 3 hours – advanced Macbeth. Studied till late. Wish the day were 48 hours instead of 24.

February 4. Painted vigourously for 6 hours. Got into Lady Macbeth.

April 1. There cannot be a finer subject in the whole world than Macbeth the moment before he murders Duncan. In the foreground are the grooms, drunken & drowsy; one has sunk down on his knees, oppressed with sleep; the other has fallen back without power, his hands resting on the ground on each side, his face flushed, his jaw dropped – immediately behind, between them and the bed, stands Macbeth, the victim of imagination and terror, his chest heaved up with agony, his mouth gasping for breath, with spasmatic effort, his nostril open, his eye glaring, his cheeks pallid and sunk – and his hands grasping the daggers.

Behind lies Duncan the King, simply lying on his back, his breast bared, his sacred cheek flushed with sleep, unconscious and innocent of the horrid scene at the moment passing in his royal chamber. There is a pathetic look which excites the most intense feelings and forms a fine contrast to the guilty horror of Macbeth – while in dim obscurity is seen his dreadful wife. Her motion seems to have arrested Macbeth; her whole soul seems wrapped, in methodizing in imagination the murder of the

King; her firmness and demoniac enthusiasm are opposed to the conscientious agitation of her heroic husband.

The colouring is deep toned and high – Shadows awful – the terror is greatly encreased by the Shadow of Macbeth englooming across the royal bed.

April 7. An old Servant of my dear Mother & her Aunt called, who excited the most pleasing & melancholy associations – I had some cold beef & Porter brought up for them and they appeared much better pleased than if I had attempted to amuse them in any other way.

May 6. Last evening Rigo, a French artist, member of the Egyptian Institute, spent the evening with me. I was curious to get out every anecdote about Buonaparte, from one who had been with him repeatedly, seen him repeatedly, & was always at his table during the Egyptian expedition.

He said the night before the battle of Aboukir, where Buonaparte beat the Turks, he lay on the ground in the same Tent with Buonaparte; (Rigo's brother was interpreter to Buonaparte with the Turks – they were all in the same Tent.) Rigo said he never was with or near Buonaparte but he was always attracted by his Physionomy; there was something so penetrating, so acute, so thoughtful, so terrible, that it always impressed him, and that this night when all the rest were buried in sleep, he could not avoid watching him. In a little time he observed him take the compasses and a chart of Aboukir and then measure and then take a ruler and draw lines. He then arose, went to the door of the tent and looked towards the Horizon. He returned to his seat, looked at his watch; after a moment he took a knife and cut the table in all ways like a boy – he then rested his head on his hand, looked again at his watch for some time, went again to the door of the tent, and again returned to his seat. There was something peculiarly awful – the time of night, his generals soundly sleeping, Buonaparte's strong feature enlightened by a lamp, the association that the Turks were encamped near them, that before long a dreadful battle would be fought. In a short time Buonaparte called to them all – they sprang up – ordered his Horse – and asked how long before day break. They told him an hour. The army were under arms. He rode round, spoke to the colonels & Soldiers, told them in his energetic manner that a mile from them there existed a Turkish army, and he expected by ten o'clock that they existed no longer.

Before ten they were annihilated.

Rigo said [when] Buonaparte was Consul, he dined with him. He is never more than ten minutes at furthest at Dinner. His two valets, the moment he eat one dish, put another; he eat that, then drank a few glasses – and retired to his cabinet. They all arose when he got up, and then staid two or three hours.

His private secretary is a young man about 29. He sleeps above the Emperor; the Emperor goes up to him at two & three in the morning and begins work – he, the Emperor retires to bed at nine generally and is always up before day break. He is grown very fat lately.

May [no date in original]. Painted 4 hours & ½, and went two hours and studied the Titians at Lord Stafford's. Nothing can equal the exquisite lucid colours but the fleshy softness of the forms. Felt weak & relaxed. May I never think of form, draw a line or paint a touch without instinctive reference to these exquisite refinements.

June 6. The first six months of the year 1811 are now on the eve of closing. If I review them with rigour, what will they exhibit? I have been at times energetically employed, but I have not so conquered my habits as to have that invincible pertinacity of soul, to be so independent of circumstances, as to make them bend to me, tho' vice tempt me, tho' sickness overwhelm me. God in heaven grant that this may be my lot – when I lie in expectation of Death may my expiring eye glisten with delight at the reflection of my efforts from this moment – and may my senses close in silence here, to open to eternal harmonies in another existence.

June 19. Arose at ½ past five; in my painting room by Six – at work till eight; began again at ten. Seguier called, on whose judgement Wilkie and I so much depend.

He thought my Figure better than it ever has been – in short he congratulated me on its being right.

I have not time to gain the affections of a woman; I have not time to suffer the petty interruptions of love, to be harrassed by the caprice of my mistress, or the jealousy of my own disposition – all this is delightful, no man on earth would enjoy it more than myself, but all this distracts attention and disturbs thought. I have not time to devote to it – and relinquish it I will.

July 5. I called last night on a Sister of my dear Mother's who married with every prospect of fortune & happiness but who by the carelessness of her husband has been reduced with 8 children to want and distress. My Father assisted them for some time – paid 80£ to bind out the eldest Girl – and the husband again altered his conduct and lived with & supported his wife. After innumerable changes and ruin, after living at Bath, Bristol, Worcester, and half the cities in England without any settled scheme – he is again in Town at 55 years of age with 8 children ignorant of tomorrow's fate or whether he shall be without a loaf for his next breakfast. It was a melancholy thing to see my dear Aunt lying [in] sickness in a little bed, up in a second floor with her family about her – to see the tear start into her eye as I approached and took her hand – and to hear her tongue faintly falter 'My dear Benjamin, I wish to die. My dear Sister is gone before me – I hope I am also going. At my time of life to be so harrassed, to have no settled home.' I sat down by her and tried to keep up her spirits. The whole room had the silence and faintness of sickness. Her face was enveloped in a white bordered cap – a white bed-gown encircled her arms to her wrists with ruffles.

I went home in silent reflection, and hoped to die before age had weakened me – or misfortune reduced me – I hoped to acquire the highest fame and to die like Nelson, when it blazed brightest.

July 9. She is dead. My poor Cousin called on me this morning and told me she died quietly – with scarce a breathing heard. I declare I felt not regret – I had a sort of feeling come over me as if she was released from misery and trouble – God grant her spirit that calm repose that was denied it in this dim, groveling spot.

1812

February 2. When a man becomes an Academician he suffers as great a change as if he had undergone chemical transmutation; however noble in feeling, however high his notions however grand his ideas before his election, he instantly becomes cautious, timid, silent, politic.

To be an Academician is [the] height of a young Student's ambition, and to qualify himself by cringing intrigue the object of his wishes, and those precious moments that should be spent in painting by day and drawing by night.

February 3. How Homer raises you by degrees to the fury of the battle. Every thing he describes has a beginning, a middle, & an end – as well as his whole poem. Milton has perhaps a more elevated gloomy sublimity that belongs to hell and chaos – but no man equals Homer and Shakespeare in that *inspired spirit*, that raciness of nature, which animates and distinguishes every thing they mention. Every thing in Homer is enlivening and vigorous – you *fancy* all glittering in the heat of day, gilded by the setting or silvered by the rising Sun; but all Milton's mighty cherubin or seraphin seemed to draw their flaming swords, or clash their sounding shields, as if they shone through a darkened glass – dingy, red, solemn, terrible.

March 27. As I was lost last night in sullen meditation on my troubles, 'Trust in God' said a voice within, and I shook with agitation. I had a feeling as if I saw 'Trust in God' written in glittering letters in the midst of an awful misty darkness. I do, I will trust in God from the bottom of my Soul – God only give me strength compleatly to depend on him.

O God Almighty, thou who so mercifully assisted me during my last Picture, desert me not now. I forgot thy mercy and was vicious, I neglected my promises of amendment and fell into my abandoned ways – but O Lord, thy mercy is infinite, to thee I will again cry. Assist me then, O God; my difficulties are again accumulating and will yet accumulate. O God, grant me the power to make so fine a Picture as may create such a sensation and give such a shock to Art, that the nobility and the people may be roused and high Art have that assistance and that protection adequate to reward its difficulties and worthy of its grandeur. Grant these things for Jesus Christ's sake.

O God, spare the lives of my dear Father & Uncle till I am independent, and able to take my Sister, and much longer if thou pleasest. O God, let me not die in debt! (At the end of 1811, I scrutinised my debts before beginning a new work and found they were £616, 10s., of which £200 was due to my landlord for rent.) Grant I may have the power to pay all with honor before thou callest me hence, grant this for Jesus Christ's sake. Amen.

April 3. My Canvas came home (for Solomon) – a grand size. God in heaven grant me strength of Body and vigour of mind to cover it with excellence. Amen, on my knees.

April 4. Began my Picture – prayed God sincerely for Success – perspectivised the greater part of the day – felt a sort of check in imagination at the difficulties I saw coming, but, thank God, instantly a blaze of enthusiastic perseverance burst into my brain, gave me a thorough contempt for my timidity, and set me at rest.

October 3. Made a[n] accurate study for Executioner for Solomon from my old and faithful model Salmon, Corporal Horseguards, who goes Wednesday next to Spain – perhaps it may be the last time he will sit – he said so himself with a melancholy tone. I hope he may return alive. I gave him and three more who had sat to me a bottle of wine to drink my health before they went and success to themselves – they are fine fellows and will do their duty.

October 7. The idleness, the wasteful idleness of this last year, I shall repent to my dying day. I have gained experience, but at a dear rate. Had I exerted myself as I ought, my Picture would have [been] well advanced; but I loitered, got entangled with an infernal woman, which shattered my peace of mind, before I could extricate myself, and tho' I came off, thank God! without vice (for she was married), yet with my habits so broken and my mind so agitated that till now I have not had command of myself as usual. What a warning have I had!

Whoever you are that read this, when I am dead, beware of the *beginnings* – fly from vice – think not it can be argued against in the presence of the exciting cause – nothing but absence & *actual flight* –

beware of *idleness* which leaves you at the mercy of appetite – employment – employment – and you must be safe.

November 30. Went to the House of Lords to hear the Prince open Parliament in State. It was a very grand affair – the beautiful women – educated, refined, graceful, with their bending plumes & sparkling eyes – the Nobility, the Chancellor – I could not help reflecting how long it was before society arrived at such a pitch of peace & quietness, that order & regulation such as I witnessed existed. What tumult, what blood, what contention, what suffering, what error, before experience has ascertained what was to be selected, or what rejected.

The Prince read admirably, with the greatest perspicuity, not the slightest provincialism, pure English. He appeared affected at the conclusion.

December 14. Made a last application à mon Père pour argent. He frankly tells me c'est impossible – that what J'ai eu is rather beyond ses moyens. I am au milieu d'un grand tableau, sans sous pour les nécessaires de la vie, ou pour modèles; however I never felt more enthousiasme, more vigour, more resolution. I have no doubt of subduing my Tableau with honour and come out of la bataille invigorated & ready pour les autres combats. En Dieu Je confie, qui a été toujours mon protecteur & mon ami. Amen, ginocchione.

1813

January 9. Drew at Lord Elgin's all day and evening till eight. How delightful is the exhausted faint feel after a day's hard work with an approving God within. Sincerely do I thank God that I have compleatly recovered my tranquillity & conquered the agitation from that infernal woman, that wholly & undivided am I again devoted [to] my Art & my glory. I cannot sport on the borders of Pleasure without plunging within the circle. I will therefore keep off altogether as the only mode of salvation. I had feet to prepare for to-morrow. However, before I sleep tonight it shall be done.

January 29. Spent the evening with Hunt, at Westend; walked out & in furiously after dinner, which has done me immense benefit. Hunt's Society is always delightful – I don't know a purer, a more virtuous character, or a more witty, funny, amusing, enlivening man. We talked of his approaching imprisonment [for libelling the Prince Regent in an article]. He said it would be great pleasure to him if he were certain of going to Newgate, because he should be in the midst of all his Friends, and then we both laughed heartily.

February 5. I have [been] studying attentively these two last days the

Bacchus & Ariadne of Titian, & [the Judgement of] Paris by Rubens. There is a gentility in Titian that borders on insipidity, but give [me] the rich, racy, careless, teeming energy of Rubens, an energy that is driving after something beyond this dim spot, and tho it may carry him beyond bounds of *propriety*, who is there that would hesitate at being so carried? It is a delight [to] me to know I see & can prove errors, fundamental errors, in such men as Rubens & Titian – to know too that I have kept them to myself silently to benefit by them, and not obtruded them on others for the sake of shewing my skill. The Elgin Marbles have so refined my eye (I thank God daily) that errors strike it instantly.

February 20. Tom Jones is a delightful novel. It lets you into all the little follies and amiable weaknesses of Nature. It shews you that the most virtuous, the most pure, the most innocent woman may have little imperfections, little vanities, without corrupting her heart. It sends you into the World prepared for it, and renders you more satisfied with human Nature. Richardson always separated vice from virtue, & rendered the one always contemptible by associating it with contemptible qualities. Fielding has mingled both, and undoubtedly reconciles us more easily to vice, by shewing that many fine qualities may unite with it. You relinquish Fielding with hope, but Richardson leaves you in a gloomy trembling, a pathetic agitation, hopeless horror – you regard your own failings with fright and promise amendment in terror. Fielding painted men as they are; Richardson as they ought to be. Fielding is the Hogarth of novelists, while Richardson may be called without exaggeration the Raphael of domestic life.

March 10. I dined on Friday last with a man of Genius, William Hazlitt. His child was to be christened, and I was desired to be there punctually at four. At four I came, but he was out! his wife ill by the fire, nothing ready, and all wearing the appearance of neglect & indifference. At last home he came, the cloth began to cover the table, and then followed a plate with a dozen large, waxen, cold, clayy, slaty potatoes. Down they were set, and down we sat also; his chubby child, squalling, obstinate, & half-cleaned. After waiting a little, all looking forlornly at the potatoes for fear they might be the chief dish, in issued a bit of overdone beef, burnt, with a great bone sticking out like a battering ram; the great difficulty was to make it stand upright! but the greater to discover a *cuttable* place, for all was jagged, jutting, & irregular. Like a true Genius he forgot to go for a Parson to christen his child, till it was so late that every Parson was out or occupied, so his child was not christened. I soon retired, for tho' beastliness & indifference to the common comforts of life may amuse for a time, they soon weary & disgust those who prefer attention & cleanliness.

As I was going to bed last night, my Picture had an imposing and grand look. I felt impressed by it.

April 25. I felt this morning an almost irresistible inclination to go down to Greenwich and have [a] delicious tumble with the Girls over the hills. I fancied a fine, beamy, primy, fresh, green spring day (as it was), a fine creature in a sweet, fluttering, clean drapery, with health rosing her shining cheeks, & love melting in her sparkling eyes, with a bending form ready to leap into your arms. After a short struggle, I seized my brush, knowing the consequences of yielding to my disposition, & that tho' it might begin today, it would not end with it.

May 8. Sir Joshua's exhibition opened. The first impression on my mind was certainly that of flimsiness. They looked faint, notwithstanding the effect was so judiciously arranged. Sir Joshua's modes of conveying ideas were colour & light and shadow; of form, he knew nothing. The consequence was he hinted to his eye & untrained hand, and with great labour & bungling, modeled out his feelings with a floating richness, an harmonious depth, and a gemmy brilliancy that was perhaps encreased by his perpetual repetitions, and which renders him as great a master of colour as ever lived. Of poetical conception of character as it regards Portrait, he had a singular share. How delightful are his Portraits, their artless simplicity, their unstudied grace, their chaste dignity, their retired sentiment command us, enchant us, subdue us.

The exhibition does great credit to the Directors of the British Gallery. It will have a visible effect on Art; it will raise the character of the English School; it will stop that bigotted, deluded, absurd propensity for Leonardo Da Vincis & insipid Corregios, and as men who shared Sir J's friendship and been soothed by his manners, it does credit to their hearts as men.

June 22. In going this morning to the Reynolds gallery, they looked careless, slobbering, unfinished, in short, they are only beautiful sketches. Sir Joshua's mind triumphed over the ignorance of his hand. He knew effect, but his means of attaining it were inadequate; his breadth was emptiness.

June 23. Fuzeli said to me once at [Samuel] Johnson's that People generally went to Church in proportion to their profligacy. I had it on the tip of my tongue to say I wonder he did not go every day.

July 9. I do not recollect feeling greater pleasure than when I read of the capture of the Chesapeake, American Frigate. I turned my eyes to Heaven & thanked God. I recollect from infancy seeing French Frigates sailing into Plymouth Harbour, dismasted, and running along the Sea Shore, cheering till my throat was parched. People bred up in London have not those feelings so strongly.

July 22. I was at the Wellington fête last night [celebrating victory at

Vitoria, the decisive battle of the Peninsular War] and affected extremely. It was a grand scene. Under the bust of Wellington stood a British Grenadier with the flag on the 100 Regiment, 2nd Battn. and the Baton of Marshall Jourdan. I was peculiarly interested at the sight. While the rich dresses of the Visitors, the variety of character – here was the Turkish Ambassador, then came the Russian, then followed the Duke of Sussex in a Highland Dress, then the Marquis of Wellesly, here a group of Hussars, with their golden tassals and rich boots, were bending down to whisper to lovely women. The crimson, golden, beaming dress of the Soldiers, the satinny, creamy, feathery lightness of the delicious women gave it an air of chivalrous enchantment or fairy land – to my dying day I shall never forget it.

August 3. My Soul yearns to see the Vatican & Capella Sistina. My enthusiasm for Michel Angelo & Raphael hourly & daily encreases. O great illustrious immortal pair, may I be worthy to meet thee in a purer existence! My frame trembles at the idea. I feel the want of kindred spirits – there is not an Artist to whom I can pour out the enthusiasm of my soul, who will listen & participate.

August 8. Walked to Hampton Court. Tho Michel Angelo could not do what Raphael did, what he did was of a higher kind.

Raphael's women did not strike me yesterday in so lovely [a] manner as before. They are full of naïveté, simplicity, & artlessness, but they are not beautiful.

August 9. Saw by accident Rubens' Luxembourg. What glittering, tawdry impotence in point of character & expression, after dwelling, as I have been lately, on Raphael's purity – it disgusted one. Except Mary looking affectionately at her new born infant, which is very sweet, all are fat, disgusting beasts. Yet what power in arrangement, what painting, I daresay, what colour. One only laments the perversion of such powers.

How inadequate is allegorical painting. It is, I think, upon the whole an excuse for impotence of mind.

August 26. The great difficulty is to find a woman of exquisite susceptibility, curbed & directed by principle. Many there are who tremble with love at every pore but whose very feeling is a cause of their vice, whose susceptibility renders them liable to be affected by every one of beauty or intellect. Happy is he who can find one that will be satisfied with his attentions, and lock up her heart against the attentions of another. God in heaven grant I may find one such, who would encourage & participate in my efforts for grandeur, who would solace & refresh me after the day's fatigue with her general & tender endearments, who would shrink with horror at cruelly trifling to prove one's affection by rousing a needless jealousy. Let me but find such a creature, and I am her slave, her devoted, enraptured, impassioned lover while existence lasts.

I begin to be weary, to be heartily weary, of vice. There may [be] 'glowing pleasure' in guilty enjoyment, for fear of discovery, from apprehension of detection at the moment, & snatched in the hot, icy fury of passion, yet surely the confidence, the rapture of legitimate pleasure with a lovely creature, pure & depending, is a million times more exquisite.

September 4. 'The mental disease of the present generation is impatience of Study, contempt of the great Masters of ancient wisdom, and a disposition to rely wholly upon unassisted genius and natural sagacity.' The wits of these days have discovered a way to fame which the dull caution of our laborious ancestors never attempted.

October 29. I think the great reason of the superior manner of the Nobility is their elevation in rank above others, so that in whatever company they fall, they are at ease. Who is not polite, witty, affable, when he fears no competition? When he thinks he descends, when he is among those who are ready to laugh, and who feel honour at being noticed?

As I looked at the different animals today at Pidcock's [a menagerie], who were so different in character, so decidedly divided by impassible bounds, I could not help asking, 'are not Men equally as distinctly separated & confused by natural powers or natural deficiencies?' Surely they are.

December 31. This year is now fast approaching conclusion. Upon the whole I have exerted myself with true energetic vigour. My knowledge of art also encreased but not so much as it might have been. O God, when I reflect on the truly miraculous manner in which thou hast supported me and enabled me to bring my Picture to its present state, I bow down in gratitude. O God, may I always deserve such unexampled mercy & protection. Amen, Amen, with all my soul.

1814

January 7. I had not met Fuzeli for one year and a half till the other evening, and being left entirely to converse with Raphael and other delightful beings in the interim, was more enabled to estimate him. He really shocked me. All his feelings & subjects were violent & horrid & disgusting. I returned home with an inward gratitude to God that I escaped in time, that I had purified my soul from the influence of his dark & dreary fancy.

January 9. I have been four years without receiving one sixpence from my professional exertions. I began this Picture [The Judgment of

Solomon] without a farthing and have brought it to a conclusion, now & then assisted by my friends and now & then by disposing of my books & property supporting [myself]; those who have trusted me know that I payed them faithfully & honorably when I had the means, and they have given me credit, with the full conviction that when I have again the means I will be again faithful & honorable.

January 26. After all, what are the difficulties of life in comparison with the rapture of a successful effort to realize a poetical character? Who would change the difficulties of an historical painter for the luxuries of a Portrait painter? Give me one moment of the delight after succeeding in pathetic beauty or sublime majesty, and I'd bear all the miseries of want & debt. God spare me my intellect & health, and what shall subdue me?

Many complain of the cruelty of the World. God knows I have never found it so. I have been peculiarly blessed with Friends who, conscious of my honor and admiring my intentions, have trusted to the one and promoted the other, with zeal & confidence.

March 16. There are a set of Men who groan against the powers of the country in Painting, as there were a set who groaned against its genius as generals, but Lord Wellington, with vigorous contempt of a great mind, overthrew the one; let the patrons give opportunity and Painters with equal energy [will] crush the other.

April 30. My object is not my own aggrandizement on the ruins of others, but to reform & direct those who have the means of aggrandizing the Art. Let me but see a desire in the Academy to foster instead of crush, let me but see a feeling in the Directors to patronise great works for their Halls & their palaces, instead of cherishing little ones for their parlours & drawing rooms, and that instant will I forget & forgive all my own paltry oppressions and back them with all my might & mind.

May 4. O God Almighty, permit me on my knees to thank thee for thy mercies; the great work [The Judgment of Solomon] to which two years of anxious study was devoted is finished, exhibited, sold, & has succeeded. O God, it has given that shock to Art that I so anxiously prayed it might give at its commencement; it has roused the people; it has affected the Artists; it has excited the nobility.

May 7. My Canvas [for Christ's Entry into Jerusalem] up & ready. God in his mercy support me & grant me power to cover it with excellence and to advance the great cause.

May 16. My Sister came up to see me. There is something so pure & correct, so unassuming & unsinful, so delicate and lady like in her manners & feelings, that she has done great good to my own mind & habits. Really the contrast with the women in London is palpable, and it has shewn me the beauty, the value, the comfort of virtue in so striking a light, that the thought, the mere perception of vice, grates against my soul.

May 26. Wilkie & I left Town for Brighton in order to embark there for Dieppe and then push on to Paris. After a pleasant voyage, we landed at Dieppe, and certainly the contrast between the two Countries was extraordinary. The high caps, rich crossed shawls, their lively black eyes, struck amazingly. The Women are beautiful but [of a] stern nature, the children with exquisite features, but not rosy. The French appear to me active, ingenious, unwearied people, polite yet persevering in an object with politeness, bowing, smiling, yet keeping their object in view.

The town of Dieppe old & gothic & fine like Vanderheyden's views in Holland. A great proportion of Women. Climate mild. Shops open airy, & every thing looking elegant. The French Sailors noisy, awkward, theatrical; boats dirty & rusty. The Inn clean, neat, & comfortable.

May 28. Nous partimes de Dieppe pour Rouen dans un Cabriolet. Le chemin fut très bon, très large, avec les arbres des pommes, fut fleuris sur chaque coté. La Campaigne etoit fort riche, et les maisons de manufacture, et les chateaux des Gentilhommes etoient très beaux, bien batis, et très fort avec les briques; en un mot, Je n'ai jamais vu en Angleterre plus de bonheur dans les peuples, plus de propriété dans les habits.

At Equi [Anglicization of Ecouis, a village near Rouen], ou nous dinons, Je rencontre un vieux prêtre. I never saw a family of more kind feeling. They seemed delighted to see an Englishman. They called in all their acquaintance, in slipped one, then another, then he wispered to go to such a one, &c. He took me upstairs and shewed me a cabinet of stuffed birds &c. The people seem glad to get [rid] of Buonaparte's oppression, and yet they regret that they have lost also with it their military grandeur.

We left in a Cabriolet in high spirits and slept that night at Magny, and the next morning again proceeded and arrived at Pontoise to breakfast. About two we entered Paris by the Rue St Denis. The Gate of St Denis is very grand, but the first appearance of Paris to a stranger is that of inextricable confusion, houses, figures, carriages, men, women, & children, all huddled together in dirt, mud & filthiness.

We drove to Hotel Villedot which was uncomfortable & extravagant. After paying, as all must pay, for a little experience, we got lodgings in Rue St Benoit, Fauxbourg St Germain, and became settled.

The next morning [June 1] I went down to the Louvre before breakfast and enquired of a National Guard at what time it opened. With the manners of a Gentleman, he told me every thing I wished, and at ten down we went. Certainly my sensations were very grand as I approached this celebrated Gallery. I darted up stairs through all obstructions, and was in, instantly, but I must own it disappointed me. It is too long – it has too much the look as if one was looking in at the wrong end of a spy glass.

Tintoretto looked dashing & careless, spotted & unfinished. Of all men that ever lived, for sensitive, trembling, sweet sensitiveness, Corregio is the most extraordinary. There is a magical, refined, almost imperceptible beauty. He has realized those fleeting, momentary expressions, which scarcely have existence, and yet affect us with their beam. He has caught them & kept them, with a harmony, a poetry, a refined delicacy, an enchanting grace. No one in England is aware of Corregio's power; he is a most extraordinary man, and I never think of him without having a musical harmonious strain undulate over my brain.

The Country round Paris is vast, dreary, & melancholy – old chateaux, dilapidated – and Paris itself has the look of misery in the People & splendid despotism in the princes.

June 10. I went to the Theatre Vaudeville & saw Cupid & Psyche. Wretched singing, and by the company it seemed a very inferior affair. As I was crossing the Thuilleries and saw Buonaparte's triumphal Arch towering darkly against the twilight sky, I could not help stopping & thinking how little good all his industry had done to the World or himself. All his monuments will serve now but to remind one of his folly, & his vice, his cruelty & tyranny.

June 12. As this was the first Sunday on which the Shops had been shut since the revolution, it was therefore a remarkable Sunday, and we arrived just in time to see the effects in religious matters of that tremendous convulsion. Last Sunday the people were at work, the Shops were open, the inhabitants dirty & dissipated. Today the shops were shut, the people happy & clean. No one can conceive the difference unless they had seen it.

June 13. Went to Gerard's the Painter's, and was certainly very much affected at the Portraits I saw there. Buonaparte 10 years ago. Good God, what a [picture!] Heavens, a horrid yellow for a complexion, the tip of the nose tinged with red, his eyes a watery, dull, fixed, stern, tiger like, lurid fierceness; his lids reddish and his mouth cool, collected, & resolute. Never in my life do I recollect being so horridly touched. All the other heads in the room looked like the heads of children in comparison. Josephine was [in] the middle, looking interesting & good natured, and Maria Louisa on the other side, young & full. Murat was in the outside room, with Lannes* with his wife & fine interesting children, a gallant Soldier, who lost his life at Aspern. I felt regret & interest in his heroic character, and his wife with six sweet children by his side. How could they suffer Buonaparte to deceive & sacrifice them all, one after the other, is to me extraordinary. Poor Maria Louisa! married to the Emperor at the time of his highest glory. Who knows what thoughts & anticipations swelled her

---

*Jean Lannes, duc de Montebello, marshal of France, killed during Napoleon's defeat at Aspern-Essling, Austria, May 22 1809.

youthful bosom? Who knows her dreams of future greatness & future grandeur, to be the empress at 19 of the Hero of the World, and to suffer nothing but agony & distress – here is the moral! She is gone, her son no longer a monarch, and her husband in exile, in contempt. O God, if ever the hand of Providence was writ in the affairs of this World, it has been visible in the conclusion of this man's career.

June 14. I declare to Heaven, that the more I think of Gerard's dreadful facsimile of Buonaparte, the more I feel as if all that approached him were destined to be his victims, Oh, that cruel, bloody, glassy eye, that looked you through without mercy, without feeling!

June 16. Saw the King at Chapel. The King has not a foolish head, but a keen, acute eye. I expect great firmness from his look. The silence was so intense that you could hear the lamps burn, with a sort of gleaming flutter.

June 17. Went to Versailles. The Chateau has a look of ruined splendour, and the Town of desolate devastation. Painted ceilings faded! Crimson tapestry torn! Golden friezes brown with age, and every thing wearing an appearance as if it had sunk & withered under the stroke of a mighty enchanter. The opera house was vast & melancholy, ruinous & dark. Here Maria Antoinette sat the night of her marriage, young, lovely, & blushing!

At the end of the great Park is Great Trianon and Little Trianon, built by Louis XIV. In Great Trianon Buonaparte occasionally resided, and here in his study were marks of recent habitation. When at Trianon, this was the study of Buonaparte. It was simply but conveniently fitted, with desks at every book case. On the one which he more used than the others, were two candlesticks and four smaller ones for other purposes. The place where he leant was rubbed; the chair where he sat was worn; the books behind were mostly military. On another desk was a candlestick with a shade for reading. The fire place had a look of recent use; the tongs and poker were black.

We then drove to St Cloud, which we could not see, as the Comte d'Artois was there for his health, but I do not wonder at Buonaparte's preference of St Cloud. It is beautifully situated, and the trees higher & more full of foliage than any I had observed in France. We returned to Paris highly amused with our jaunt.

Every where do you meet with the consequences of the gigantic wars that have desolated Europe. There is scarcely a waiter at a coffee house or a coachman of France that has not served as a Soldier, been in a battle, or received a wound. On going to Rambouillet, I took up a fine youth, [who] was going to join his friends, and had been wounded at Chaumont. He was just nineteen, delicate & slender. He came from Chartres and told me he had sat off with 60 companions from the same town, and that he was the only one alive. He really wept as he told me. He said if Buonaparte had

Study from *St Peter Martyr*
by Titian, Louvre, 1814

reigned longer, he would have murdered all the World, and then made war upon the animals.

At Versailles I saw Hamlet *traduit* and rendered fit for the French stage. Ophelia was murdered, and Hamlet literally rendered a blubbering boy. Ophelia is with Hamlet entreating by her affection to be more composed, when his Mother enters. Here, as he is talking, he sees the Ghost. The impression on the audience and the effect on me was certainly dreadful. I shall never forget it. Hamlet in the next scene brings out an urn that contains his Father's ashes. Here was true French whine & affectation. Tho when his Mother again returns, and he makes her swear she knew nothing of her husband's murder, and brings her to touch his sacred ashes, there was an awful silence and a severe agony throughout the House.

June 25. It is curious to observe in the Louvre those Pictures which have the most effect. Breadth, brightness, & size & depth bear down all opposition; greyness, Teniers, has no chance, or Rembrandt, brownness, as little.

Went to see Talleyrand's Pictures – very fine. They were hung in the room where the Peace was signed. In his bed room was the Times newspaper.

June 27. Studied Titian's Pietro Martyre with profound attention. Indeed to the Italian School you must turn for all the refinements of the Art. The expression of the executioner's head is truly wonderful; he has cut his victim down, and feels all that grating as if a razor had touched his heart; it can hardly be described – not in a brutal manner, but with a sort of ah! as if he felt for every cut.

Paul Veronese looks certainly flat, and unsubstantial; Rubens, full, vigourous, & vast. His power of handling is dashed, terrible, overpowering. His feeling of a whole as to masses & composition has given him, and will ever give him, a reputation in spite of his want of grace, beauty, expression, poetical conception of character, or any of the great requisites of Art. Surely there must be something extraordinary in a man who can obtain & keep a splendid Fame in spite of such deficiencies. Tintoretto, strawey, rushed, & careless, without the solidity of Titian or Rubens; Titian full of sweetness, feeling, & sensation.

June 28. Saw Gobelin tapestry of Raphael's works – gave me an exact idea of their size, and some of their breadth, colour, & character.

Spent the day at the private library of the Institute, copying the dresses of the Ancient Egyptians, exceedingly useful. The French expedition of Egypt has been proved a great delight to the learned, by the exposition of several cities, which no single Traveller could explore before. The consequence to us Painters is a complete series of the costumes, features, & manners of the inhabitants, copied from their temples, still perfect & uninjured.

July 3. My dear Wilkie set off this morning for England; in spite of Wilkie's heaviness of perception and total want of spirit as to gentlemanly feeling, his simplicity & honesty of manner, his good sense and natural taste endear one to him. I feel low at his departure, tho' I shall soon see him.

July 4. Saw the Cartoon Raphael, the original cartoon for the School of Athens – exceedingly fine. Not remarkable for drawing but for breadth and a whole. The heads of the boys talking to Archimedes beautiful, the hands finely sketched, the whole composed in a masterly manner, and with true feeling. It was really delightful to see something in this way after the insolent imbecility of the present French pictures. Some Spanish Pictures also, two very fine Murillos, and a fine sketch by Velasquez.

July 6. I strolled out in the evening to see the Imperial Guard on foot parade. More dreadful fellows I certainly never saw. Their appearance really impressed me. They have the look of thorough bred veterans, a disciplined banditti, without the irregularity but with all the depravity.

Conducted by the talents of Buonaparte, what would have become of the World if they ruled it? Principle and intellect would have vanished from its surface. A sight of his guards would cure his admirers.

July 17. Again do I touch the Shores of Old England. My sensations were grand. Never did she stand higher, or on a more glorious point. As I approached her sacred shores, and France vanished from my view, I felt as if my journey had been a dream. I have seen many, many virtuous women, good wifes, the tenderest Mothers, but in the men there is a careless ferocity of feeling that stamps them. A Frenchman will tell you of a murder as a joke, an Englishman with a natural horror, because War is never felt in England, but the great business of the Continent is fighting.

September 24. Hastings. I cannot help being amused when I reflect sometimes at my own restless spirit. What incessant raging & craving activity I have undergone for these last two days! The first thing in the morning I bathed in a stormy sea, for it blew a gale, and amidst the breakers, where I was almost suffocated with surf & foam, & beat down upon the sand by a gigantic wave, I dived through it and reared my head on the other side, as it raised me to the top, & then sunk me with a long sweep into the valley between. How my heart beat with real enthusiasm when I was on the top of a wave and saw another coming as if to overwhelm me (however there was no danger; it only required firmness & skill). The first wave left me & passed with roaring dash in upon the shore; the other caught me up & passed on like the other. I felt like a God. Ulysses himself never behaved more like a Hero.

September 29. I this day received communication from the Mayor of my native Town that the Freedom of it had been voted me by the Commonalty. I do not ever recollect being so acutely affected at any success as at this. It sunk deeply into my heart, made it beat, and my cheeks flush & eye fire, as it beamed across my mind. God grant that my next production may shew me worthy of such distinction.

October 28. I saw Kean's Hamlet last night, and totally disagree as to its being his worst part. The fact is we are ruined by the ranting habits of the stage. To me his whole conception & execution of Hamlet is perfect. You see him wander silently about, weary, in grief, disgusted; if he speaks, it is not to the audience; if he feels, it is not for applause. No, he speaks because impelled to utter his sensations by their excess. He weeps because his faculties can no longer retain themselves. The longer he acts, the more will he bring the World to his principles, and the time is not far distant when his purity, his truth, his energy, will triumph over all opposition.

December 2. I have lately been amongst Actors & Actresses. I never refuse invitations that will afford me opportunity of seeing human nature in all its varieties.

Those who have once violated any of the great principles of Society & live in the practice, however surrounded with splendour & luxury, can never rid themselves of the aking whisper of conscience. I have been introduced to a Lady adopted or kept by a rich [a word is scratched out]. She is surrounded by every pleasure, by gold, silver, & precious stones; every want is anticipated, every wish gratified, her invisible & keen & restless monitor tells her with a bitter laugh she is a slave! She feels it, she knows it. Alas, I looked at her with pity as I dined off her silver plate & drank from her golden goblets. She met my silent investigating look & blushed! It spoke volumes to me! She was pensive the whole of dinner and then suddenly seemed to burst out with an internal flash, and fled from thought in the most violent gaiety.

December 31. The last night of 1814, a year to me in which I have suffered the extremities of misery, & want, & enjoyed the greatest success; in which I have enlarged my mind by seeing another Country, & studied the productions which the World have for 300 years looked up [to] with reverence & delight. O God, from my soul I bless thee for thy goodness. Grant I may reform & rear the Art of my glorious Land; grant my exertions during the next year may make a great stride to their accomplishment. O God, spare my eyes and my intellect, & continue my strength of mind & vigour of body to resist every vicious inclination, & accomplish every great, good, & glorious wish, for Jesus Christ's sake, my Saviour, my Redeemer. Amen, Amen, O God.

1815

January 7. At the moment of execution, one suffers agony, at the impossibility to compleat the idea; the imagination fired at the moment goes so much beyond the efforts of the hand that not till days afterwards, when fancy has cooled & Nature is absent, do you begin to relapse into approbation. I never was satisfied with any effort till I had forgotten what I wanted to do.

January 18. Certain delightful qualities in a Woman are usually attended with certain tendencies to vice. If you love the one, you must put up with the other & risk your peace. If you will not risk your peace by marrying the one with such delightful qualities, you may secure your tranquillity by marrying those of decent inanimateness, without gaity or playful fascination, but with fire side, stocking-mending moping, and hot plain work, breathy stench.

April 10. I painted a Portrait of a Friend, a long promise! Then did I miserably feel the different sensations after concluding the one to those after a day's work on my Picture. The one was all the timid, mean sensation of a face similist; the other all the swelling, bursting glories of realizing a [host] of visions of imaginations. There is at this moment more talent in this Country than any Country in Europe. The right encouragement is giving employment to it. Payne Knight* was envious of Lord Mulgrave bringing forward Wilkie & I, as a man could be. From the first moment of my appearance in Public, Payne Knight attacked me and my whole system, in the grossest manner, and then the Directors refused me the prize for Macbeth, and set their faces against great Pictures, and the year following advised great Pictures to be put into their halls, and in the same preface, attacked me for painting them. What is the meaning of this exquisite boggling and fogginess?

April 15. My perpetual sicknesses from weak eyes greatly break in upon my habits. It is a long time before I recover my regularity of application.

April 16. What a delightful moment is that of declaring a passion which has long possessed one to a pure, delicious girl, who owes to you her first excitement. In a silent evening, accidentally alone with her, the flutterings of heart, the longings for disclosure, the trembling approaches! She sits – you venture to sit near her! You slip gently from the edge of your own chair to the edge of hers, which you affect to conceal! and which she affects not to see! an involuntary sigh; you put your arm on the back of her chair without daring to touch her lovely shoulder – awed, for fear of offending, you dare, agitated & shaken, to touch her soft hand! She withdraws it not! You press with a start of passion the gentle, helpless hand to your full & burning lips! Your floating eyes meet hers, looking out under her black locks with lustrous tenderness. Down sinks her lovely head under your heated cheek, and you feel her heavenly breath, breathing quickly into your neck! You move your lip gently to meet hers, but are unable to reach it, buried as it is in your neck. O God! with the look of an Angel she turns up her exquisite mouth, & as you kiss it, your lips cling, with a lingering at every little separation and you suck extasy till your brain is steeped in steam! You press her with an intensity of grasp. She suffers all, trembling, depending, smiling. Does not this speak all a man would wish? No cant, no dropping on knees, no speaking to Fathers, – not even a word to her dear self! Perhaps a noise – the Servant with candles! She starts up, with her hair each side of her forehead, and with a dreaming sort of distraction at having been kissed by a Man!

These are the sweet sensations of life. At tea with the family not a word spoken to each other, hardly venturing to treat her with common politeness; when unwatched, when the rest are occupied, a stolen look,

---

*Richard Payne Knight, governor of the British Institution, with whom Haydon was frequently at loggerheads.

and an exquisite smile from her exquisite lip, assures one of approbation. What ages of doubt does *this* obliterate. One bounds home like a deer, and rushes to rest that one may dream.

April 20. I have two hundred pounds to pay the twenty-first of next month. As yet I have not a sixpence towards it, but in God sincerely I trust, who has always relieved me. Let me but be successful in realizing my conception & wishes in my day's labour, and what shall subdue me but extinction?

Enable me, O God, to conclude grandly & magnificently my present Picture of Christ's triumphant entry into Jerusalem, in spite of all obstructions, however great. Grant its effect when finished may compleat the feeling Solomon has began. O God, let me not die in debt, call not me hence till I have paid all I owe with honour. Spare my eyes, invigorate my intellect, grant me capacity to discover my faults & energy to correct them, strengthen every requisite that thou has blest me with, and supply those thou hast not. Amen, Amen, in humbleness & gratitude.

April 21. I met two melancholy instances of the fate of life. My sweet Gipsey Girl, whom I had not seen for 3 months passed me in the Street. I knew her lustrous black eye, which looked up as usual with its accustomed sparkle, but she shaded her face, and seemed conscious of something she was ashamed of. I went up and to my infinite horror, her lovely features were totally disfigured by the small pox! And as she blushed & felt pain at my presence, I left her. Poor girl. As if this evening was destined to melancholy sights, I called on a Friend. The Servant shewed me into a Parlour, and giving me a chair, walked down to her Master. As I sat musing, the door slowly opened and a delicate, slender creature entered, who had the remnants of beauty still glimmering on her faded cheek, enveloped in a black, long veil, which she held under her chin with her bony hands. As she advanced, she perceived me, and was retiring. I instantly rose. Good Heavens, this was a young Lady, whom I had known; young, plump, active, & beautiful, dying in Consumption! I could scarcely refrain from tears, as I touched her feeble hands & shook them. She had not strength to speak or to bear questions, so she withdrew like a spirit, and looked a friendly & eternal farewell, with her yet gentle eye, into which some tears had started. Dear Soul – old age & disease! What terrific enemies ye are to human vanity! I remember her always sweet, lively, & interesting. I was then 17, gay, volatile, & boyish. Death was then to our young thoughts in long perspective. She, alas, is now almost arrived at the end of it. I went home & spent the evening in mournful meditation. There is something extremely interesting in sickness. I think I should love my wife more tenderly then than at any other time, so keenly was I affected at this young creature's state. I looked at every thing with a double interest. I felt the humming of silence in my brain! and mused till midnight, hating the noise even of a dropping cinder!

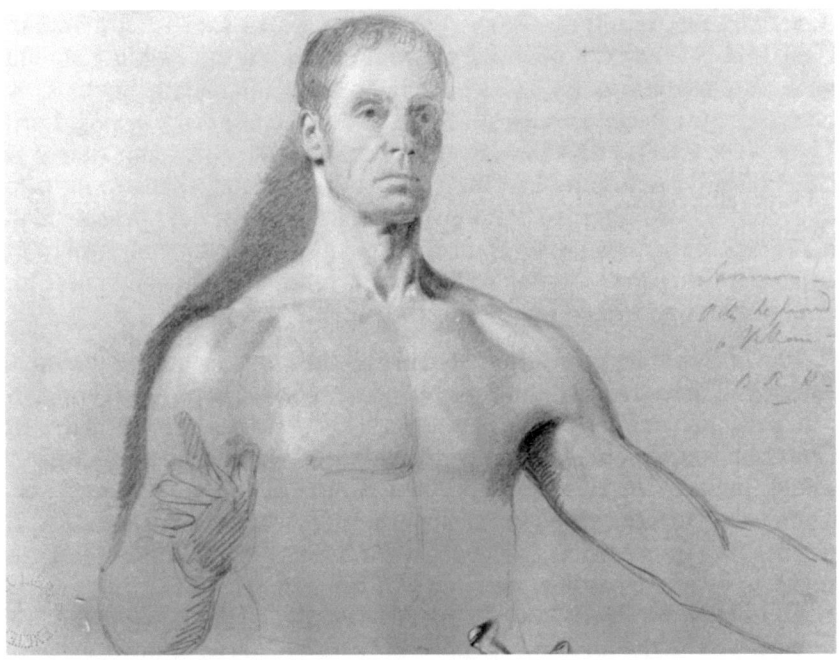

Study for Christ for *Christ's Entry into Jerusalem*. The model was Sammons of the Life Guards ('Pity he proved a Villain!', B.R.H.)

May 2. Went to the Institution to see the Vandykes & Rembrandts lit by lamps. Was amazingly impressed with the care, the diligence, the compleat finish of the works of these great men. Came home & looked at my own Picture. It must be done so, and there's an end.

May 5. The Directors are always guiding Youth but never think of rewarding maturity. Academicians, to be sure, are pretty fellows to scrutinize the purity of principles. I never think of belonging to the Academy but I feel as if I should instantly become from a healthy looking, pure, wholesome being, a yellow, jaundiced, poor, shrivelled creature, as if I had been dipped in a bilious puddle.

May 6. Why does not Payne Knight put forth his reasons for doubting the originality of the Elgin Marbles? Shall a mere connoiseur's opinion be put against the opinion of an Artist? Shall the idle, superficial, conceited, vain glance of a dilettante be of more value than the deep investigating principles & practiced search of the Artist?

Genius enables a Man to conceive events & the passions likely to be called out, & practice & study enables him to execute by the above means the passions he has conceived. When I see this great principle in every figure however small in the Elgin Marbles, is a Connoiseur, a mere man of doubtful taste, to tell me or the public that works with such marks of Genius & Science are doubtful productions? That the Nobility should suffer themselves to be led by such blurred, infatuated, envious, & prejudiced intellects! Dr Clarke too has joined the hue & cry against Lord Elgin – Dr Clarke, who took away all he *could* take away, and sneers at Lord [Elgin] because he had the power to take & did, thank God, take away more. Lord Elgin, to him I owe every principle of Art I possess & to his energy & vigour & perseverance, the Country will ultimately owe right notions & firm principles that will extricate it from the perversion of truth & dereliction generated by the Royal Academy.

May 13. No other professions are cursed with connoiseurs but Poetry & Painting. There are no connoiseurs in War, in Physic, in Surgery. No man will trust his limb[?] to a connoiseur in Surgery; no sweet Girl in Consumption, with her lovely bosom wasting & her sparkling eye sinking, would believe in her recovery if a Connoiseur was her adviser. Connoiseurs never existed in finest periods of Art. They are beings who rise like flies from carrion, in the decay & rotteness of its Works. They are curses to living Artists because their very origin & nature instigates them to value only the dead. Poor Painters & Poets are the beings who are supposed to be the mere mechanism of these creatures' thoughts.

And yet the direction of the public taste and the direction of the native genius in Art is to be left not to those who have spent their lives in the study, but to those who take it up for their amusement to fill an idle day and afford chatter for a dinner.

May 20. For the first time in my life, I have [been] obliged to borrow money of a money lender. A Friend went first & asked him to do it. He consented & appointed me the next morning. I went & shook at the degradation as I entered the door. He received me with a sort of sob, a little, low fellow, with red eyes, his lids hanging down over his pupils so that he was obliged to throw his head back & look at you through the slit, as it were, his eye lids made. I could not speak to him, so he began, 'Well, Mr Haydon, you want to borrow [a] hundred pounds.' 'Yes. I will give a bill endorsed by a Friend so that you will be secure.' He hummed & said he had respect for my talents, but that he feared he could not do it. I really blazed with indignation; he had induced me to come by promising to do it, and now drew back to see what further I could offer. He now said, 'Sit down, Sir.' I sat down. He was shaving. 'You see, Sir, I never like to deal with Gentlemen. I only do business. I have no objection to cash the bill, provided you will take some goods of me.' 'Certainly,' was my reply. 'Walk up stairs in the Front room & look about you. Choose what you like & let me know.' I went up, & found a room full of every thing on earth – Pictures, books, shirts, leather breeches, shoes, hats, jewelry, &c., &c. A rascally sketch of Rubens was placed [so] as to catch my eye, *knowing my love for him.* I saw it at once. I went down & told him I liked that sketch. 'Well, what you'll give?' 'What d'ye ask?' 'Twenty guineas.' 'It's mine,' said I. His little skinny lips drew back & smiled. He became gracious. He talked of my nearsightedness, begged to look at my glasses, tried them on, asked me to try on his, enquired where I got mine, & then wondered that I should be nearsighted as well as he. 'Well,' said he, 'draw out the bill of 122.10, that is, including the interest, and it shall be paid you tomorrow.' 'At what time?' said I. '*My* time is *your* time,' said he. '½ past Seven in the Morning,' I said. 'Yes.'

May 23. I breakfasted with Wordsworth & spent delightful two hours. Speaking of Burke, Fox, & Pitt, he said, 'You always went from Burke with your mind filled, from Fox, with your feelings excited, & from Pitt with wonder at his making you uneasy, at his having had the power to make the worse appear the better reason. Pitt preferred power to principle,' he said.

May 27. I have worked this week intensely & advanced my Picture delightfully, my eyes strong, my mind in fine tune.

June 13. I had a cast made yesterday of Wordsworth's face. He bore it like a philosopher, sitting in the other room in my dressing gown, with his hands folded, sedate, steady, unable to see or speak.

When he was relieved he came into breakfast with his usual cheerfulness. Wordsworth's faculty is describing all these intense feelings & glimmerings & doubts & fears & hopes of Man, as referring to what he might be before he was born & to what he may be hereafter. He is a great Being, and will hereafter be ranked as one who had *a portion* of the spirit of Homer, Virgil, Dante, Tasso, Shakespeare, Chaucer & Milton, but as one who did not possess the power of wielding these feelings to any other purpose but as referring to himself. This is, in my opinion, his great characteristic distinction.

I afterwards sauntered along to Hampstead with him with great delight. Never did any Man so beguile the time as Wordsworth. His purity of heart, his kind affections, his soundness of principle, his information, his knowledge, his genius, & the intense & eager feelings with which he pours forth all he knows affect, enchant, interest & delight one.

June 14. Mr Philips, a member of Parliament, called and seemed much delighted with my Picture. After a little time he said with apparent feeling, 'I have no doubt from your long devotion to historical painting, it is probable you may not be quite easy in pecuniary matters. I intend to have a picture of you, and if you will allow me to present you with 100£ in advance, you will do me great pleasure.' I was really quite affected at such conduct. O God, thy kindness to me is unvarying & steady. Spare my eyes & intellect to the latest gasp of existence.

June 23. What times these are! [The Battle of Waterloo was fought on

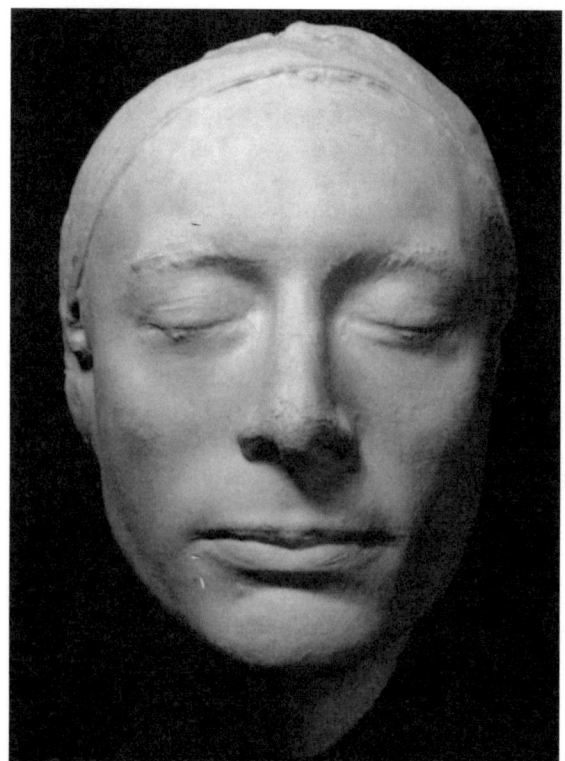

Mask of John Keats

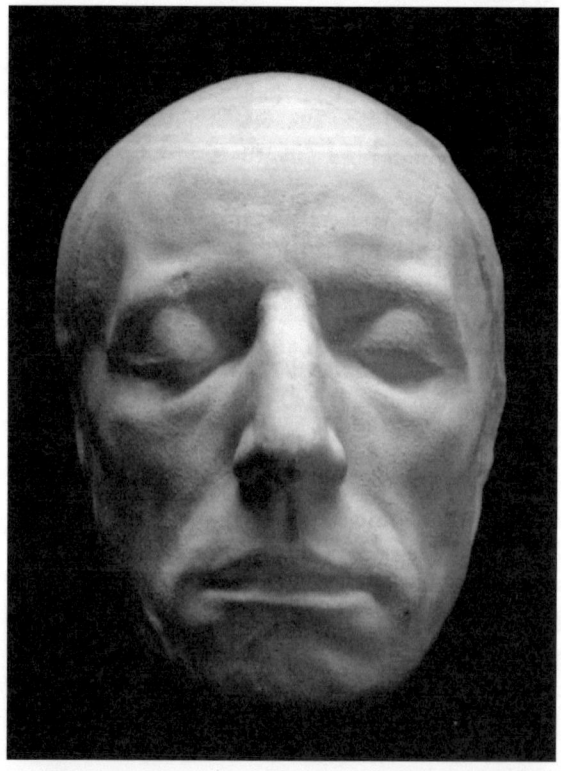

Mask of William Wordsworth, 1815

June 18, 1815.] How often lately has my mind been haunted by Buonaparte. How singularly success operates on our minds. When he was at Moscow, and it was burnt, one thought of him as a tremendous being. When he abdicated one felt a contempt. When he escaped and rushed to Paris, you imagined him like a comet. Now he is again beaten, one knows he will yet struggle, but yet one's apprehension is gone. Really, one cannot think of Wellington & the British Troops without tears. Their constancy & firmness, his genius & prudence. Now will the Imperial Guard say again, 'Napoleon n'etoit jamais battu'? I believe not.

Wellington will truly be considered by Posterity as the Saviour of the World's intellect, for the age would have been brought back to ignorance & barbarism had the Demon succeeded in his despotic system. Great & Glorious Man, my heart beats when I think of him. I only fear he has not a sympathetic heart, and he is not capable of feeling the sensations he excites in others.

I have heard he is now exceedingly affected at losing so many friends. He says nothing but seems exceedingly touched. I shall be happy if it is so. This is only what he wants to render him interesting.

June 28. Sir George Beaumont [called] & settled about the Picture he wishes me to paint for him & paid me 50 guineas in advance. The Academicians who envy this conduct of Sir G. as it relates to me, are beginning to affirm I must have been submissive. Pitiful fellows. No. I have not deviated one wit from my principles of Art, nor will I to my death. Sir George has made the concession to me. I told him I would not paint less than life. He consented & said he had no wish I should. Was I to behave pert & uncivil when a man of his rank behaves with such politeness to me? Surely not. The fact is, the Academy hoped my destruction and urged me on as they thought blindly in the contest, by saying 'Go on, Haydon, you are the Champion of Artists' rights.' Did they imagine I did not see through their motives? Poor fellows. They thought I was young, inexperienced! I played off my age & youth against their weakness. Ha, ha. They felt not the fire I felt within my own breast. At the very time these poor creatures were urging me on in my presence, they were saying at table, behind my back, 'He thinks his talents will carry him through; he is mistaken!' Honourable Gentlemen! I knew all this – & more! Amiable Friends! disinterested Painters! in a word – Academicians!!!

June 30. Went to Hampton Court to study the Cartoons and to ponder upon a National subject. I mused in a hay field till the sun had set and twilight was coming in saffron silence.

July 11. There is something to me infinitely imposing, sublime, & overwhelming in the present degraded state of France & Napoleon Buonaparte. English troops in the Champs Elysees! What a change! What

Benjamin Robert Haydon asleep, by Sir David Wilkie, 1815

a punishment for their presumption, what a glory & reward for our forbearances.

July 15. Saturday. Painted this whole week with intense application. Finished my corner figure. Painted yesterday till I had excrutiating pains in my optick nerve from continued staring.

July 19. It is a melancholy thing to see one makes so little improvement. Drawings I did two years since are just as well as any thing I can do now.

August 6. All my old Friends who remembered me a rosy boy just come to Town but always felt my genius, drank tea after 9 years separation, and we all spent a happy, happy evening. One had been in the Spanish War, another had been to India, & I had been to Paris, and we all listened & Participated in turns. We got into such a humour for laughing from repeated funny stories that the Table shook. When they departed & I came back & felt the silence, where wit & humour & jollity were just before, I relapsed into a muse, a painful muse of why is variety necessary to our enjoyments? Why must we separate to relish meeting? Why must we sleep to relish waking?

What a delightful sight it is, after a shower of rain, to see the dear Women tripping along and tucking their drapery round their lovely hips, now & then giving one a glimpse of a lovely ankle & part of a full leg.

November 19. Sunday. Last night I was introduced by Mr Hamilton to Canova, [the leading sculptor of the period] and was extremely interested. He has a fine Italian head, & when he smiles the feeling sent forth is so exquisite that one fancied music would follow the motions of his lips.

He behaved to me with great affection. He looked at my casts & appeared to take an interest in every thing I had done. He was feelingly & deeply impressed with my present Picture, & at the Gipsey's head in it he repeated 'charmante, charmante.' In shewing some drawings of hands, 'parfaitement bien, vous êtes un brave homme.'

What a paltry set of beings are the R. A.'s, never to pay him any honor, but to vilify & pretend he is coming over here for work! He told me, he had all his life had too much work. 'Come to Rome, vous y verrez la veritable democracie de l'Art,' said Canova. I promised I would. One had a feeling about Canova as if he was, as it were, a descendant of the great. His opinion was an opinion formed at a place where every thing great & good & grand in Art had nursed it; it was coming from head quarters, and I cannot help saying I felt extreme delight in finding principles and conclusions which I had attained from observation on Nature in England, sanctioned by Canova, who had drawn them from both Nature [and] Art at Rome.

November 20. Dear Maria* sat again today and tormented me as I painted, with her lovely archness & wicked, fascinating fun. After sitting some little time, she insisted she could paint the hair better than mine, & taking the brushes out of my hand, she dabbled a lock over the forehead, & then laughed with a rich thrilling at her own lovely awkwardness. I looked at her as she leant over, my hair & cheek accidentally grazed the silk that covered her exquisite bosom – I could have eat her bit by bit – but her Father had trusted her to my honor, & I would have split with passion rather than ventured to have touched her hand. She sat for three hours, with perfect good humour, sometimes singing sweet airs with a honey voice, sometimes mimicking ballad singers. Sweet, Sweet Girl. She found some pretence to go shopping in Bond Street, tho I taxed her that it was only to shew her new flounces to the Bows, which she denied with a blush. Peace & happiness for ever attend her.

November 28. Spent the whole of this day shewing Canova the Duke of Devonshire's &c., &c. He had seen a Picture of Northcote's at Guildhall of Wat Tyler & he asked to see him. We called about half past three, took him quite by surprize. He was in all his glory of filth & beard. It would have been better for Northcote had he never called, I doubt not. He kept bringing out wretched Portraits & at last, conscious what a figure he cut

---

*Maria Foote (later Lady Harrington), daughter of Samuel T. Foote, theatre manager. (See also diary entry April 16, 1815.)

before such a man, he looked up as he spoke, with a twist of his body and a mortified insignificance in his face, his whole air, as it were, assuming a withered littleness, 'we can only paint portraits here.' Poor fellow, I would not have had thy wealth if at the expense of thy feeling at that moment.

December 3. I think Racine in his Iphegenie has lost an opportunity of shewing the deep secret struggles of passion against the consciousness of duty. This decides his inferiority to Shakespeare, who would never have suffered such an opportunity for truth to pass without exhibiting it. The character of Achilles is passion for Glory. When he was told that the oracle has said the Greeks should never proceed to Troy if Iphegenia was not sacrificed, what would have been his first sensations?

What an opportunity to exhibit the glorious struggles in a great breast, those secret whisperings of self, which gleam across the mind and are concealed beneath the smile of — As I read it my heart beat as I approached this crisis, and I was miserably disappointed in finding common place chit chat.

December 5. The Engines in Fuzeli's Mind are Blasphemy, Lechery, and blood. His women are all whores, and men all banditti. They are whores not from a love of pleasure but from a hatred, a malignant spite against virtue, and his men are villains not from a daring desire of risk, but a licentious turbulence of moral restraint. Such a monstrous imagination was never propagated on lovely woman. No. Fuzeli was engendered by some hellish monster, on the dead body of a speckled hag, some hideous form, whose passions were excited & whose lechery was fired at commingling with fiery rapture in the pulpy squashiness of a decaying corpse.

December 31. The last night of this wonderful year. January, March, August, Sep., Octo., Nov., Dec. – seven precious months at this precious time of my life was I wandering about in weak eyes, unable to apply myself a moment, nearly a whole year lost, in consequence of imprudent excess during the latter part of Solomon, when I painted sixteen hours a day six days without ceasing. I hardly slept, and could my strength have lasted, I should have gone mad. My reward was an irreparable injury, I fear, to my constitution. Regular hours of application are more conducive to continuance, tho' I look back on this effort and think it has given me the practice of internal deduction. I made a study of a head & found my hand improved. Thank God. I close this year in humble hope that at the conclusion of the next, my present great Picture will be well near a conclusion. O God grant it, grant no longer weakness of sight may check or harrass me. In thee I trust, Amen. *Finis.*

1816

January 3. I remember after in my own mind I had resolved on being a Painter, I went to a Sale at the Naval Hospital, Plymouth, resolved to buy an edition of Albinus [*Tables of the Skeleton and Muscles of the Human Body*], tho' I had not a farthing. With a beating heart I bid for it and got it. The great thing now was to get my Father to pay for it, so I went and told my dear Mother, and begged her interference, which she promised me & obtained. The next day I copied away swearing I'ld master Anatomy, my head whirling at the idea of going to London to begin life. I remember shewing a pen & ink drawing to my Father, who looked into my face & smiling said, 'how can you be such a blockhead to loose your time so?'

As I learnt the names of the muscles I used to make my Sister hear me, to try if I was perfect. We used, dear Girl, to walk about with our arms round each other's shoulders, I repeating 'levator Scapulae arises – inserted, &c.,' with 'now don't tell me' if I was out. Our house was a house of business and confusion; there was never any solitude or any place for study. I have been routed out of the shop, with my Albinus & drawings, then took refuge in the parlour, then the parlour was wanted to lay the cloth, then I have sat on a landing place close to a window in the staircase, then a good scolding from my Mother for making the stairs in *a litter* has sent me up into the attic, where I made a little hut with large pasteboards enclosing a Window.

January 20. Sir George Beaumont, in answer to a letter, began the old cant, tho with kind intention, about Portraits & his fears & that my Ambition was a laudable one but that Houses were small & fortunes not large and all the old story. I directly fired away one evening after a day of glorious labour, told him I was determined to sacrifice myself, that we must be great in Art or our greatness would ever be incomplete, that if he owned my ambition was a laudable one, it would not be my disgrace if with a *laudable* ambition I was suffered to be ruined.

February 20. The mortalities, the filthy mortalities of life, are enough to make one's heart sick. *I* that should drink nothing but nectar, sleep only upon fleecy clouds, waft with angels by day, & kiss only such by night, *I* with a keen, cutting relish for all the beauties of divine being, who would live & quaff the glories of godhead, have been obliged to have a nasty, filthy, stinking, putrid, ulcerous blister! Yah – to relieve a nasty, thick, puddled, slimy sore throat, I was sick at heart.

March 2. The only model of mine that returned alive from Waterloo called last night. He was made Corporal Major for his gallantry and declared to me he killed 10 cuirassiers and a lancer. I believe it from my heart. He is the most powerful young man I ever saw – six feet three nearly, and a complete instance of what I would wish an English Soldier to be, disgusted with slaughter when left to his reflections, but fierce & terrible & blood thirsty as a Lion when roused! and when fighting was over helping them he had been so dreadfully killing an hour before.

June 2. I rode yesterday to Hampton Court round by Kingston & dined at Richmond. The day is delicious, the hedges smelling of may blossom, the trees green, the leaves full & out, the Thames shining with a silvery glitter, & a lovely girl who loves you, [in] the dining room of the Star & Garter at Richmond, sitting after dinner on your knee, with her heavenly bosom palpitating against your own, her arm round your neck playing with your hair, while you are sufficiently heated to be passionately alive to the ecstasy without having lost your senses from its excess – Claret on the table and the delicious scene of Nature in Richmond Park beneath your open window, moaty, sunny, out of which rises the wandering voice of the cuckoo, while the sun, who throws a silent splendour over all, sinks into the lower vaults & the whole sky is beginning to assume the tinged lustre of an afternoon.

June 4. Went to the Institution by night. Really when I reflect where I was a few years since, and now to see the nobility bow to me & approach me, & beauty whisper & smile with its rosy loveliness, as it speaks & listens,
when I reflect on my innumerable inextricable difficulties, without a farthing in the world of resource, and yet always paying my bills of 200, & 100, & 50 regularly, and always money in my pocket; when I remember that one evening at the time of my deepest want, in the midst of melancholy reflections, an awful voice said within my breast 'Go on,' and on opening the Bible by hazard, with an intention to consult my fate, the first passage I saw was the following one: 'Fear thou not, for I am with thee; be not dismayed, for I am thy God; I will strengthen thee.'

June 30. O God, this is the most trying period of my life. Oppression, desertion, misfortune, were stimulants to effort, roused one's pride, & fired one's energy, but success & praise & perpetual smiles & perpetual public notice are more fatal enemies to manage.

July 3. Imitation of Nature is not the end but the means of conveying intellectual associations. Do you go & look into a lovely woman's face after being satisfied she is beautiful at the distance where you can most conveniently and most effectually see the effect of her form? Certainly, if you go nearer it is not to see but to touch. Skin is a disagreeable object when examined, and to make it the same surface when near as when afar off, would be to produce disagreeable sensations; facility of expression is more delightful than exactly delineated skin.

July 4. A day of the greatest possible enjoyment. I painted 7 hours without fatigue in my eyes. My body is never fatigued; was I not afraid to do too much again for which I have so often suffered, I would have painted 14.

September 11. The Academicians now say I am an artful designing politic fellow; first I was a rash, thoughtless fool, now when they perceive I am likely to stand my ground, I am artful, designing, & politic. Thus it is with envious impotence. They always attribute the actions of those they envy to any cause but principle, & the excellence of their works to any cause but talent.

October 9. Went to Dulwich. Watteau's Pictures always look as if his colours had been the blushes of a beauty, as if he had dipped his brush in the nectar of her lips and never painted till he had warmed his soul with the luscious sparkle of champagne or the fire of bodied Burgundy.

October 19. We are prejudiced, you say, in favour of Xtianity by education, and are not fair judges, and you are prejudiced, I say, with the prejudiced fear of *having been* prejudiced by education, and therefore you are equally in the other direction. My intention of putting in Voltaire by the side of Newton [in the crowd of Christ's Entry into Jerusalem] is naturally making a stir amongst all the Deists in the country.

But why? Surely it is giving Voltaire fair play. I paint the triumph of the author of that religion in whose divinity I firmly believe. I put this author's opponent and ridiculer looking on with a sneer. If Newton is right, Voltaire will be as he ought to be, ridiculous. No, no, my dear Deists. The noise, the bustle, the irritability, the mere intention of putting him where he ought to be put, before my Picture comes out, is a proof of the palpable hit I have made. And rely on this – *he goes in! I'll* risk Posterity.

October 25. Voltaire seems of that order [of] minds which are always mortified that the World should have come to any conclusion on Religion, Art or Science before they came into the World. Thus Mankind are always unjust, ignorant, & superstitious, their decisions are all wrong, & must be all set aright. Such men pass their lives in defending the neglected, and levelling the established, in ridiculing the opinions of ages and substituting others more absurd than those they wish to conceal. The vanity of setting up is as exquisite as the pleasure of pulling down. The contemptibility of the Jews as a nation is all an argument in favour of their inspiration. Why has a nation so little, so contemptible, so mean, been the origin of the Religion of all the civilized part of the Earth?

November 5. Punctuality in money matters involves a great many virtues. To be punctual you must be active, industrious, provided, & foreseeing, whereas neglect of punctuality always is united to indolence, carelessness, & selfish indifference to the inconveniences [of] others. If a man is moral, energetic, & deserving in England, no men are more open & kind than

Bankers & Commercial men. But they must have first something to calculate on, & where they cannot calculate on capital as to money, they are content to do it on good character and principle, as to morals. And are they not right? What is the use of giving with profusion when it would be spent in heartless thoughtlessness? No, no, first of all prove what you are by doing great things with inadequate means, and then you will find plenty rush forward to help you to do greater things with means more adapted.

[The next two pages have been cut from the diary and are now in the National Portrait Gallery; they contain Haydon's profile of Keats, dated 'Nov. 1816' and the 'vile caricature of B. R. Haydon by John Keats'.]

December 3. Wilkie past the evening. He seems to be getting rid of his prejudices and not too rigidly to command his feelings. Never saw him so affected by my Picture. He dwelt on it with mute eagerness, & at last, completely conquered, he said 'It will make a decided impression.' 'God grant it may,' said I. 'It is *very imposing*,' said Wilkie, 'and a great advance beyond Solomon.' We then examined every head with a candle, and criticised each with the severity of the most acid criticks. This is true human nature. It is what we always do to each other the moment that either has expressed a *decided approbation* of what the other has done. When one has acknowledged the success of a month's labour, the other joins in with every censure, and adds notions of error, which escaped the other (wretchedly written).

1817

January 5. It is extraordinary what an influence Genius & reputation have on Women. Without affectation, if I did not perpetually struggle against it, I might do nothing else but doze on lovely bosoms, & sigh out my convulsive soul on rosy lips. Can it be wondered at that men so often fail in their views on the road of life, when these lovely creatures start up from every cluster of flowers, to touch one's heart and chain one's feelings? Then the agony of lost time! Oh, my pangs afterwards are, I hope, the yearning eagerness of high intellect, disgusted with the fierceness of an appetite and tortured at its incapacity to controul what in its beaming perceptions it feels it ought [to] have conquered. How convinced must every man be as he grows older of the truth & soundness of that advice which tends to keep the passions in subjection. Appetite uncontrouled deadens the intellect, pollutes the imagination.

January 20. Dined at Horace Smith's*. Met Hunt, Shelley, & young Keats; became excessively irritable at Hunt's brutal ridicule of Christ and his divine doctrine. I have known Hunt now 10 years, during which we

*Horatio Smith, poet, essayist and novelist.

Sketch of Benjamin Robert Haydon by
John Keats

Sketch of John Keats by Benjamin
Robert Haydon, 1816

have scarcely ever met without a contest about Christianity. I have ever listened patiently to what he has said, and he has ever listened so too, but agitated to what I have answered. After such perpetual contests without effect on either side, one would think he as well as myself must see the uselessness of tormenting each other on a subject in which we cannot from the constitution of our Minds ever come to a similar conclusion. But of late my resolution to put in Voltaire's head into my Picture seems to have brought up all Hunt's bile & morbidity.

My only refuge now is in personal insult, and that I will make a point of inflicting whenever I meet him. This [is] a man who can scarcely talk of a principle he has not violated. Let him look round on his Friends; is there one he has not ill used in money matters? Did [he] not induce his Brother under a sacred promise to put his name to two bills of 250 each, and while *I* and his Brother were fagging about all day in the dirt, in order to raise the money that John might not go to prison, he never came in till three hours after his promise, because it was likely to rain! In domestic matters to his wife he is a tyrant. His poor wife has led the life of a slave, by his smuggering fondness for her Sister. He likes & is satisfied to corrupt the girl's mind without seducing her person, to dawdle over her bosom, to lean against her thigh & play with her petticoats, rather than go to the effort of furious gratification. His wife's Sister, the Aunt of his four little children – is it not cruel to keep his wife on the perpetual rack of waning affection, to praise the Sister for qualities which his wife has not, and which he knew she had not when he married her? This private conduct *must* be mentioned because in private conduct a man shews his real character, being the situation in which he is uncontrouled.

He will do the most dishonorable things. I put my name once to a bill for 45 which I owed him (he scratched out 45 & made it 55, because he wanted more, and then appealed to my friendship after the bill was gone!).

He affects contempt for ribbons & Stars, yet I have seen his face shake at the mention of Lord Erskine bearing a title. If there is to be a revolution and such men are to get at the head of affairs, God help us. A revolution is often talked of by them. How I have smiled in my sleeve. Leigh Hunt's personal cowardice would ever keep him writing instead of acting, & Hazlitt's apprehension of being killed would keep him quiet except with his pen.

I write these faults in a passion, but it is a passion that in its heat pours forth truths which have for a long time been collected.

January 22. Was introduced to Lord Yarmouth at his house, and saw his Pictures. His manners seemed very pleasing. He made himself the person honored, & never you. The great secret of manners is to make every thing *felt* and nothing palpably expressed. He held out every Picture himself in the best light, took my hat out [of] my hand, ran down stairs after a Print, instead of ringing the bell, and when I went away, opened the door & putting his body flat against it to keep it back, called for his Servants with a *suppressed loudness*, as if to say, '*he is coming*'.

January 23. Was introduced to the Grand Duke Nicholas [of Russia] at the Elgin Marbles. He is a fine young, tall, elegant Prince, frank & with good taste, for he was deeply impressed by their beauties.

Before he came in, as I first entered, I was so impressed that after taking off my hat, as I always do when I enter among them, I gave three cheers. 'You are a historical Painter,' said the Duke Nicholas. '*Where are your Pictures?*' Ah, thought I with a sigh, what would have been my answer in Italy or Greece? I told [him] 'Chez un Monsieur in Hanover Square.'

Shelley said he could not bear the inhumanity of Wordsworth in talking of the beauty of the shining trout as they lay after being caught, that he had such a horror of torturing animals it was impossible to express it. Ah, thought I, you have more horror at putting a hook into a fish's mouth than giving a pang to a Mother's bosom. He had seduced Mary Wollstonecraft's daughter & enticed away Mrs Godwin's own daughter, to her great misery. He has now married the former, but this only shews the nature of his mind, and of all such minds who strain at a knat and swallow a Rhinocerous.

January 27. From the specimen I have had of the anxiety attendant on the knowledge of Royal Personages, a Courtier's life must be like the lover of a coquette. The Duke Nicholas promised to call & kept me for two days in a fever of anxiety, starting at every knock, & never came! Alas, he was so inundated with visitors that he could not, but by Heavens, what a life is his that depends on the smile of Princes!

Adieu to his Imperial Highness, an end of my Royal hopes & expectations. After all, what an extraordinary influence Royalty has on a man & on the World. It seems to rub off some of its gold dust on you, as a Butterfly does the down from its silky wing on your fore finger. I said to myself, 'I must be a little more distant, & not be so easily seen or so frank!!!'

January 29. Because Wilkie did not visit Leigh Hunt in Prison, he never forgave him. How did he bear it? Did he nobly forbear in silent contempt? No, but took the first opportunity to make a cowardly attack on his genius and reputation. This is the way he always does. Only tell him home truths and lay open his faults, and the next Examiner will contain a cowardly stab at you. Every Examiner has these assassin stabs levelled at all who have hurt his vanity during the week.

[A portrait sketch, entitled, 'My lovely Mary, when first I saw her', is attached to the diary, with the lower part folded under. On it, however, may be read the following:

> O God that we had met in time
> Thy heart as fond, thy hand more free
> Then thou had'st lov'd without a crime
> And I'd been less unworthy thee.
>   B. R. Haydon.

According to the *Autobiography* (I,240), BRH had met his future wife (1793–1854) in 1816. Born Mary Cawrse, in St Neots, Cornwall, she was at this time married to Simon Hyman, a jeweller of Devonport. BRH said that he fell in love with her at first sight, that he haunted the street by her house for a furtive sight of her, and that he sympathetic treatment of her dying husband and her gentle reproof of his impassioned manner won him for ever. They were married in 1821.]

March 17. Leigh Hunt called & caught me reading Rimini. Old associations crowded on us, & we soon forgot our irritations.

Keats has published his first Poems, and great things indeed they promise. He is a sound young man & will be a great one. There are parts in his 'Sleep & Poetry' equal to any thing in English Poetry. Never was there a truer call! The interest I excite amongst the genius of the Country is certainly very singular. There must be something in me too. I have always wanted one of that furious energy & enthusiasm to pour my heart into, to sympathize with, to comprehend me. Keats is really & truly the man after my own heart. We saw through each other *at once*, and I hope in God are friends for ever. I only know that if I sell my Picture, Keats shall never want till another is done that he may have leisure for his effusions – in short, he shall never want all his life while I live.

April 7. I got some interesting particulars of [Keats'] early life from his Brother Tom, who had them from a Servant, [from] whom they were obliged to find out to ascertain Keats' age that he might come to his property.

He was when an infant a most violent and ungovernable child. At 5 years of age or there abouts, he got hold of a naked sword and shutting the door swore nobody should go out. His mother wanted to go out, but he threatened her so furiously that she burst into tears and was obliged to wait till somebody through the window saw her situation, came, & released her.

An old Lady (Mrs Grafty, Craven Street, Finsbury) told his Brother George, when she asked what John was doing, and on his replying that he had determined to become a Poet – that this was very odd, because when he could just speak, instead of answering questions put to him, he would always make a rhyme to the last word people said, and then laugh. This is true Genius, innate capacity. As he grew up he was put as apprentice to an Apothecary; here he passed a wretched life, translated all the Aeneid without ever having been regularly educated, reading Shakespeare & Spenser & Chaucer, & some times telling his Brothers & in an agony he feared he never should be a Poet, & if he was not he would destroy himself. His master at last continually weary of his dislike to the business, gave him up his time. Before his Mother died, during her last illness he sat up whole nights in a great chair, would suffer nobody to give her medicine but himself, or even cook her food; he did all, & read novels in her easy intervals of ease.

Keats is the only man I ever met with who is conscious of a high call and is resolved to sacrifice his life or attain it, except Wordsworth, but Keats is more of my own age.

May 6. Hazlitt sat to me for a head. I never had so pleasant [a] sitter. He amused me beyond all description. I told him I thought him sound on every thing but Art, that he appeared to me to think there would never be another Raphael. He said, 'Am I not right, *bating* the present time?' 'Certainly,' I said. 'Then,' said he, 'I have nothing to do with the present time; my business is with what has been done.' 'Very true,' said I, 'and if you have nothing to do with the present time, why attack it? Let it alone, at any rate.' Thus his real thoughts were evident. The success of Painting is to Hazlitt a sore affair after his own failure.

May 28. On Monday last there were one thousand and two people visited the Elgin marbles! a greater number than ever visited the British Museum since it was established. It is quite interesting to listen to the remarks of the people. They make them with the utmost simplicity, with no affectation of taste, but with a homely truth that shews they are sound at the core. We overheard two common looking decent men say to each other, 'How broken they are, a'ant they?' 'Yes,' said the other, 'but how *like life.*'

June 28. Dined at Kemble's farewell dinner. A more complete farce was never acted. Many, I daresay, regretted his leaving us, but the affectations of all parties disgusted me. The Drury Lane actors flattering the Covent Garden ones, the Covent Garden flattered in turn the Drury Lane. Lord Holland flattered Kemble; Kemble flattered Lord Holland. Then Campbell, the Poet, flattered Moore (whom I knew he hated), but Tom Moore, like an honest, sensible genius, as he is, said not a word, drank his wine, and flattered no one. This gives me a higher opinion of Moore, would make me feel more inclined to know him, than any thing he has ever written.

Young (another actor of the regular ding dong propriety) made a flaming speech about Mr Kemble &c. and assured the company that nothing but such a system of acting could secure public praise, however *other methods* might produce *temporary* effects, that he had humbly pursued this plan, and hoped he always should &c. Any one would have thought that the English Stage had taken its origin from Kemble – Garrick was never mentioned – when all that Kemble has done for it has been to improve the costume. Yet Kemble is really & truly the Hero of all ranting; all second rate ability find it much easier to imitate his droning regularity than the furious impulses of Kean, who cannot point out when they come or why, but is an organ for Nature, when she takes it in her head to play on him.

October 10. I doubt whether too intense a perception of the identity & colours & substances of Nature is not a clog on the futility of the Invention. Titian took 8 years on the Pietro Martyre, 7 about the Last Supper, not because he was all the time thinking or varying his inventions, but because he did every plant & tree & stump & cloud & distance from Nature, that the means of conveying his ideas might be as perfect as the conception. While Michel Angelo painted Capella Sistina in 20 months, because he was utterly regardless of truth of imitation, except in form, and was satisfied if the mind could comprehend his intention by a hint.

October 13. Hazlitt spent Sunday evening with me.

December 2. Wordsworth is in Town again & looks better than ever. He sat to me today for his head & I made a drawing of him.

December 12. After praying to God to assist me in my present temporary distress, for all the money advanced last Summer had been swallowed up in removal & expences & I then found myself in a delightful house without a farthing to support it. This tortured me, having known the blessings of ease. I wrote Mr Coutts, the rich Banker, who married Miss Mellon, the Actress, & to whom I had been introduced by Mrs Coutts after she had married him.

Sir,
I have had the honour of being introduced to you by Mrs Coutts, and as within this last year I have lodged the money which I possessed in the Bank of which you are the head, my writing to you at all, tho' so great a liberty, will I hope be in some degree palliated. May I proceed at once to detail to you the cause of my conduct?

I have been engaged on a large Picture for three years; thirteen months of that time I have been unable to apply myself from ill health and weak eyes, brought on by intemperate application in the early part of my studies, and by living in a confined situation. During the last Summer I was obliged to remove to a more commodious house, and a better air, or risk by remaining where I then was, the probability of [n]ever being able again to finish another Picture; the means I had thus accumulated to complete my present great Picture of 'Christ's triumphant entry into Jerusalem' were thus swallowed up in the expences of removal, and by procuring the necessaries requisite in household affairs, and I am, Sir, at present with every comfort about me, with a large Painting room, with my eyes & health restored by better air, but all these blessings nearly rendered ineffectual by the prospect of pecuniary want. It is painful when my great Picture is so near completion and fame & reward so nearly within my grasp, to be thus in danger of losing both by the want of temporary assistance. The liberty I thus take with you, Sir, is not and cannot be from any supposition that I can have the slightest right or claim, but from the conviction that you have ever displayed a willingness to assist those, who are disposed to assist themselves. I do not want any sum of money at once advanced but to be allowed to have credit at the Bank, to the amount of my anticipated expences required to bring my Picture to a conclusion, all of which I would by bond promise and undertake to replace within one year. For such credit I would make over my Picture as security; I would insure it, to the amount wanted, and lodge the policies in your hands. The sum I fear I might require would be 400£, which should be repaid within one year with interest. Should you think, Sir, the Security sufficient, and should you be disposed so to favor me, you would thus brighten every prospect of my future life. That you will honor me by an early answer is my sincere wish, and with every hope I may not have marred my own expectations by the daring liberty I have taken.

Believe me to be, respectfully,
B. R. Haydon.

After imagining all sorts of visionary obstructions, a letter came. I sincerely & inwardly prayed for success & opened it. It was as follows.

Strand, 6 December, 1817.

Sir,
I have considered with attention your letter, and I confess tho' my feelings tell me I ought not to consent to the request it contains, considering the great number of a similar kind that are at this very time before me and the impossibility of satisfying a quarter part of them, & the great doubt of any of them succeeding in any adequate manner to the expectations of the Partys, or the hopes I can even imagine myself, yet I feel an inclination to put the sum of Four Hundred pounds in your powers, and to indulge the flattery of seeing by that means your Picture finished, & your fortune established in the manner you have pictured, & the sum I have advanced repaid.

On the other hand past experience almost blasts all my hopes, as I have assisted several in your line in the course of a long life, & have never succeeded; on the contrary I have seen *their prospects disappointed, and my money lost.*

That your case may prove contrary, & that I may see you successful, will give me great pleasure, but indeed I must look to it with very doubtful eyes. But the tryal shall be made. All depends on your exertions, and I shall say no more on the subject now, but conclude with my good wishes.

Sir, your faithful, humble servant,

T. Coutts.

This letter mixed melancholy with my gratitude. Mr Coutts was 80 yrs. of age! Here was the letter of a benevolent man. How different from [the name is scratched out] – him I had known 10 years. He refused. Mr

Coutts not one. The inference is obvious. The next day I received this note.

Sunday, 7 Decem, 1817.

Sir,
   One thing I intended by my letter but unfortunately forgot, which was to request you would never mention to *any person whatever* my having consented to assist you, as it is particularly my wish to avoid being spoken of in matters of the sort and besides it is sure to embarrass me with new applications & complaints from People connected with [me] for my refusing them & granting my aid to a Stranger.
   Your obliging attentions will truly oblige me . . .

I had of course been quite silent.

December 22. Wordsworth sat to me today & I began to put his head into my Picture. He read all the book of 'Despondence Corrected' in his Excursion in the finest manner.

Wordsworth's great power is an intense perception of human feelings regarding the mystery of things by analyzing his own. Wordsworth tries to render agreable all that hitherto has alarmed the World, by shewing that Death, the Grave, futurity are the penalties only to go to a happier existence. What we hope he assures us of. What we fear he exhibits without apprehension; of what we have a horror he reconciles us to, by setting it before us with other associations. Wordsworth is the Apostolic Poet of Piety & Pure thoughts, because his intensity of purpose is so strong. His object is to reform the World, by pointing out to it how it *ought to be.*

December 26. Got in Newton's head. Voltaire, Newton, & Wordsworth make a wonderful contrast.

December 28. Wordsworth dined with me; Keats & Lamb with a Friend made up the dinner party, and a very pleasant party we had. Wordsworth was in fine and powerful cue. We had a glorious set to on Homer, Shakespeare, Milton, & Virgil. Lamb got excessively merry and witty, and his fun in the intervals of Wordsworth's deep & solemn intonations of oratory was the fun & wit of the fool in the intervals of Lear's passion. Lamb soon gets tipsey, and tipsey he got very shortly, to our infinite amusement.

He then attacked me for putting in Newton, 'a Fellow who believed nothing unless it was as clear as the three sides of a triangle.' And then he & Keats agreed he had destroyed all the Poetry of the rainbow, by reducing it to a prism. It was impossible to resist them, and we drank 'Newton's health, and confusion to mathematics!' There was something interesting in seeing Wordsworth sitting, & Keats & Lamb, & my Picture of Christ's entry towering up behind them, occasionally brightened by the gleams of flame that sparkled from the fire. I never passed a more delightful day, & I am convinced that nothing in Boswell is equal to what came out from these Poets. It was an evening worthy of the Elizabethan age.

December 31. The last day of 1817. In reviewing the year, I have more to thank God for than during any year of my life. I still remain ignorant, nearly so, of the anatomy of the horse. I do not know enough of perspective, but in power of painting, I am visibly improved.

This year I changed my habitation and on the whole the Art is advanced. My pupils have made drawings which have astonished all. Of young Bewick I have the greatest hopes; he will be the honor of the Country. I have another in training I picked up at Oxford last summer, & I think he will shine also. I hope my own Picture may create a sensation and give a shock, and that the prejudices of the Country may be effectually destroyed.

Finis – ¼ past eleven at night. Lisson Grove.

TWO

1818–1825

1818

January 15. Wordsworth sat to me for a chalk sketch of his head. He sat like a Poet and Philosopher, calm, quiet, amiable. I succeeded in a capital likeness of him, and when it is framed shall send it to him as a mark of my affection – he was the first who wrote me a sonnet – when such a thing was indeed an elevation.

January 24. From January 15th to this day – I have been laid up in my eyes and have done nothing.

January 26. This is my Birth Day – I am thirty two, and now 'pour toujours s'est passée la fleur de ma jeunesse.' Adieu! adieu! I have passed half of the ordinary extent of man's life. I must now decline imperceptibly to the grave, but O God, spare my eyes for 10 years & I will make myself eternally remembered. Spare them, I humbly entreat thee, Amen.

January 27. I don't know when I have been so melancholy [as] at finding myself thirty two, thirty two, thirty two, thirty two. I'll shave my head & be cropped. I went out to Wilkie yesterday and we condoled on our altered health – on the passed glories of our youth. My youth has been passed in Love, Study, Fame, & Fighting, & now I am reaping the reward of each; my constitution is shaken by the two first & my mind balmed by the two latter.

March 27. Dissected the fore half [of] an ass, & gained immense knowledge. My head now beginning to be cleared of my ignorance of the animal.

March 31. I drew 9 hours again & the next day my eyes were strained. All that day I was obliged to lay by steaming & fomenting.

April 2. I bless thee in gratitude that my health is improving. Amen. O God have mercy on me – grant my present picture compleat & glorious success, and that a new & a glorious Aera in British Art may begin. Grant me the means to keep my present happy & healthy situation. Grant I may die at the right time.

April 5. The English are the people perhaps the soundest in feeling as to proprieties in the World. No nation has a stronger or deeper feeling of the rights of domestic happiness & sympathy, no nation will sooner rise with one voice to repel any intrusion on the privacy of Domestic rights, yet no nation feels greater disgust at a man's obtruding on the World what regards his domestic concerns only; and as they will not suffer others to intrude on him, so they shrink from any attempt of his to intrude upon them.

May 8. The progress of one's manners to one like myself not educated like a Nobleman is a curious matter of reflection. 9 years ago a great many ladies of rank called on me to see Dentatus; being then a secluded student, I behaved awkwardly, timidly & contemptibly: instead of handing them to their carriages with a manly and a frank air of confidence, I stood with the fore door in my hand & peeped at them through the doorway. At the Institution today a Lady of high rank was going to her carriage; another Lady said, 'Mr Haydon will attend you.' I flew instantly, offered her my arm which she took, and [in] the presence of all, I handed her out, & into her carriage perfectly at ease and retiring stood at the entrance till she drove off, bowing to her as [I] caught her eye. On reflection I found my address improved.

May 11. Keats, Bewick, & I dined together, Keats brought some friend of his, a noodle. After dinner, to his horror when he expected we should all be discussing Milton & Raphael &c., we burst into the most boisterous merriment. We had all been working dreadfully hard the whole week. I proposed to strike up a concert. Keats was the bassoon, Bewick the flagellet, & I was the organ & so on. We went on imitating the sounds of these instruments till we were ready to burst with laughing, while the Wise acre sat by without saying a word, blushing & sipping his wine as if we meant to insult him.

May 12. O God, in thee I trust; spare my sight to finish my Picture, humbly, humbly beg thee. Amen.

[The next five pages of the diary are not in Haydon's handwriting, but were, as he wrote at the end, 'Dictated to Bewick while my eyes are ill.']

May 29. The greatest curse to society is the delicate irritability of medical men. Many a wife, many a mother, many a child and many a sweet girl have been sacrificed from the apprehension of their relatives to offend a medical attendant by hinting at a wish for further advice. It is quite interesting at first entering an Oculist's room to wait for your turn, a crowd of blinded people filling the room makes one melancholy and musing; however after a little while it is quite laughable to see the vanities and weaknesses of human nature bursting out even under the influence of complaint. Some people whom you talk to took care to inform you there was nothing the matter with their *eyes*, only their *lids*, while others quite hopeless of any triumph let their vanity take refuge in the very hopelessness of their situation. Old ladies would whisper to you what Sir Wm. [Adams] thought of *their* complaint and mothers would stand with their children upon the table and taking off the bandage from their eyes, explain to us what *little martyrs* they had been. Oh, human nature! thus are thy vanities and follies a balm and a salve for thy *miseries and complaints*.

July 9. Such is the propensity in human beings to become objects of interest to each other, that when they cannot excite attention by their virtues or their talents, they make no scruple of boasting of their crimes; when neither crime, virtue, or talent are of sufficient consequence to attract attention, you will find them claiming precedence on account of their diseases.

December 31. This Year has been the Year of the greatest glory & greatest misery united, perhaps greater than 1814.

For six months I have been laid up in my eyes in torture of mind & body, but what of that? I had a light within which ever animated me. I always feel as if my heart beats in a sunny ray. All these troubles & hindrances are but judicious obstructions of my leading Genius, to cause such a working up before I again appear before the public, as will greatly enhance & encrease my future fame! I am sure of it & Time shall shew it. My mind is greatly encreased in strength & capability to resist vice. This is a blessing. Grant me always, O God, an eternal sensation of thy eternal presence. Protect me, grant I may live to see the glory of England in Art, as it has ever been my object from sixteen to now. Amen, Amen, Amen.

1819

January 11. O God, I bless thee for the effectual blessing I have received at the beginning from one who was my early employer & Friend. I wrote him. In consequence of my illness my means had wasted & my Picture was yet to do. I asked him to assist me & he sent me £200 which he said he did for the sake of the Art; & insisted I would not consider it a debt, for he knew how much the feeling of a debt incurred must impede the progress of an Artist. This was Thomas Hope & he shall not repent it.

There is an instinct existing in the World of what a Genius ought to do in order to develope his powers to their full stretch. If he is found with a bottle of wine accidentally, drinking one glass for his health, the *world fear* he drinks! If he is met walking with a fine woman, they begin to be alarmed at his *probable dissipation*! It seems to be a wise remission of nature to act as a check upon the weaknesses of great men. A Man of Genius is never forgiven if he does not succeed, from *whatever cause*.

I must own I get more & more estranged from Wilkie every day; his nasty detestable heartlessness, his mean sacrifice of his feelings to his interest, render him a very disgusting man. Wilkie never changes his shirt without first reflecting whether he may not commit himself by so doing in the eyes of the World. Wilkie is a man who never puts on his night cap without first reflecting with due consideration the way he must place it, with the least injury to his personal interest and the least chance of committing himself in the eyes of the World. He never calls, from any pleasure he feels in being with you, to relieve the irksomeness of illness, to chat in friendly intercourse, to pass an hour. No; he finds himself in your neighbourhood on business too early for the tea of the person to whom he went; he so arranges that your tea hour shall suit his convenience – he calls, – as soon as tea is over, you can perceive he is masking his eagerness to be gone that he may pay another visit. Cut open his bosom when he dies – do you expect to find a *heart*? Alas no, you will discover after searching a cold, icy, hard, impenetrable Scotch pebble!

(The opposite observations on Wilkie were written after my illness, and when I was cut deeply by Wilkie's shameful neglect – but they are too severe. Since then I sold one of Wilkie's small Pictures for him to a friend of mine, and this seems to have made a visible impression on his heart; he left off his unjustifiable behaviour entirely & we are now better Friends – in short excellent Friends. October 1819.)

January 31. On Saturday last was the proudest day of my life. [BRH opened a private exhibition of eight cartoons by his pupils Bewick and Charles and Thomas Landseer on Saturday, January 30.] When I returned home I had nothing to do but retire to my closet & humble myself in the presence of my Creator. I can write no more at present.

March 17. O God, grant me patience to bear up under my calamatous debility of sight. Amen.

April 10. Fuzeli says my dead Child in Solomon is stinking. Perhaps it may be. There is at least some excuse, it is *dead*, but which excuse can we find for those who make their living figures *stinking*?

He says my two Counsellors are Jews, that they would be incongruous in Ananias, & that none of the Apostles have that appearance. In Ananias Jewish Counsellors would be incongruous, so would a crown on St Peter's head! But are there not Jews in the Transfiguration? and ought there not to be Jews? What short sighted cavilling.

April 11. There is something in the Fate of Servants that always makes me melancholy. Born to a lower station, destined to have their views narrowed to the will of others, considering as much a necessity their habits & hardships as that the sun shall rise or the stars set. They breakfast after us, dine on coldish meat & colder potatoes, rise earlier & go to bed later. How their hearts beat at a holiday! How carefully are the best gown & white stocking & new bonnet & pink ribbon & yellow gloves put on; how anxiously do they contrive to know if their masters want anything before they go, *after they are dressed*, in order that they may have an excuse to shew themselves! Poor creatures. No doubt there are exceptions, but I talk of the principle in which a race of beings are born & live & die for ever an inferior one! Once when I was in the Kitchen in the House came a thundering rap at the [door]. All the Servants started up, with 'there's *master.*' All stood still, for all expected each would go. 'Why don't you go, John, & Sally,' went from one to the other. At last one went. Why should a set of human creatures start up when another knocks? When they are ill, how long they bear it without complaint, working daily, when [they] should be nursed & brothed & flannelled. Such is the condition of life; some must work & some play. They have their ambitions & their hopes, their jealousies & their loves & their emulations. They see us daily take our wine & eat our tarts, and yet their minds are so influenced as to act under the impression that such things are not for them. Poor souls. Peace to them.

April 14. The reason why men in general obey the orders of others, is that they are happy for an opportunity to display their power when they are not responsible for the consequences. This will also account why men are always found to execute the most cruel orders, as there are always numbers who are willing to tyrannise, in a belief that as they did [not] originate the cruelty, they will not be answerable for doing it.

I have puzzled at this for these two years & have not got it yet.

All men have a love of power, but not equal capacity to gratify it. They therefore will submit to be directed by others, if in that submission, others must be directed by them.

July 7. My pecuniary difficulties are now more dreadful than ever. My Friends, my rich ones, tired of helping me because sickness has so long delayed my Picture, yet I thank God I never felt in better spirits, never had more confidence in my great Protector, never had higher urgings!

July 25. Piety & belief must be to Byron the most dull & leaden of feelings. The torture of doubt, the agony of crime, or the anticipated horrors of damnation are necessary to make him think of Religion at all. He must prefer the Satanic grin of a fallen devil to the lovely mildness of a cloudless face. The great error of such minds is that because this World is scarcely worth more than a laugh, they distrust the goodness of God for putting them into it, and with a desponding curse, relinquish all hopes of another.

October 3. Wilkie, Scott & Otley dined with me and a very pleasant day we had. After dinner we insisted that Wilkie the tory, the cautious tory Wilkie, should drink success to Reform! He resisted a long time, kept putting his glass up to his mouth, & begging for mercy. We then affected great candour, appealed to his gentlemanlike feelings, and with a face like Pistol when he was forced to swallow the leek, he said 'Must I eat?' 'To be sure,' said I. He said 'Success to Re – re – form, (but very moderate, remember).' We roared at our triumph.

October 6. Wilkie sat to me for Christ's hand, & seemed full of remorse for his imprudence on Sunday. When you do not touch his interest or his professional passions there is not a more delightful fellow for amiable feelings than Wilkie.

October 4. The three great grounds of my belief in Xtianity are as follows: I believe & can prove to my own mind the truth of the prophecies; 2ndly, I can prove to my own mind the truth of the miracle of the lame man; 3rd, I can prove that in no system of Ancient Philosophy is a future life so decidedly stated as in Xtianity, or repentance & charity so essentially made the means of converting the wicked & miserable. Hume and these men say they will not believe a miracle; therefore if they are determined not to believe what might happen, of course they would not believe it if it did, and their minds are not in a state for conviction; their minds are in an unnatural state, & have not the full exercise of their perceptions, because they set out with premising that a thing cannot be which we know *may* be, because nothing is impossible with God.

If the evidence in favour of the miracles is adequate to prove & would prove a common historical fact, no man has a right to deny assent and if he does, his mind is not in a fit state to judge of the probability.

October 8. Sir George & Lady Beaumont called on their return from Antwerp, full of Rubens in which I heartily & cordially joined. He is the most glorious fellow living. His touch always goes into my marrow with sensation. What they said about my Picture had double value in consequence of being so fresh from such fine things.

Because the Apostles disagree in the relation of the events of Christianity, is this any proof of their falsehood? Suetonius says Nero witnessed the fire of Rome; Tacitus denies it; does either invalidate the truth of the fact that Rome was burnt?

December 4. It is a calumny, a vile infamous calumny, that the character of the people of England has changed. The character of their rulers have changed from continental connection, but the people of England are the same loyal, religious, great, energetic, glorious people as ever.

Did not the people of England prove themselves the same great people at Waterloo as at Agincourt, Cressy, & Poitiers? Did not they make for 20 years the most tremendous sacrifices, for the safety & liberty of themselves & Sovereigns of Europe? & ought they not after such sacrifices & such forbearance to have had their petitions for reform, respectfully drawn up & legally presented, treated with common respect? Most assuredly they ought, but how have they [been] treated? In a way that disgraced the Government & the Sovereign. The Ministers of the country, unable to meet the legal & just demand of the English people, conjured up a plot in the metropolis, the great share of the liberties of this grandest people in Europe suspended in order, as it was affirmed, to secure the traitors to the Constitution, traitors which the Ministers themselves created. Exasperation was the consequence, the press teemed with blasphemy & passion, because its first appeals in terms of reason & forbearance were treated with contempt & neglect.

& now taking advantage of the very irritation which the Government has fomented, the constitution is violated, restraints imposed, and all the glories of that Freedom dimmed by those who, by their Grocer's shop talent, would never have risen to distinction. Consider for a moment to what a period we are come, when Whigs, Tories, Reformers, & Methodists could hear Castlereagh mention a Censor on the British Press and not start from their seats as if a viper stung them. Consider this of Englishmen, and then you will see to what a pitch of degradation your minds are arrived.

The Freedom of the English press was the great cause of complaint with all the Sovereigns of Europe, because whenever they might blind their own subjects as to their conduct, in England they were sure to be scrutinized with truth.

Any man knows that when he has been in intercourse with the higher order of Society for any time, a sort of contempt for popular rights creeps insensibly on his mind. The good sense of the middle classes alone can save us. The higher order are so cramped by false delicacies, & the lower so stimulated by inherent passion that unless the middle classes sacrifice their temporary interests to the safety of their religion & constitution & firmly & temperately insist on reform, the day of England's greatness is past, past for ever! & the day of infidelity or despotism, civil blood & desperate struggle will succeed; France must rise as we sink & at last will step in & complete our ruin.

Napoleon has done an irreparable injury to liberty by shewing the feasibility of complete & systematic despotism. He has given the clue to those already in power by his principle of training the mind.

December 31. As I always have reflected a little at the conclusion of every year, I must not let this conclude without returning thanks to God for his mercies during this one, which is now on the point of ending. I thank him from my heart for having so recovered my health as to have been able to devote myself to my Picture, and bring it under his goodness to a state of forwardness that borders on completion. Continue to me the same vigor & activity of mind, bless my pupils, enlighten their understanding, & grant them equally sufficient firmness to resist & conquer the difficulties they may meet. I am engaged in a hazardous plan; as far as it is consistent with virtue, bless it, bless it with success!

This last year of 1819 has been on the whole the year of most delight and vigorous activity of mind & body since I began the Art, and I am really in better health at this moment than I have been for years. I am more regular, have greater command of my passions, & on the whole am better pleased than ever before at the conclusion of any preceeding year.

Thee, O God, I bless & hope I shall not deserve punishment by any obtrusive confidence, Amen, Amen, Amen.

1820

January 3. I plunged into the city today and after five hours incessant walking, returned light hearted, having by God's mercy arranged all my difficulties for the coming month, & tomorrow I go to the back ground like a Lion to his prey after a day's fast.

January 7. I think I have succeeded in the back ground, for which I thank God.

It is not the common expression of grief & pathos that I wish to represent, but some thing at this moment higher, the feeling of unknown martyrdom, calm, prophetic, resolved. At this moment the Pharisees told him to rebuke his disciples & [about five illegible words] he replied if they were silent the very stones would cry out.

February 20. O God, who has so wonderfully protected me through my difficulties to the end of my great Picture, accept now my heart felt gratitude that thou has listened to the prayer I uttered at its commencement, viz., that in spite of all obstructions thou wouldst be pleased to let me conclude it in a grand & magnificent manner. I have under thy mercy brought it to a conclusion. O bless it now it leaves the house this day, bless it when exposed to public view, grant it may keep alive Christian feeling, grant it may meet success & enable me to discharge those debts incurred during its progress. Amen, Amen, with all my Soul.

March 31. It is singular & glorious that after having so thanked & prayed, I sit down to recount one of the most glorious triumphs of my life! The Picture got safely down, was safely put up, after great effort. The frame weighed 600 lb. weight, & snapped an iron ring at the attempt. I glazed it in a week, my eyes & strength keeping invincible, but positively worked my shoulders & body to exhaustion. On Thursday before the Saturday, the private day, the stuff to hang the room with could not be got for colour. I started away into the City, obtained it at a wholesale house, brought it back in a coach, made the upholsterer bring up all his women, six, promised them a guinea to work hard, & by Friday night all was sewed, nailed, & the whole Picture ready!

I came into the room! All was still. The sun shone on my Picture, which really looked impressive! The chairs were all arranged in battle array. What, thought I, if nobody comes! I could not bear the idea, so I walked into St James Street & read the papers without remembering a word. I now went back & Salmon told me Sir William Scott had gone in. I felt relieved! By degrees People dropped in & before four o'clock all was bustle, anxiety, admiration, & enthusiasm, especially with the dear, dear women, whose hearts & souls are always open to pathos & passion. A great many were wavering about Christ, when Mrs Siddons, in her solemn & sublime tone, said, 'It is decidedly successful! and its paleness gives it an awful & supernatural look.' This was not said to me, but reported. I sent back my everlasting gratitude, & was introduced.

The day was indeed glorious, & I retired home oppressed with a roar of sensations.

March 30. Today I was introduced to Walter Scott & was exceedingly interested. His expression denoted a kind, keen, prudent, deep man, his conversation great relish for Nature, & for no part of her works more than for those of vice & humour mixed. He told us stories of Dick, a smuggler who had broke his arm & always had it shorter, had one eye, & was so well known to the Magistrates as to be rather in sympathy with their good wishes. Dick was transported and was found a year or two afterwards in the Country. On being brought before them, they seemed half pleased to see their old acquaintance, & yet with awful anger asked Dick how he dared return, to which he answered, 'please your honors, I did not like *the Climate!*'

April 16. The impertinence of the Scotch writers since the success of Walter Scott & Wilkie, two men of solid genius, only proves how new success is to the nation, & how unaccustomed they have been to produce men who deserve it. Having been for years a sort of rejected people, despicable for the love of money, pitiable for the poverty, & hateful for the [two illegible words], they are [in] such extacies to find themselves not as stupid as the Beotians, that they flourish their maiden swords with the random rashness of young recruits. Scotch have the vanity of the French without their liveliness, the pride of the Spaniards without their generosity, the avarice of the Jews without their necessity, the filthiness of the Russians without their ignorance to palliate their beastliness, & the cunning of the Italians without their sensibility to excuse its excess.

If a man has met with public sympathy in success, he should appeal to it. Twice has the public approbation saved me from ruin, & I appeal to it at this moment as my last resource. I do not want provision for the decline of my life, I wish only the common means of subsistence.

Notwithstanding it has been received with enthusiasm by all classes, notwithstanding the press has burst forth in unanimous approbation, not one individual or public body or nobleman has even from curiosity enquired the price. Do they imagine without fortune [I] can devote six years to one work & exist without food? Does not an historical painter have the same wants as any other individual? Had the subject of this Picture been a dutch boor making water in a corner or disgorging the contents of a filthy stomach in his mistress's lap, how would Courtiers & King, Ministers & Nobility have crowded forth to become its eager purchasers – but Christ entering Jerusalem in triumph was not for them.

July 8. How any one who has slept on the bosom of a sweet woman can ever use any woman, but especially *that* woman *ill*, is to me extraordinary!

Perhaps the most delightful moments on Earth, that is the most delightful thing as to calm consciousness, is the chat that takes place with a lovely woman in bed, after having proved vigourously your manhood to her, when you begin to recover from the perspiring stupor of intoxication & rapture. This book is a picture of human life, now full of arguments for religion, now advocating virtue, then drawn from chaste piety, & then melting from a bed of pleasure, idle & active, dissipated & temperate, voluptuous & holy! – such are the elements of that mysterious, incomprehensible, singular bit of blood, bottom, bone, & genius, B. R. Haydon!

August 9. Had the Directors purchased my Picture this year they would have given an impulse to the Art of which they are not aware, but they suffered private pique to operate against their public duty. I am born, I now see, to have all my virtues elicit themselves by opposition & difficulty. God only grant me health. I am at this moment in as much want as ever, & have paid £1300 since 1st of April, & though my exhibition brings 6 & 8 £ a day, it goes like lightening.

August 14. Oh! If my mind & Soul could but once get clear from that leaden clog, pecuniary difficulties. If my mind could but once act without anticipating obstruction, it would act with more power than it has ever done yet.

September 21. I have passed the most enchanting fortnight mortal creature ever passed on Earth. I was sitting musing one evening, alone as usual, when a Coach turned into my road, & stopped at the door. I heard a sweet female voice enquire if I was home, & before I could collect my senses the loveliest creature that ever was created darted into the room with the air of an angel; my heart filled with nervous pulsation. I thought I knew her; the shades being over my candle I could not see distinctly, when in a tone of voice melting with tenderness she said 'don't you know me?' 'Good Heavens – Mary!' I could not say more – it was the sweet creature with whom I had been on the Thames 3 years ago, to see the opening of Waterloo bridge! On that sunny lovely day, when we glided away up the glittering river & passed the evening in sunny shade & sweet conversation! My poor heart opened as if by the touch of a talisman – she was the only creature I ever really loved – & totally subdued by her loveliness & her frank throwing herself in my way the instant she arrived in London, I concealed nothing; she told me her feelings for me were the same & ever would be, & so we kissed & swore eternal fidelity. The next day we strolled into a lovely meadow near Kilburn, and affected by the beauty of day, sat down in the sun and disclosed our feelings to each other in the tenderest strain. By the next evening I was totally subdued by her witchery & willingly so; for she is the only woman I ever knew but one who has not a particle of the devil in her – if God bless my efforts in a year I will marry her. I spent a fortnight in painting her sweet head, in making studies from her lovely face for my next Picture; her fun & humour are natural & undesigned & ten times more effective. She is an Englishwoman & a perfect one, & though as full of love & sensibility as an Italian, has a frankness which renders her superior – tender, gentle creature! I have never seen thee but in sun shine, the very air & atmosphere seem to breathe about thee as if they felt thy influence. During the fortnight she was with me, the weather was enchanting, as it looks in Claude's Pictures, and shone on her lovely face with a sort of sleeping quiet & love. She acknowledged I had her heart, she consented to marry me whenever I thought fit – & having it thus settled, the day came for separation! I caught the last flash of her divine head & turned away; she drove off. I felt as if a part of my side had fallen off, & taken half my sensations. When I entered my house, my poor, forlorn, & miserable House, it looked as if a lovely meteor had disappeared & left it dim & wretched; there stood the chair that she had sat in, the books she read, the glass she had looked in – Dearest Mary, her presence this last fortnight has fixed me as to marriage; with my habits it would be a great blessing & relieve, delightfully relieve, the anxieties of thinking. About two evenings before the last, we drove round Highgate & Hampstead, and on entering the Heath the sun was gloriously setting. What moments these are, Good God! – they must be momentary anticipations of a higher state of existence! I slid one arm round her lovely waist, touched & pressed her hand, perspiring & warm; she looked round like an angel, with that sort of grave intensity of passion one sees when it is deep! trembling from head to foot; I slowly approached her breathing mouth, & kissed lips that pouted, warm, tender, moist, & soft! Overpowered, she acknowledged I had her heart & that she had never known so dear a moment. As if smiling at our love the sun dropt from beneath a golden cloud & shone out on the joyous landscape! Birds, sheep, all nature seemed to partake of our sensations, the very trees waved & sighed. Sweet creature! Her private History is as affecting as her beauty is enchanting. At 16, she was such an exquisite girl & so persecuted by men of fortune, that her friends hurried her into a marriage with a man old enough to be her Father, because he was rich; – he was ruined and died! I knew her before, but she kept me at a distance, though I saw I had touched her heart. The way she did all her duties to this man doubled in my eyes the effect of her beauty. She is now single. At her husband's death, feeling my precarious & dangerous situation, I thought it my duty not to involve a lovely creature in my perils, & kept my passion to myself till I had better prospects; her conduct during this time was unexampled. For two years, beautiful & pestered to death, uncertain of my real intentions, she suffered. At the end of that time she determined on a journey to Town; & strange as it may appear, I was thinking of going down to see how she was going on, and if she was the same creature, to make her an offer. Dearest Mary, may no unlooked for event obstruct our intentions!

September 23. Heard from my dearest Mary, who arrived safely. O God, grant no unforeseen obstruction may hinder our marriage, but grant, I humbly pray thee, we may be married.

The scenes I have passed with this dear creature shine inwardly & suddenly in my brain with such intensity that I start up! like one caught up by something supernatural.

September 26. Heard again today to the full extent of my wishes. The leading Star in the Horizon of my life has hitherto been *ambition*; Love has now lifted its glittering & beautiful head, into the mild Heaven, where without weakening the power, it softens the fierce shine of the other.

She is a Juliet in Love, an Imogen in sweetness, & a Miranda in openess of disposition; but herself alone in adding to these delightful requisites a voluptuous tenderness, without which no woman interests me. May she be my wife. May my wife be as Mary is, a mixture of Penelope & Sappho. She would not hurt a fly & would rather injure herself than give pain to a human Creature.

September 29. Every hour & day adds strength to my feeling for this dear Girl; as I walk along it comes over me like as if I suddenly ascended into a hot cloud! O God, do not let any accident prevent our marriage. Why did I ever let her go till it was done – I declare to God if I did not think it would take place, my relish of life would be gone. Society is better off with marriage than without it; it keeps up appearances, but then it ingenders intrigue, hypocrisy, lying, meaness, & deceit. The consequence of *lawful*, unrestrained intercourse would be ruin; so that marriage is the best method of regulating that intercourse.

Men never look at Women without the association of intercourse immediately following; it is not so with Women. The habitual restraint of their early lives checks this feeling & when they submit it is really from sentiment & not from mere wantoness of appetite.

Men wane first in love, especially in England, get fond of eating, drinking, or hunting, and leave their wives to nurse & read novels. Women in the heat of blood have feelings as well as us, especially after marriage. If men & women would but keep up a little of the art, after marriage, they used before, they might live longer in delusion, in tranquillity & peace.

But what pangs does a Young Man suffer as the vices of those who pass in the World for virtuous open upon him; when he meets in Society Women passing for examples to their sex, received by others & respected by all; than whom, he knows in secret, 'none go to it with a more riotous appetite.' What must he think of the World? I wonder any pure young Man keeps his senses at the first winters in London.

As a matter of curiosity, what a spectacle the Day of Judgement will be! when all disguises will be torn off; when all concealments laid open! As much good will come as evil, many crimes in the eyes of the world will be ameliorated by an all-wise judge from circumstances, how many culprits will be pardoned! how many hypocritical judges condemned! How many dear Women who have sunk slandered from envy, will freeze their slanderers with a look, before him who knows all hearts, all motives.

There is in this World such a continued tendency to perfection, both morally & physically, & such a continued check from imperfection of material, that there must be a higher state of existence, a day [of] retribution, to set all to rights.

A Woman remembers when her husband was a lover, when he sprang for her gloves, sighed at her looks. A Woman never forgets this delicious time & *always* regrets it. The lover as husband is immersed in providing means for his children; he has no time to be alive to the pleasure or fancies of his wife. This is the history & origin of half the adulteries in the World.

November 1. I saw a Snyders today enough to make one's heart & soul leap with ectacy! it was a Picture of grapes, cabbages, pumpkins, cucumbers, rosy apples, a snub nose boy, an ugly Flemish woman, a wheel barrow, & a wicket basket! – a Scarlet jacket, & purple petticoat, but oh, what painting! What colour! luscious white cabbage leaves dying into emerald green & ending in deep crimson – velvet tinted grapes wet & moist! green gourds with golden streaks & silken apples, ruddy, tawny, mellow, & shining! painted as if the tip of his pencil had tasted the sweets of each & had bathed its long hairs in their juicy liquour! I never saw tints so exquisite, colour so delicious, tone so fresh without rawness, or execution so daring without crudity. I declare to God I shall never forget it – its beauties are burnt in on my fancy.

I left Town Nov. 18th in the mail & got to York* the next night.

November 26. I dined with Sir W. Scott [in Edinburgh] last night and was exceedingly delighted with the friendly unaffectedness of his reception. I saw it was genuine nature. He said the Scotch, he feared, were more revengeful than English & Irish, & that in their number of crimes revengeful murder predominated in their proportion. I told him I had walked that morning over Salisbury Crags, & admired the prospect, 'Ah,' said he, 'Mr Haydon, when I was young I used to delight in that walk, but that time is over.'

December 8. Left Edinburgh for Glasgow. Glasgow fine streets, fires enormous, houses hot, same smell as in Edinburgh, the look of manufacture & abomination. Set out again after securing a room for my picture [Christ's Entry into Jerusalem] for Penrith. Travelled all night, & on rolling over a bridge near Gretna Green into England, all of us inside passengers gave three cheers. Breakfasted at Carlisle & got to Penrith, & set off in a chaise for Keswick. Caught a view of distant mountain scenes on the hills, dark blue hills & sun clouds rolling over their tops as if bursting with light – the whole scene grand & impressive. The first hint of Keswick Lake & hills exquisite. Wrote Southey, had a hearty answer, spent a day with him – he is like an enchanter. Set off for Ambleside, called at Wordsworth's; he at Sir George's beautiful situation. Southey's fitter for a poet. At Kendal walked about with a little Whig hater, loyal but a Queen's man – picture of English healthy independence. He hated Radicals & sinecurists – he loved a man who worked for his own & eat it like an Englishman! He asked me who made my hat, & thought it a queer shape!

I shall return to London greatly improved in mind & health.

December 31. The last night of the most glorious Year of my life. I have at last lived to see my talents publickly acknowledged by the whole country; O God, thou who hast so mercifully brought me through such difficulties, desert me not now; great trials are yet to come but support me through the whole of them to triumphant independence. Grant I may live to pay my debts with honor; & grant I may make my art subservient to strengthen the manly & moral feeling of my glorious Country. And when it pleases thee to call my spirit to a purer region, grant I may yield my breath with the consciousness of having done my duty *here* and of deserving thy awful approval *hereafter*. Amen with all my soul.

---

*En route to Edinburgh and Glasgow to exhibit 'Christ's Entry into Jerusalem'. *Blackwood Magazine* (Nov. 1820), commenting very favourably on the Edinburgh showing, said, 'It is quite evident that Mr. Haydon is already by far the greatest historical painter that England has as yet produced.'

1821

January 1. O God Almighty, permit me to bless thee for thy innumerable mercies during life; enable me to conclude my present Picture of 'The Resurrection of Lazarus' and my small Picture of 'Christ's agony in the Garden' in spite of all obstructions. Grant their effect when finished may entirely compleat the feeling my two last have begun, grant they shew the nation the value, the beauty, the morality of the highest species of Painting, and rouse the Patrons and the Public to a clear and just sense of its defective support, and to a determination to devise & compleat some plan for its national encouragement. O God, let me not die in debt. Spare my eyes, invigorate my intellect, strengthen every faculty which thou has blessed me with, and supply me with those that thou hast not. Accept my deep gratitude for the triumphant success of 'Christ's entry into Jerusalem' and for its having advanced the public taste, Amen.

At the conclusion of my Picture in spite of my success, I became melancholy at its not selling; wishing to get rid of all petty harrassings, I grew furious & desponding. My dash upon Edingburgh relieved my mind by changing the scene and I returned, braced for another campaign. I now see difficulties are my lot in pecuniary matters, and my plan must be to float & keep alive attention to my situation through another Picture.

March 1. Spent the evening at Mrs Siddons to hear her read Macbeth; was exceedingly interested; she acted Macbeth himself better than either Kemble or Kean. It is extraordinary the awe this wonderful woman inspires. After her first reading the men sallied into a room to get Tea. While we were all eating toast & tingling cups & saucers, she began again. Immediately like the effect of a mass bell at Madrid, all noise ceased, and we slunk away to our seats like boys, two or three of the most distinguished men of the day passed me to get to their seats with great bits of toast sticking out their cheeks, which they seemed afraid to bite. It was exquisite! At last I went away highly gratified, and as I was standing on the landing place to get cool, I overheard my own Servant in the hall say, 'Why, is that the old lady making such a noise?' 'Yes,' said another. 'Why, she makes as much noise as ever.'

What a bit of nature! It awakened me out of a Dream, and made one think perhaps that the old Lady *was* making a noise.

March 7. Wednesday. Sir Walter Scott breakfasted with me with Lamb, & Wilkie, and a delightful morning we had. I never saw any man have such an effect on company as he; he operated on us like champagne & whisky mixed.

It is singular how success & the want of it operate on two extraordinary men, Wordsworth & Walter Scott. Scott enters a room & sits at table, with the coolness & self possession of conscious fame; Wordsworth with an air of mortified elevation of head, as if fearful he was not estimated as he deserved. Scott is always cool, & amusing; Wordsworth often egotistical and overbearing. Scott can afford to talk of trifles because he knows the World will think him a great man who condescends to trifle; Wordsworth must always be eloquent & profound, because he knows he is considered childish & puerile. Scott seems to wish to seem less than he is; Wordsworth struggles to be thought at the moment greater than he is suspected to be.

This is natural. Scott's disposition can be traced to the effect of Success operating on a genial temperament, while Wordsworth's takes its rise from the effect of unjust ridicule wounding a deep self estimation.

Yet I do think Scott's success would have made Wordsworth insufferable, while Wordsworth's failures would not have rendered Scott a bit less delightful.

March 9. Poor John Scott! [editor of the *London Magazine*]. For a fortnight before his burial & death, I exhibited in my nature as fine an instance of wounded pride struggling to keep down the urgings of former affection as ever Man shewed. I held out to an hour before his funeral, & then a sudden blaze of light shone inward on my brain and shewed me his body, stretched out, helpless, inanimate, and dead! My affections burst in like a torrent & bore down all petty feelings of anger & irritation. I hurried on my black clothes, after thanking God in a hurried prayer for the alteration! and drove down to his door. Poor Scott – upon my soul I loved thee once with all my heart; why did you ever use me like a traitor? As his Friends dropped in & the room began to fill, my feelings became too strong to be commanded. I hung back in the shadow. All our conversations on Death and Christianity and another World crowded into my mind.

Scott was a man of singular acuteness of understanding & power of mind, but he was not what might be called a Man of Genius. His power of conversation was very great, his knowledge considerable; he had been badly educated & badly brought up. The curse of his life was a rankling consciousness of his inferiority to some of his Friends. He was very entertaining, had a good heart at bottom, but it was so buried in passions that its native goodness had seldom power to force its way.

Scott was an unhappy man & had ill used every body he knew. He attacked Byron to gratify his spite because Byron took no notice of him at Table, & abused him for ill using his wife, at the very moment he had beat his own!

He attacked Hunt with indignation at his politics after having offered to write in his paper & was irritated by rejection – & assailed me on his return from Italy, from mere spite at my success. Instead of being rejoiced, he became angry, and making use of my own remarks on historical painting, which he begged as a favour I would give him, he tacked them on to a degrading attack on myself, thus making my own power of mind back, as it were, & give force to his own abuse of my character.

There really never was such treachery, and it really is not to be wondered at that I felt angered & inflamed!

God forgive him, he is gone to his audit, and if he ever loved any man he loved me.

March 29. Keats is gone too! He died at Rome, Feby. 23rd, aged 25. Poor Keats – a genius more purely poetical never existed.

In conversation he was nothing, and if any thing weak & inconsistent. Keats was in his glory in the fields! The humming of the bee, the sight of a flower, the glitter of the sun, seemed to make his nature tremble! his eyes glistened! his cheek flushed! his mouth positively quivered & clentched! He was the most unselfish of human creatures; he was not adapted for this world; he cared not for himself, & would put himself to any inconvenience to oblige his Friends, and expected his Friends to do the same for him; having no regular habits, he broke in on all the regular habits of others; he was proud, haughty, & had a fierce hatred of rank; but had a kind heart, and would have shared his fortune with any man who wanted it. His knowledge of the Classics was inconsiderable, but he could feel their beauties. He had an exquisite taste for humour, & too refined a notion of female purity to bear the lovely little-sweet arts of love with patience; he had no decision of character, had no object on which to direct his great powers, was at the mercy of every pretty theory Leigh Hunt's ingenuity might start.

One day he was full of an epic Poem! another, epic poems were splendid impositions on the world! & never for two days did he know his own intentions.

Leigh Hunt was in my estimation the great unhinger of his best dispositions; latterly, poor dear fellow, he distrusted his guide. Keats saw through Hunt's weakness, but thinking him ill used, he would not cease to visit him; this shewed the goodness of his heart.

He began life full of hopes! fiery, impetuous, & ungovernable, expecting the World at once to fall beneath his powers! Alas, his genius had no sooner began to bud, than Envy & hatred spat their poison on its leaves, & tender, sensitive, & young, it shrivelled beneath their putrid effusions. Unable to bear the sneers of ignorance or attacks of envy, he began to despond, flew to dissipation as a relief. For six weeks he was scarcely sober, & once he covered his tongue & throat as far as he could reach with Cayenne pepper, in order as he said to have the 'delicious coolness of claret in all its glory!' This was his own expression as he told me the fact. Ah Keats, how soon art thou passed!

The death of his Brother [Tom Keats, died December 1, 1818]

wounded him deeply, and it appeared to me from that hour he began seriously to droop. He wrote at this time his beautiful ode to the nightingale. 'Where Youth grows pale & spectre thin & dies!' – alluded to his poor Brother.

As we were walking along the Kilburn meadows, he repeated this beautiful ode, with a tremulous under tone, that was extremely affecting! I was attached to Keats, & he had great enthusiasm for me. I was angry because he would not bend his great powers to some definite object, & always told him so. Latterly he grew angry because I shook my head at his irregularity, and told him he was destroying himself.

The last time I saw him was at Hampstead, lying in a white bed with a book, hectic, weak, & on his back, irritable at his feebleness, and wounded at the way he had been used; he seemed to be going out of the world with a contempt for this and no hopes of the other. I told him to be calm, but he muttered if he did not soon recover he would cut his throat. I tried to reason on such violence, but it was no use; he grew angry, & I went away very deeply affected.

Poor dear Keats! Had nature but given you a firmness as well as a fineness of nerve! you would have well directed your great powers & have been an honor in your maturity as you were a glorious hope in your younger days! May your glorious spirit be now mingling in converse high with those immortal beings Shakespeare & Milton, before whose minds you have here so often bowed! May you be considered worthy of admission to share their musings in Heaven, as you were fit to comprehend their imaginations on Earth!

April 26. My eyes are wonderfully better, Thank God, & seem to bear all fatigue.

There is what all admirers of his [Lord Byron's] Genius must lament, & but ill becoming the mouth of a reformer, a Patrician insolence & contempt of the people of England. He says he was *bored* with the travelling English. He says there is a soi disant poet who goes to bed & dictates while he eats bread & butter; now this is a falsehood, & Lord Byron knows it is one; eating bread [and] butter must be to Lord Byron the most insipid of food, but surely this is better than ill using an innocent man & drinking brandy to get rid of the devil within him in consequence of such conduct.

If Byron had eat a little more bread & butter & drank a little less brandy, he would not have been such a curse to others & a torture to himself.

April 28. As I stood last night in the midst of a conversazione of celebrated men, I thought of Johnson's reflection, viz., that there was not one of those who would feel pain at their own reflections before midnight. I first encountered Soane, smiling & talking to several, a man of a good heart & caustic temper which renders life a burthen. Then I saw the Duke of Sussex, with a star on his breast and an asthma inside it, that made him wheeze out his Royal opinions. I went through the greater part of the company, and ended with myself and what secrets could I tell, beneath my own healthy face. My mind was then aking, and just at that very moment a young man came up & congratulated me on my Picture with a smiling face. Dressed like a flower, he looked like one in mind & fluttered about from person to person, when I *knew* at that moment he was miserable about a young girl who had ran away from her Parents on his account, and *I* was *tortured* at my pecuniary difficulties. Away we all went to our respective pillows, and our Host to his, flattered by his brilliant conversazione, and he enraptured that we were gratified.

And must there not be a World of justice, of peace, of truth hereafter, where souls may shew themselves what they *are*, without bodies to disguise their real essence? There must be! Ah! Scott, you know it by this time, *you* who used to writhe your faculties with scrutinizing its hopes and chances. Poor dear Keats too. I strolled the Kilburn meadows last evening. The influence of my two Friends seemed breathing about me. I never felt so strongly the insignificance of life as I have lately; I see through its pretences thoroughly. Perhaps my highest days are over.

April 30. Worked in the morning for a short time & then went out to the different exhibitions and to arrange some pecuniary difficulty & met with great insolence from an attorney. Thus the day has passed! I am sorry to say my mind is in a very unhappy state; the truth is I want to marry the Woman I have loved & who loves me, & I cannot. This really weighs on my spirits. I have gone on year after year restraining the urgings of a delicious passion in schemes of ambition & restless activity of mind, but her dear image haunts me, as Clarissa's remembrance haunted Lovelace; and between every interval of exertion presses me to agony! I am now in the prime of my manhood; a few years will destroy it and if I do not marry her now it will never take place & this I see. The last time she was with me, she said one night in low spirits, as the tears stood in her eyes, she had a presentiment it would never take place – & I have latterly had the same sensation.

May 9. Went to Angerstein's & Stafford's, and studied deeply. Compared Raphael's Julius the Second in colour with Vandyke's Govertius. The first looked red in the flesh; though beautifully painted it wanted cool tints. Vandyke's head looked no colour in particular, because no colour predominated, but all being broken, gave that look of variety which flesh has. In Character Vandyke's had an air of *looking* characteristically with a consciousness, while Raphael's thought & looked unconsciously as Nature, deep, intense, penetrating, & powerful. Vandyke's characters always border on *something* affected, Raphael's *never*. Nothing can be finer in Art than this Portrait of Raphael's.

Nine days have passed in May, & I have not touched a Port crayon or pencil but once. I wish to God I could keep up but alas! pecuniary difficulties are sad obstructions to regularity of study. Exhibitions and business I ought to have nothing to do with; in short, I should be left free, unembarrassed, & quiet, and if God for once in my life does leave me so, my genius will then really devellope itself which it never has yet.

May 10. The head of Christ again poses me before beginning. His mildness of character is so inconsistent with Depth of thought; the form that gives the one destroys the other; the sunk eye which gives depth of thought has an air of severity.

May 11. Not yet began. Why? I cannot tell. My conscience at me all day. I go out & slink home as if all the World was looking at me.

May 12. Idle the whole day. All this whole week has been passed in sheer inanity of mind, fiddle faddling imbecilly & insignificantly. I don't think at this moment I could draw a great toe.

May 13. Sunday. Passed the day without a religious feeling, though I ought to have thanked God sincerely for the blessings of the last week.

May 14. Did nothing but walk about with a sort of fury as if my life depended on it. When I came in the Strand, I said, 'where shall I go? I'll go to my Tailor's.' I walked to my tailor's, knocked with a thundering roar, sent for him, found great fault with my coat because it was not as I wanted it; he promised to alter, & I went away, & determined to go & see Smithfield! Poor human Nature! Poor human Nature! Thus the day has passed & this is the conduct of one who has 12 pupils that look up to him with a sort of awe!

May 18. Never shall I forget when I borrowed 400£ of Mr Coutts! I was appointed to meet him & was received with distinction and affectionate interest. I signed a bond, was shewn his bust, & rooms, &c. I withdrew, and as I was going out of the door a poor negro, lame, came up to beg for something. 'Get away,' said the Servant, '& let this Gentleman pass!' Poor fellow! he asked for 2d. & was spurned by a Servant, I for 400£ & was received like a Prince! but there was a being watching us both at that instant, which was not to be imposed on by appearances, who penetrated to the innermost heart, & saw & comprehended the first glimmerings of thought; to him were we both impaled. I trembled & walked home and began to think if I did not pay Mr Coutts that I was the greatest beggar of the two.

May 20. The most triumphant thing for the Art of this Country and that has taken place for years was the great success & spirited competition at the sale of Sir Joshua's Pictures during the last week. The eyes of the

Nobility & men of property seem really to be open to the merits of native genius, and it was a curious circumstance to witness the comparative indifference at the sale, with which a fair Teniers & a respectable Titian and an *undoubted* Corregio were put up, knocked down, & carried off, in comparison with the eagerness, the enthusiasm, the competition roused by the elevation of a Picture by Reynolds.

The excellence of Reynolds was not grandeur, or expression, or form, but delicacy of character, elegance of air, harmony of colour, and such was his intense feelings for these qualities in nature, and his great power of transferring them to his canvas, that to whatever height Art will rise in this Country, there can be no period however refined, no time however pure in taste, or altered in principle, when Reynolds' genius will not be acknowledged, in spite of his gross defects.

On the principle above stated, I prefer Charity to [any] of his large productions. The innocent purity of her look, the length and grace of her form, the beauty & sentiment of her action & air, the golden & strawberry tone of her colour, the breadth of the effect & richness of the surface, would enable this exquisite [picture] to keep its place triumphantly by any Corregio on Earth!

The result of this sale is a most gratifying promise of living Artists. When they see men of feeling & rank stepping forward with such spirit to the support of English genius, it ought to [give] the most consolatory & stimulating effect.

I went to the private view of the Institution after Reynolds' sale was over, and though I thought as high of Reynolds as ever, I thought higher of Titian [and] Rubens. The firm solidity & masterly drawing of Rubens, the clearness, precision, & strength of his effect, struck me deeply.

There is one great excellence in the Christian Virtues of Reynolds. Every figure looks as if fitted to an extended composition, and is not an unconnected figure *fit* for itself alone. This is done with great skill.

May 22. The greater part of May has passed & yet nothing done. I finished the Agony 26 of February, was occupied till the end of March in Exhibitions, from the 1st of April till now with common energy I might have done wonders. I worked a little till 20th, & then have idled ever since. A man is always the same. I despair of ever altering till I am dead. [The reason I was so idle at this time was from my uncertainty of being able to marry & tho deeply in love. Aug. 1822. B.R.H.]

May 23. Spent the day at the Gallery again. Met Wilkie there, & complained to him that Portrait Painters by the necessity of being ready for their sitters get into better habits of application. He differed, & said it must be recollected that their thinking ended with the sitter's departure, while our thinking never ended. This was consolatory but not quite true.

What is the use of this groaning daily? Why do I not begin? I cannot conceive how Wellington after his furious life, exists in peace & quiet.

May 26. Strolled about in agony of mind, torture of body, and racking of conscience. Went to the Gallery in the evening. As the women were sweeping round, Mothers with their daughters, husbands with their wives, lovers with their mistresses, brothers with their sisters, & sons with their mothers, I looked at them all and thought strange how little of life is passed in intercourse, how much is occupied in meditation & discussion & anxiety & depression & self reproach; and then we dress, paint, & sally forth to meet others dressed & painted; go home & die.

May 31. Began at last at the head of Christ.

June 4. Since I began to work I have not had an uneasy moment. Wilkie & I had a grand consultation yesterday about my Picture, and from the combined consequences of his advice & my own thinking, I have improved it amazingly today.

June 22nd is a remarkable day in my [life]. I was arrested. After having passed through every species of want & difficulty, without often a shilling, without ever being touched, now when I am flourishing, I become a beacon, and a tradesman proud of an opportunity to shew me he is as good a man. Here was a man, to whom I had paid 300£, but, because I employed another to fit up my last room, out of pique arrested [me] for the balance! The officer behaved like a man. I told him I must shave & begged he would walk into the painting room. I did so, and when I came down, I found him perfectly agitated at Lazarus. 'My God, Sir,' said he, 'I won't take *you*.' (This is a fact.) 'Give me your word to meet me at twelve at the Attorney's, & I will take it.' I did so. At the Attorney's we argued the point, & I beat him in the presence of the Officer. I proved the gross injustice of the proceeding, & the officer let me free till night. At night I settled everything. The expenses were eleven pounds! Alas, alas, how things will be one day changed!

Laws are solemnly made that seats shall not be sold in the House of Commons. Castlereagh sells them; Hunt tells him so; Castlereagh dines with the King, eats off plate; Hunt goes to Prison, is confined with felons, refused his wife, sleeps in stone walls, & dines off pewter, but J. Hunt pays his debts, never violates a law in his life, assists his Friends, is faithful to his wife, never gives suppers after the opera to trespass on the sabbath.

A poor boy is born in St Giles, is never educated, & left to strole till grown up, his Mother a strumpet, his Father a thief. He grows up, with irregular habits; he is hungry, he has never worked to get a living, he does not understand; he steals, he is caught, he is hung! Castlereagh is born in a velvet bed, is drawn into the world by the perfumed hands of a gold caned Doctor, is washed, frilled, dandled, cradled, kissed, & clouted in fine linen & roses, grows up, goes to College, leaves college, goes into political training, represents the nation, takes his oath of preserving the purity of the Constitution, knows there is a law against it, & sells a seat, thus breaking the oath *he* has taken, and dines with the King & has his Picture hung, by a Knighted Painter. Very well, J. Hunt, the boy of St Giles, & Castlereagh die, are raised by the last trump, appear naked, & silent, & astonished before the great Redeemer of mankind. Who, think you, will *then* have the best chance of reward, of applause, of having said, 'well done, thou good & faithful Servant.' Will not the Boy be pitied & pardoned, J. Hunt applauded & lifted up, & Castlereagh hurled to Hell, hissed at as he falls! This is truth, & truth he will most likely find it. But on the other hand, will not an unerring judge say, 'poor Creature! are you not to be pitied like the poor boy? Poor creature, poor glittering creature! with your satin shoes, with your velvet robe, your silver dress, your perfumed ruffles, your quivering plumes, have you not had also your examples to influence your mind?' You have, & probably an unerring judge will pity & pardon both. An unerring Judge will know how much is to be attributed to habit, how much to the errors of others, & how much the organization of ourselves.

What a day was yesterday, what a Picture of human Nature. From the bailiff's house, I walked to Lord Grosvenor's, & my mind was extremely affected, after the insult I had just received, to enter a room full of lovely women, splendid furniture, exquisite Pictures. All was gay, breathing, animated, voluptuous! I strolled about amidst sparkling eyes, musing in the midst. I then went home, where I found the son of an old Friend of my Father, *without [a] shilling*, having lost a situation from his eccentricity. He had come by the coach, & left his trunk for his fare, & wanted me to pay it. I lent him what I could spare, little enough, God knows, & away he walked as happy as I did from the Sheriff. Here's just a picture of a human day, of human beings, human delusions, human absurdity, & human *law*! – and then we all put on our best cloaths, and talk of the respectability of our situations, go to Church, kneel down & pray to God, get a cold, die, & hope we shall be *happy* in a better world, after having made a beautiful creation a mass of filth, comic hypocrisy, & folly!

July 4. I thank God my mind is now in the right tone, and not till lately has it been so. My error has been always expecting every Picture I brought out to do every thing I hoped, & put me above anxiety. I have made up my mind to do as well as I can, when I can; if free from trouble so much the better; if not so, to do all I can in spite of trouble. This is the true state of mind to act in. I thank God for it! Wilkie drank tea with me tonight, & brought me news Napoleon was dead! Good God! I remember 1805, as we were walking to the Academy, just after the battle of Jena, we were both groaning at the comparative slowness of our means of acquiring fame, in comparison with his. He is now dead! a captive! and we have gone quietly on, rising in daily respect, with no bayonets & cannon to carve our way to fame & honor, & have no cause to lament our silent pathway.

July 6. 'Although,' said he (Buonaparte), 'I feel my strength decaying, I am *not yet so prostrate* as to take refuge in spiritual remedies.' Times, July 5.

July 10. My dearest, dearest Mary came to town for a short time.

July 12. Spent the most delightful day of my life yet, with her! at Richmond! The sun was descending, the air warm & still, the water glittering, the trees rich, shady, and trembling with sun beams! We opened the windows & enjoyed this delicious landscape together. I then turned my head back & looked up – a face hanging over me, full, rosy, smiling, & devoted! that pressed my lip with inside kisses, ripened! amorous! & moist! May God bless me with health & fortune to make thee, dearest creature, the tenderest husband! Amen. She has the simplicity of a child, the passion of an Italian Woman, joined to the wholesome tenderness & fidelity of an English one.

July 21. What a scene was Westminster Hall on Thursday last! [The coronation of George IV.]

It combined all the gorgeous splendour of ancient chivalry with the intense heroic interest of modern times; – every thing that could effect or excite, either in beauty, heroism, genius, grace, elegance, or taste; all that was rich in colour, gorgeous in effect, touching in association, English in character or Asiatic in magnificence, was crowded into this golden & enchanted hall!

I only got my ticket on Wednesday at two, and dearest Mary & I drove about to get all I wanted. Sir George Beaumont lent me ruffles & frill, another a blue velvet coat, a third a sword; I bought buckles, & the rest I had, and we returned to dinner exhausted. After dinner with the playful, bewitching elegance of a beauty, she put on my coat & sword & marched about looking at herself. *She* staid up; *I* went to bed at ten, & arose at twelve, not having slept a wink. I dressed, breakfasted, & was at the Hall Door at half past one. Three Ladies were before me. The doors opened about four, & I got a front place in the Chamberlain's box, between the door and Throne, & saw the whole room distinctly. Many of the door keepers were tipsey; quarrels took place. The sun began to light up the old gothic windows, the peers to stroll in, & the company to crowd in, of all descriptions; elegant young men tripping along in silken grace with elegant girls trembling in feathers & diamonds. Some took seats they had not any right to occupy, and were obliged to leave them after sturdy disputes. Others lost their tickets. Every movement, as the time approached for the King's appearance, was pregnant with interest. The appearance of a Monarch has something [of] the air of a rising sun; – there are indications which announce his approach, a whisper of mystery turns all eyes to the throne! Suddenly two or three run; others fall back; some talk, direct, hurry, stand still, or disappear. Then three or four of high rank appear from behind the Throne; an interval is left; the crowds scarce breathe! The room rises with a sort of feathered, silken thunder! Plumes wave, eyes sparkle, glasses are out, mouths smile. The way in which the King bowed was really monarchic! As he looked towards the Peeresses & Foreign Ambassadors, he looked like some gorgeous bird of the East.

After all the ceremonies he arose, the Procession was arranged, the Music played, and the line began to move. All this was exceedingly imposing. After two or three hours' waiting, the doors opened, and the flower girls entered, strewing the flowers. The exquisite poetry of their look, the grace of their actions, their slow movement, their white dresses, were indescribably touching; their light milky colour contrasted with the dark shadow of the archway. The distant trumpets & shouts of the people, the slow march, and at last the appearance of the King under a golden canopy, crowned, and the universal burst of the assembly at seeing him, affected every body.

After the banquet was over, came the most imposing scene of all, the championship & first dishes. Wellington, crowned, walked down the Hall, & was cheered by the Officers of the Guards. He shortly returned with Lords Howard & Anglesea, and rode gracefully to the foot of the throne; they then backed out. Lord Anglesea's horse became restive. Wellington became impatient, and, I am convinced, thought it a trick of Lord Anglesea's to attract attention. He backed on, & the rest were obliged to follow him. This was a touch of character.

The Hall doors opened again, & outside in twilight a man in dark shadowed armour against the shining light appeared. He then moved, passed into darkness under the arch, & Wellington, Howard, & the Champion stood in full view, with doors closed behind them. This was certainly the finest sight of the day. The herald read the challenge; the glove was thrown down; they all then proceeded to the throne. My imagination got so intoxicated that I came out with a great contempt for the plebs, and I walked by with my sword. I got home quite well, & thought sacred subjects insipid things. How soon I should be ruined in luxurious society!

December 4. I am married! Ah, what a crowd of feelings lie buried in that little word. I cannot write or think for the present. I thank God for at last bringing me to the arms of the only creature that ever made my heart burn really, & I hope he will bless me with health & understanding & means to make her happy & blessed. Dearest, dearest Mary – I cannot write.

December 31. The last day of 1821. I don't know how it is, but I grow less reflective as I get older. I seem to take things as they come without much care. Here I sit sketching, with the loveliest face before me, smiling,

Sketch of Mary Haydon, the artist's wife

loving, & laughing! Marriage has encreased the happiness of my mind beyond expression; in the intervals of Study, a few minutes' conversation with a creature one loves is the greatest of all reliefs. God bless us both! My pecuniary difficulties are still great, but my love is intense! my ambition intense! & my hope in God's protection cheering! I am really & truly in love, and without affectation, I can talk, write, or think of nothing else. Amen.

Painted 5 hours. End of 1821.

1822

January 5. Painted 6 hours. Dearest Mary came in at intervals like an Angel to sooth & encourage me. It is impossible to express the raptures I feel on seeing her divine face peeping about, behind my canvas, fresh, full, voluptuous, & tender! Sweet creature! She is really a reward for all my anxieties.

January 10. Painted 4½ hours, & half finished the other sleeve. The naked arm would not do. Many things very fine to imagine as after thoughts are found inconsistent with the first arrangement, and are therefore given up.

Dearest Mary ill – agitated me the whole morning. It is extraordinary the sympathy excited by the helplessness or illness of a beloved being.

January 12. Out all day to pacify creditors, & succeeded.

January 21. 10 days I worked hard, 11 I have worked idly, yet I have advanced. I have now 10 left, and if free from pecuniary difficulties, I could finish my principal figure.

January 25. My Birth day – 36 years old! One year more & I shall compleat Raphael's age! My influence on English Art has certainly been radical. Edwin Landseer dissected animals under my eye, copied my anatomical drawings, and carried my principles of study into animal painting! His genius, thus tutored, has produced solid & satisfactory results. Bewick & Charles Landseer will do always good things, and I can perceive at last a willingness to concede the point as to the soundness of my methods.

March 18. I call[ed] on Phillips, my kind, kind Friend, this morning, but he refused to advance me a sixpence more. I left his House braced to a tensity of feeling I never felt for years. I called immediately on some turbulent creditors & laid open the hopeless nature of [my] situation. Having relieved my mind, I walked furiously home, born along on the wings of my own ardent aspirations. I never felt happier, more elevated, more confident! I walked in, went to my dearest Mary, kissed her lovely face, & then to my Picture, which looked awful & grand. 'Good God,' I thought, 'can the Painter of that feel trouble? can *he* be in difficulty!' When I look at a figure that is complete, and remember from what difficulties it has issued, I am astonished! I am born to be the sport & amusement of Fortune, to be put up in one freak and bowled down in another.

On this day I write this without a single shilling in the world, with a large Picture before me not half done, yet with a soul aspiring, ardent, confident, trusting in God for protection & support. Amen, with all my being.

I shall read this again with delight – and others will read it with wonder. March 18th, 1822.

March 19. My situation is worse than it was during Solomon, but my reputation greater. I have my health, am in a good House, have a sweet wife, and more experience in my Art; but Fortune has deserted me this year and involved me, 'Go on,' I still hear, and go on I will, until arrested by calamity or Death. God grant me success.

April 22. Went to Richmond with dearest Mary, the scenes of our love & courtship. The trees were budding, the birds deliciously singing, the place wanted the rich warmth of summer, but I was affected as we sat on the same bench [on] which we had sat two years before. We were then trembling with passion & restrained by principle; every leaf, every Zephyr, the air, the Sun, all nature appeared floating in love & voluptuousness! Now – our love relieved, our passion gratified, we sat down calm, collected, & tender, and talked of the days past like a rich dream, passionate & musical. Dear little Orlando [BRH's elder stepson] was going to School for the first time, and as we sat, he bounded about light, active, healthy & happy, with a face round as an apple, & rosy as a rose. Dear little fellow! God protect him & make him a good man!

May 1. My dearest Mary is with child! I always prayed God I might know the sweet name of Parent before I died and I hope God will bless my prayer. God protect & bring her safely through her danger, for Jesus Christ's sake. Amen.

May 16. Worked hard lately. My Picture much advanced. By the 21st of next month I shall know when it will be finished. Dearest Mary sat, impudent, beautiful, naughty, & funny. Upon the whole she behaved rather more as she ought than at other sitting times, & I contrived in the midst of all her wickedness to get a sweet head of her done.

June 1. Took dearest Mary to the review of Cavalry on Hounslow heath. It was the finest sight in the World, and completely English. All Classes mixed. You would see the sun burnt errand man turning his cart &

horse into vehicles of pleasure for *that* day, by the side of the crested Barouche filled with beautiful women, and while they tasted their light Champaigne out of a taper, graceful glass, he swilled porter from a white jug, wiping the sweat from his brown forehead, as they sweetly absorbed the heat by touching their lovely faces with delicate lawn! The Duke of Sussex drove in the front of the line & immediately deprived us of our view. 'That is not *fair*,' said the People, though he was the King's son, and a rush took place to see as well as his Highness. It is curious that though the English have such an instinct for personal right, how soon they are brought to their senses if a word convinced them they have trespassed on the right of another. 'Why surely you will let the *Duke* see, won't you?' said a voice, and instantly all seemed convinced the *King's son* ought to have some distinction.

July 19. Hard at work. Got the foot too large from carelessness.

July 30. In spite of all my difficulties, what a happy fellow I am! in health, with a lovely wife, and a divine Art. O God have mercy on me and grant I may bring my great Picture to a most glorious conclusion; grant no sickness or difficulty or want may obstruct me, and no amorous tenderness seduce me from accomplishing this great object.

August 3. The foundation of all good colour is a judicious preservation of your ground at rubbing in, & the certain means of colouring badly is to obscure it by dashing thick painting.

I am convinced that Titian's brilliancy is entirely owing to an *artful* use of his ground.

Obliged to leave off the early part of the morning from strained eyes. Notwithstanding my great difficulties I have been pretty quiet lately. If they would only leave me quiet I will pay all.

August 5. Out the whole day on business. Dearest Mary accompanied me, & took Shakespeare to read in my occasional absences; she solaced my mind & delighted me as we rode along.

Painting room carpet taken up after being down for three years – loads of dust under it.

Called on John Hunt. Found him deeply afflicted at the loss of Shelley. There certainly is something in Shelley's death! When one considers his early writings, his rash unbelief, there is something in his being whirled off in that way into eternity, awful & mysterious. The first time I ever saw him was at dinner. I could not think what little, delicate, feeble creature it was, eating vegetables only, when suddenly I was roused by hearing him say, 'as to that detestable religion, the Christian religion.' He knows by this time the great secret.

Hazlitt too has been disgracing his character & reputation. The Genius of this day really all seem to have a wrong feeling as to duty. Hazlitt married some years ago; his wife had property, she produced him a child, a fine boy. As he got into Society, the manner of his wife appeared unpleasant. At last he got so in love with a young coquette, he remembers adultery in a man can procure divorce in Scotland. He advises his wife to let him go down & commit adultery, & then for her to come down & proceed against him. Down he goes, sleeps in a brothel, with a strumpet *one eyed from disease!* (his own acct.), his wife brings her action, & he [is] divorced!

One has heard of people being caught in adultery, & few are proud of it, but here is a man who goes 500 miles to break a commandment of God, & brazenly enters a brothel – it is no use writing about it.

August 9. Rossi threatened execution. I endeavoured again to get time, & went to work in rapture. Rossi is a man with a large family, & I feel for his wants, but he ought to have a little sympathy with me, as I was always regular for the first 4 years. Finished the sleeve & hand & veil of the other, which looks well.

Hazlitt called last night in a state of absolute insanity about the girl who has jilted him. Poor Hazlitt, his candour is great, & his unaffected frankness is interesting.

August 19. Monday. Unable to work at all these last ten days, from deranged health, by imprudently indulging in fruit after hard work. Such is human Nature!

September 16 and 17. Dearest Mary. I said, 'Let us go to Windsor,' as we awoke. She agreed, and away we went with hardly money enough, but full of spirits. We got there at six, dined at the White Swan, and sallied forth to the Castle. We walked to Eton, & sat & lounged in the shades of its classical play ground. Our money lasted well, but unfortunately, a Barber who shaved me, as he was lathering, talked [and] so praised his Windsor soap, that I, victim as I was, took 6 cakes, spent 4 shillings out of the regular course & thus crippled our resources. The great thing was now whether we should pay the Inn bill, or pay our fare to Town & leave part of the bill to be sent. Mary was for paying the Inn & part of the fare, and leaving the rest to be paid when we arrived. We paid our bill & part of the fare, & I was reduced to sixpence when we took our places on the top. Before the coach set off I took out the sixpence as if I had 50£ in my pocket & said, 'Porter, here's sixpence to you.' The man bowed & thanked me so much that all the passengers saw it, & without sixpence in my pocket I got as much respect all the way home as if I had had 100£.

October 26. Finished the last bit of foot left to do. Huzza!

The Picture will be put on a new frame on Monday, & then I shall finish the massy parts, background, &c.

October 27 and 28. Picture restretched.

October 29. Idle, as the ground was not dry, and I could not do any thing else, of course.

November 6. At the Background like a tiger. I think it will do! How difficult it is to put action into a background without disturbing the action of the foreground. This is the great art.

November 12. Out the whole day on business & settled every thing. Came home to relieve Dear Mary's anxiety. Just as I was beginning to finish the right hand corner, in came a man with 'Sir, I have an execution against you,' & in walked another little sedate looking fellow & took his seat. I was astonished, for I had paid part of this very matter in the morning, tried as I was. I told the man to be civil & quiet, & running up stairs to kiss Dearest Mary, told her the exact truth. With the courage of a heroine she bade me 'never mind,' & assured me she would not be uneasy. Tried as I was I sallied forth again, telling the little Cerberus that I hoped he knew *how* to behave.

I went to Evans, a miserable apothecary, who [was] the cause, & asked him if this was manly, when he knew my wife was near her confinement, and told him to come to the Attorney with me. He consented, evidently ashamed. Away we went to the Attorney, who had assured me in the morning nothing of the sort should happen, as he had not given the writ to an officer. He now declared the man had exceeded his instructions, & wrote a letter to them, which I took. Away once more I rushed to Dear Mary, & found my little sedate man with his cheeks rosy over my painting room fire, quite lost in contemplating Lazarus. In the interim some Ladies & Gentlemen had called to see the Picture, & he insinuated to me he knew how to behave. Dearest Mary, quite overcome with joy at seeing me again, hung about me like an infant, kissed & wept on my shoulder. Ah, sweetest creature! my heart beat violently, but pained as I was, I declare to God no lovers can know the depth of their passion unless they have such checks & anxieties as these. For thy mercies, O God, this day, accept my gratitude! – my rapidity of extrication I attribute to thy goodness. Amen.

November 16. One's life is one perpetual struggle with ideal perfection & inherent tendencies that obstruct attaining it. Here I sit today, knowing I ought to be finishing my foreground, and yet sluggish, croaking, & imbecile, despising myself for not doing what I ought to do, and yet feeling a sort of pang at the idea of touching a brush and despising myself for feeling so. I shall pass the day in fret, fidget, shivering by the fire, cursing the Climate, groaning at the Government, the King, the people, and looking gloomy at every thing but the face of my dearest, dearest Mary! she is now entering the room, floating, smiling & looking like an Angel – bless her. I must shut up.

At night, *December 12*. Never to my dying day shall I forget the dull, throtled scream of agony, that preceded the birth, and then the infant cry that announced its completion. Tatham, the Architect, a worthy man, was in the painting room, and Mrs Tatham, who had had 14 children, was with my dearest Mary. I had been sitting on the stairs, listening to the moaning of my love, when, all of a sudden, a dreadful, dreary outcry announced intense suffering, and then there was a dead silence, as if from exhaustion, and then a puling, peaked cry, as of a little helpless living being, who felt the air, & anticipated the anxieties, & bewailed the destiny of his irrevocable humanity. I rushed into the antechamber; Mrs Tatham came out & said, '*It's a boy!*' I offered to go in, & was forbidden. I ran down into the Painting [room] & burst into tears!

December 20. I passed an anxious night, dreaming all sorts of horrors about my dear Mary. I went up twice to listen, but all was quiet. Today how shall I express my gratitude to God? I found her nursing her babe & nearly recovered. God be thanked.

December 31. ½ past eleven at night. The last day of 1822. For thy mercies, O God, in bringing me through a year of such difficulties, accept my gratitude with all my soul. For the delivery of my sweetest Mary from the dangers of child-birth. O God, I bow to thy goodness. Amen. *Finis.*

1823

January 8 to 15. All occupied in incessant activity to keep my ground against pecuniary pressure. O God, thou hast helped & supported me, help & support me to the end. Amen.

February 5. Moved it today, and the colours brightened out so that the workman exclaimed! Lazarus made me tremble! It is now lighted by the south.

O God, bless this last Picture with triumphant, undeniable, & complete success! Grant in addition the success by exhibition & grant I may sell the Picture, so that by the joint reward I may pay my debts with honor & secure for ever the security & tranquillity of my dearest Mary & child & of her children. Amen. ½ past ten at night, Feby. 5th, 1823.

February 10. I began to glaze today, & got over St John, Martha, the Jews, Pharisees, & St Peter, & Mary's head, with pitcher. My arm aked.

Dearest Mary and I have scarcely seen each other these three days. She has been occupied with the child & I with my Picture. The dear boy grows apace & seems to be more pleased with colour than any thing. He will lie for hours quietly looking at a variegated shawl. God grant he may [have] the genius for the Art, that he may compleat what I leave unfinished.

February 20. The Boy continues to look at nothing but Pictures & busts;

and what is curious, he pays no attention to noises or singing, but laughs with delight the moment he sees any bust. A fragment of three horses' heads from the Elgin Marbles rivetted him, & he kept talking for a half an hour in his way. I hope he has genius.

March 1. The private day was today, & the success complete & glorious. O God, accept my gratitude! No Picture I have painted has been so applauded. The approbation was universal, and Lazarus affected every body, high, low, & learned.

March 7. O God, I have this day began the Crucifixion! Bless me through it! My difficulties are again accumulating, to thee I again cry. Enable me to conclude grandly & sublimely my present Picture of the Crucifixion, in spite of all obstructions, however great!

March 8. Proceeded to oil the ground of white preparatory to rubbing in the Picture. When once a man has began, how eager he is to go on. In the midst of my business today, my mind was always reverting to my canvas, & I rushed home as soon as I could. The Art is too great a delight to let any one share its raptures by employing Pupils.

April 2. I called in to the room today & found it full of dear little girls and their Mothers. The sight was really a reward. One great comfort to me is that I shall leave nothing behind me to hurt the mind of the most innocent.

April 9. Out all the morning, born down by pecuniary necessity. After arguing to no purpose with a creditor, I left him. The moment I returned I took out my colours, after reading two or three threatening lawyer's letters, which I found on my table, and made a very good sketch.

May 10. Advanced the Crucifixion gloriously by devoting a whole day – I could not resist. I was going out on business when my heart & soul got affected by looking. I put on my jacket & set to at the background immediately and never ceased till dinner. Occasionally I had piercing twinges of the consequences, viz., two executions tomorrow as sure as I am alive! God protect me. I am in the hands of Lawyers whose expences would pay half my creditors, but what can I do?

King's Bench. 22nd May. Well, I am in Prison! So was Bacon, Rawleigh, & Cervantes! Vanity, Vanity, here's a consolation. I started from sleep repeatedly during the night, from the songs & roaring of the other Prisoners. All I hope in God is that dearest Mary's strength will support her. At this moment mayst thou be at home, smiling at thy lovely baby, in peace & quiet. Ah Mary, there is a balm in thy lovely face that soothes one's soul.

May 24. Slept better, but the air is low & foul. Anxious & restless about futurity. God grant me success. After all, if my imprisonment has an effect, it will tend to my great object. Grant I may finish the Crucifixion in spite of all apparent impossibilities.

Dearest Mary came in the evening, and we spent a delicious three hours. Sweet visiting Angel! Sweet rapturous creature! what a blessing thou art to me!

May 25. Arose at seven. Not so well. Got better as I walked about. It is a severe affliction! I who have talents to be an honor to my Sovereign, to have my books, prints, casts, draperies, sketches, & drawings of years, lotted, numbered, & hurried off to a sale room! Alas, O God, though out of this will grow my substantial greatness, though this will at last awake my Country to my real situation. But I submit, remembering the unmerited sufferings of him who was without vice, and who came only to do good. Should I complain?

Dearest Mary came over with the boy, the dear boy, who smiled & laughed with rapture at seeing me. We passed a delightful day. But I am quiet & melancholy! God protect us. Amen.

May 30. Out on a day rule. I had a great mind to fly as I issued from the door. I did not dislike the idea of returning. At any rate in a Prison, if you are shut out from the World, the World is shut out from you, and this is a comfort.

Diploma of merit for English Historical Painters! [The following pass is attached to the diary:]

The Bearer, Benjn. Robert Haydon, Esq., hath this Day a rule of Court to go out of the Prison of the King's Bench granted to him to transact his Affairs & to return again before 9 O'Clock on the same day. Dated this 30th day of May, 1823. Rd. Hill, Clerk of the Day Rules.

June 15. Had my house been filled with rich furniture, with plate, with hangings & silks & satins & wardrobes, it might have been a just subject for

the service of creditors, but teeming only with studies, to excite and devellope my ideas, to sell off for a few pounds what no money can replace, to take away all the accumulated treasures of my mind & habits and leave my walls bare, desolate, & ruinous, is a disgrace to my Country. It really is so, upon my honor.

June 16. Home all day with dearest, dearest Mary.

June 19. L'adversité est sans doute un grand maître, mais ce maître fait payer cher ses leçons, et souvent le profit qu'on en retire ne vaut pas le prix qu'elles ont couté.

June 20. Lazarus sold to Binns, my upholsterer, for 350, and Jerusalem for 240! This may appear the destruction of Historical Painting in England. I say not. The very excess will advance it!

June 29. Had my old voice within saying 'Go on' as I got up. I never have this but in important crises. I resolved at once to persevere & press the point. I wrote Brougham & shall [place] a plan before him immediately for adorning the great room at the Admiralty.

July 10. Sweetest Mary came again. I kissed her eye lashes, milky forehead, her exquisite nose, passionate lips, downy cheeks, pillared neck, her arms, hands, bosom, feet. O God, with rapture!

July 23. Yesterday I went up to Court. What a day. There is something in a Court of Justice deeply affecting. The grave, good look of the robed judges, the pertinacious ferretting air of the Counsel, the eager listening faces of the Spectators, the Prisoner standing up like a soul in Purgatory, & the Evidence against him like a wronged & anguished sufferer are all calculated to give one a notion of another World!

At last up rose a grave, black robed man, & said in a loud voice, 'Benjamin Robert Haydon! Does any one oppose? Benjamin Robert Haydon!'

Nobody came, & I mounted! My heart beat violently. I put my clentched right hand on the platform where the Judges sat, and hung my other over my hat. There was a dead silence; then I heard pens moving, then a great buz. I feared to look about. At last I turned my head right facing the Spectators. First, the whole row of Counsellors were looking like ferrets, knitting their brows, & turning their legal faces with a sort of piercing half closed musing. Startled a little I turned, & caught both judges with their glasses off, darting their eyes with a sort of interest. I felt extremely agitated. My heart swelled. I was honorably acquitted, bowed low, & retired.

July 26. Thanks to thee, O God, I was this day released from my imprisonment. I went up to Court again. About ½ past eleven my name was mentioned. I stood up, when the Chief Commissioner said aloud, 'Benjamin Robert Haydon, the Court consider you to be entitled to your discharge, and you are discharged *forthwith!*' I bowed low & retired. I am now free to begin life again.

July 27. Barnes, Sir Walter Scott, Sir Ed. Codrington, Lord Mulgrave, & Hazlitt have shewed feeling throughout. John Hunt utter apathy! And Wilkie as much as was consistent with his cautious views. When John & Leigh Hunt were in Cold Bath fields & Horsemonger Lane, I sent Portfolios of Prints & had my Picture of Solomon put up for three days in each of their prisons to relieve the tedium of confinement. I wrote to Hunt for Books – I got neither answer or books. I saw him but once, & never had a line! Such is Human Nature!

August 20. I am in a most deplorable state of ennui & imbecility. Idle & weary.

September 7. Mr Tatham, a Friend and a kind one, sat to me for a chalk Sketch of his head, and paid me ten pounds. People are weary of Sacred Subjects. I will bry a Bacchanalian one; but though I know I have a taste for humour, I seem to lose the feeling of Inspiration I always feel on sacred subjects. Tomorrow I begin a Portrait! Success.

September 8. Began my Portrait career by painting a Gentleman. Before he came I walked about the garden in sullen despair. After I had got his head in, when he was leaving me he told me he was sure I must want money, and slipped a note of considerable amount into my hand! He does not come again till Thursday, and tomorrow with a light and grateful heart I will begin the sketch for my next Picture. This is advancing steadily. O God, grant I may pay all my debts before I die.

September 10. Began Sketch of Silenus subject. Humorous subjects do not fill the mind so fully. You laugh, & there's an end; but with sublime subjects you muse & have high thoughts, and think of death & destiny, of God & the resurrection, and retire to rest above the world & prepared for its restlessness.

September 23. Worked hard, but alas, on what? – a hand and drapery around it! I get excited, though, about Portraits. My devotion to Historical Painting has plunged me into vast debts. Portraits & success are my only chance of paying them.

September 24. Proceeded with my Portrait. Nearly finished it.

September 25. Finished it.

September 28. Was lent a capital Picture of the Flemish School. Compared it with my Portrait, which made it look flimsy. The lowest of the old Painters had a mode of working their tints which I verily believe is lost to the World. We equal or excel them in thinking & propriety & true taste, but in handling the brush – since Vandyke there has been no soul that knew any thing about it.

November 3. My fifty pounds being gone, I sallied forth today instead of working, to try if I could get some, but felt such instinctive disgust & degradation at *borrowing* that I returned home without attempting it. A day lost, to my great pain of mind, but what could I do? I am without any sort of employment whatever – not a Soul, but one, has ever expressed a desire to give me any, though every Patron in England must know I am without a guinea or the prospect of getting one but by their means. I must own, though, in good health and capital spirits, which my sweet Mary's face always gives me.

By the bye, it is curious to see how Hazlitt's prejudices about Painting in England, from his own practice, warp his understanding. He called *oil* the perishable vehicle of the *English* School, when Vasari distinctly says when Titian used it, as well as Lanzi, and many of Van Eyk's Pictures are as perfect as when they were first executed.

Upon the whole, then, there is no evidence from Vasari, who wrote at the time, or Lanzi, who wrote afterwards, that tempera & oil were mixed, but there is distinct evidence from their writings of the *reverse*.

November 5. Here I am this moment ready to do any thing, to the portrait of a cat, for the means of an honest livelihood, without the employment, or notice of a Patron in the country. I am determined I will find out the *impasto* mode of the Venetians & shall proceed tomorrow, relieved for the time.

November 10. Perhaps the reason that the Legitimate [*sic*] of the day don't like great works & heroic subjects is that the actions of heroes makes them feel their own insignificance, whereas the Dutch boors & English paupers are a continual assurance of their own superiority.

November 12. In a humour of apathy I took up Voltaire Dictionnaire Philosophique, but it unsettled me, made me melancholy, by its view of human Nature. I turned from its pointed satyre and witty indecency with musing disgust. I was quite unhinged for the day.

November 28. They married a daughter of the Earl of Gowrie to Vandyke to *disgrace her!!!* [King Charles I arranged the marriage of Sir Anthony Vandyke in 1640 to Mary Ruthven, granddaughter of the Earl of Gowrie.] Amiable, short sighted blockheads. To become the wife of such a being is to be disgraced! But had she married the bawdy, dull, gartered, starred heir of a large house, a coronet, she would have been elevated, though she might have been obliged to have had recourse to her Footman to continue her Lord's progeny from the inert, inefficacious impotence of her Lord's spinal marrow!

December 3. There never was a man who was so fond of devouring his Friends as Hazlitt, and there never was perhaps any individual so qualified for a meal as himself. The most impaled being alive in respect to attack, he is [a] man who exists only on the pleasure of dissecting the weaknesses of others. Yet he reconciles all by his candour, which spares neither himself or others. Born down for years by the supposition that he was disgusting to women, he prowled about the World brooding revenge; wearied by continual ill luck with women of education, he tried his power of excitement upon Sally; she, poor girl, who preferred deeds to flowery speeches, first tantalized & tried him, & then laughed at his passionate timidity, frowned, dismissed him.

Since this affair, he has tried his hand in desperation in another manner, & meeting with encouragement, his whole nature seems altered;

he goes about the World with a gay Lothario expression, which singularly contrasts with the metaphysical saturnine gloominess of his face; he seems Christian relieved of a load, or a damned soul, which after years of torture, has caught a glimpse of the Heaven to which blessed Souls are destined. Candid, unprincipled, doting, fiendish, paradoxical, unintelligible, intellectual, delightful, anti-Bourbon Hazlitt – Hail!

December 5. Worked hard, and my Silenus in order for finishing, but I have not such high aspirations, with this subject. I used to kneel down regularly before my Picture & pray God for support through it, retire to rest after striding about my solemn & solitary Painting room. These were moments worth nourishing! What pleasures have I enjoyed in that study! In it have talked & walked Scott, Wordsworth, Keats, Procter, Belzoni, Campbell, Cuvier, Lamb, Knowles, Hazlitt, Wilkie, and other Spirits of the time. I offered them the comforts not the luxuries of life. They all were pleased to come, and as they sat at table, the Entry into Jerusalem or Lazarus formed the back ground to their heads.

December 6. Sketched the whole day.

December 8. Sunday (December 7,) saw Brougham & spent a half hour with the greatest satisfaction. He explained why Long declined interfering with the Admiralty. He seemed all enthusiasm & warm heartedness and promised to do all he could again this session. Huzza.

December 9. Sketched 4 fine subjects, till I was sick of inventing. I was more fagged than with a hard day's painting. Macbeth on Stairs, Mercury & Argus, Moses & Pharaoh, Venus & Anchises.

December 10*. I painted all last week. Idle today from no other cause but the curse, the usual curse – no money. If I am to go this way, I shall die from disgust & pain of mind, that is, wanting money.

I prefer chalk sketches to pen sketches, though they rubb.

December 10. Arose in an agony of feeling from want. Driven to desperation I seized & packed up all the books I had except my Vasari, Shakespeare, Tasso, Lanzi, & Milton; got into a Coach, & drove to a Pawn
broker! Books that had cost me 20£ I only got 3 for, but 3 was better than starvation. I came home & paid my lodging.

December 14. Sunday. Worked hard for the first time for years, but if it conduces to my greater regularity of employment, I hope God will pardon me. Finished the head.

December 26. Went to Lord Stafford's for an hour & saw the Acteon [Titian's 'Diana and Actaeon'] on the ground. It is painted on a rough

---

*Diary gives two entries for this date.

canvas with a great body of colour in the centre of the limb, and diminished each side to the contour. Nothing can be so soft, & sweet, & mellow. I looked at my own picture after I returned, & it looked rosy. When this picture is complete I shall take it down before glazing & place it by the side of the Titian. To this I look forward as the most useful lesson of my life.

December 28. Hard at work. Got in another head quizzing Silenus – a little too individual. I must own, wicked as it is, I have been very happy since I have continued to paint of a Sunday. My train of thinking has been continued. I have not broken in on my days. After the idleness of Sunday (for I really did not give it up to Religion) I was feeble on Monday & dissipated in thought. I love my Art, & hope God will forgive me in so loving it as to make the excellence I attempt the best tribute of gratitude I can pay to his mercy for the talents he has given me. This is sophistication. I don't approve my conduct, but I can't help doing it. God in his mercy forgive me. Amen.

December 31. Last day of 1823! Last day of 1823. A year of more misery than any I have endured since my birth. Perhaps that of 1802, when I was blind, was more acute & melancholy, but as the sphere of my affections is extended now, of course my responsibility is more.

In the midst of such troubles as we have been afflicted with, we must feel gratitude to God for his mercies. I was enabled, by God's mercy, to provide my dear, dear Mary with every comfort for her last lying in. God in heaven grant me equal power to do that at her next, & bring her safely through it, to be a blessing as she is to all. Amen.

For myself, I was never better, in fuller practice, or happier in my Art. Melancholy as my fate seems, my very ruin & troubles (my devotion being so thoroughly known) have given that shock to the feelings of the Higher Classes which no work of Art, however exquisite, could have accomplished. As the first step Angerstein's pictures have been bought as the first foundation of a national Gallery. If Mr Brougham can only now induce the House to get into a committee for Arts, the thing will be established. He is determined. Individually, I have prospects of two commissions for large works. Every wish but two of my heart has been gratified: I have only two left, viz., to be able to pay *all* I owe, & to see the Government practically by purchase encourage Painting! O God, on my bended knees grant these two things before thou callest me hence, and I will kiss the dart in Death's merciless hand with rapture! Amen, with all my soul. End of 1823.

1824

January 5. Arose early and set to work – and got it all right. Mr Symmons called, a mild, gentlemanly connoiseur. Signed the agreement for the lease of my House [158 Connaught Terrace, Edgware Road]. God bless me in it. Amen.

January 13. Very hard at work. I painted the best feet I ever painted – certainly. I could not help thinking as I looked at them that there were 17 years continual labour & thinking in those feet & yet how it would take 17 years more to paint them as they ought to be painted – and that even after 100 years practice there would be something to do & a beauty that could not be done. I opened the window & let in the air twice. When I do not do this I feel ill – the room is so horribly small.

January 14. Completed my yesterday's work, and obliged to sally forth to get money in consequence of the bullying insolence of our old, short, bawdy looking wicked eyed, wrinkled, waddling, gin drinking, dirty ruffled Landlady – poor old bit of asmatic humanity! As I was finishing the Faun's foot, in she bounced, and demanded her four pounds with the air of an old demirep dutchess! I irritated her by my smile, & turned her out. I sat down quietly & finished my feet.

January 17. Put in the last head in shadow well. It added greatly to the effect & story. I think I shall call the Picture 'Silenus intoxicated & moral reproving Bacchus & Ariadne on the irregularity of their lives'.

January 19. Out all day to get my house ready. Shall be able to do nothing for a week, which will perhaps do me good.

January 22, 23, and 24. Exhausted with fagging to get into my house. Got in in the evening, it was a beautiful day, and we were all well fagged. Today, 25th, is my birth day, & God protect us from the misfortunes, the inattention we have endured. God protect us & save us. Amen.

January 26. Not yet settled. Last night I had a horrid dream & awoke in a profuse sweat. I dreamt I was suddenly in a crowd who appeared to be looking after a person they had lost. I asked what the people in robes were about, & some one in the Crowd said, 'They are looking for Haydon who has escaped from prison.' Instantly a set of voices said, 'There he is, there he is!' & I was seized like lightening! Instantly I felt myself between two gentlemen in red robes. At last we came at full gallop to the Walls of an immense prison, with a wide ditch. We crossed & I heard the buz of endless Prisoners. All the feelings of regret I remember were not being able to dine with Sir W. Beechey, keeping him waiting. My anxiety was so great that I awoke.

January 28. Still pestered with Carpenters, Painters, Masons, Plaisterers, & Bricklayers.

January 31. End of the Month, half of which I have of necessity idled – and settled in a nice House. God protect and prosper us.

February 1. My Great error in life was not being content with my triumph in Power by the success of Solomon. *Here* I should have stopped – but born along by the tide of success I fancied myself invincible, I fancied myself destined to be above the calamities of failure. Alas, I was no match for private intrigue, and the leader of the Institution who was too debased by the slavish habits of court to suppose any thing could be sound that did not issue from a Royal Academy.

A man who has come into Art 50 years before his time must expect the advantages as well as disadvantages of his situation. Everything he does is a wonder, and being a wonder people are ready to answer the question – 'is it any thing more?' A man with no nose is a wonder & so is a sheep with six legs, but these are no argument for their truth or excellence. After the first gape of astonishment is over, people quietly determine to rest & see what comes of it – & a man starves in the mean time.

Prince Leopold was amazingly struck with my Picture at Bullock's – he enquired about me, found I was a liberal in *Art*, & never praised me again. So it is & so it ever will be. I opposed authority, no matter what authority – it was authority and that was enough for all other authority.

February 7. Met Wilkie by accident in the Street. We hailed each other, took arms, & walked along. I agreed to call on him. He seems to have lost the King by some awkwardness & want of presence of mind. He had began the King's entrance to Holyrood House, the King was to sit, and sent for Wilkie to come to Windsor. Wilkie went down and was introduced with his Sketch. The King objected to the attitude of legs, and said, 'You wish me to sit? I'll sit now.' Wilkie replied with his usual simplicity of mind, 'I have no *materals*, please your Majesty.' The King put himself in the attitude, but alas, Wilkie took not the hint. He should have taken pen & ink or any thing rather than suffer it to pass, or his Sovereign to make an offer in fact in vain!

February 9. Called on Wilkie. I liked his composition of the King receiving the keys at Holyrood, but it wants grace & taste. The King never can like it; he has put him in Jack boots merely because he cannot do justice to his beautiful leg & foot. I could perceive throughout a desire to do something to please the King, and yet his innate hankering not to commit himself with too many heads lest he might not be paid for it.

February 27. Hard & deliciously at work. Put in the Background in an instant with the fury of a devil & stopped & gazed in delight, at its poetical, woody, sunny solitude.

I have not a pound in the World at this moment – yet I never passed a happier morning. Mary came to me for some money to pay for mangling. I said, 'don't talk to me about mangling, look at that background,' at which she kissed me with all her soul in her sweet lips & went away laughing.

February 28. Finished the back ground – the Picture is now in a fit state for glazing – huzza.

March 9. Idle & anxious for want of money.

March 17. My sweet Mary was brought to bed of a sweet little girl, just as I wished (about 5 o'clock in the afternoon). God bless them both. I had begun glazing Silenus and had just got through his figure.

March 26, 27 and 28. Continued to consolidate the glazing. Mary better & better – & the little Mary as interesting & squalling as infants generally are.

March 29. Met Moore at dinner, and spent a very pleasant three hours. He told his stories with a hit or miss air, as if accustomed to people of quick and refined sensibility. Rothschild at Paris (a Jew) asked who they would have as a God-Father for his child. 'Talleyrand,' said a French man. 'Pourquoi, Monsieur?' 'Parcequ'il est le moindre Chrétien possible,' replied he!

Moore is a delightful, gay, refined, voluptuous, natural creature, infinitely more unaffected than Wordsworth, not blunt & uncultivated as Chantrey, or bilious & shivering like Campbell – no affectation, but a true, refined, delicate, frank Poet.

April 3. Wordsworth called & said, 'Well, Haydon, you found the World too strong.' 'Stop, sir, the battle is not over'; and down we sat and had a set to. I maintained my ruin had advanced the Art, & that the purchase of Angerstein's pictures & Wilkie's, a living artist among them, was the greatest triumph since the Elgin Marbles. He acknowledged it.

April 25. Sunday. Saw Brougham after a long delay – promised to get Lambton to present a petition on History Painting. So my fears were from too eager feeling of dissappointment. I hope we shall succeed – indeed I am sure of it. God protect our efforts.

April 26. Of what use is my Genius – to myself or others? It has brought me in prison – of what use is that fame which a breath may destroy as a breath has created it? Here am I, now after 20 years' devotion in a profession that I cannot get my bread by. I conceive subjects, and sketch them, and then in the midst comes a baker's knock that carries consciousness of being a creditor in its very thump. All this was bearable when I was unknown because the hope of fame animated me to exertions in order to dissipate my wants; but now, what have I to hope? My Youth is gone! every day & year will render me more incapable of bearing trouble; at an age when I ought to have been in ease, I am ruined! I wonder my frame has born this so long – the mere agitations of the conceptions one's mind has flushing one's brain with blood, & bathing one's body in perspiration, must wear it, and then in addition the necessities of poverty are dreadful!

In the evening the nurse left us. I always feel touched when a nurse, an old creature, hardened by trouble and misfortune, and who passes the remainder of her days in ushering little infants into being, goes. She is generally an attendant in danger and risk, and has been witness to scenes of tenderness & joy & sorrow & recovery – and is somewhat mixed up with the deepest feelings of a Husband. These periods touch to vibration the deepest and most mysterious cords of our being. Peace attend her old withered soul!

April 27. Sent Petition to Brougham.

April 30. Sold Puck for 20£ to Kearsey, who so kindly interested himself for me last year.

May 3. After 20 years devotion to Historical Painting about which there was so much noise & hope at the time I began it – I have two commissions, one for a Lord Mayor and another a family piece!

Whenever the press in London burst forth as it always has in my favour, the Artists say it's owing to my connections!

A Gentleman sketching in the Highlands was approached by an old Scotch-woman, and after looking at him for some time she said, 'Ah, did ye ever see a Pector of Christ's entry into Jerusalem?' 'Yes,' said he. 'Ah,' said the old Woman, 'that was a Pector! I went to see it, and when I came in all the lads & lassies had their bonnets off, and I just took off mine and sat me *dune* and *gratt!* (cried).'

Was this owing to connections?

May 8. Saw Mr Lambton, who has promised to present my petition. He seemed fearless and independent. My feelings in Lambton's presence were curious. 20 years ago, when I came to Town, he was a child – and I who had struggled through every species of want, &c. What a curious destiny that God should give me a talent & deny me fortune, and yet Mr. Lambton must come to me if he wants a Picture, as much as I must go to him if I want protection; so we depend on each other – such is the world.

I meant to be very fine when I began but I have written puling trash.

May 15. Byron is dead! I felt deeply at reading it. Moore said the other day, when I met him, that in a letter from Lord Byron to him (Moore), he said, 'I shall fight, and if I get killed, do justice to a Brother warbler.' I never saw him and I regret it extremely. A Friend promised to bring him, but never did.

The day I dined with Miss Baily at Hampstead in company with Wilkie, Miss Baily told me that Lady Byron had told her, on the very morning they were married and were driving home through the grounds, and all the

Peasantry were cheering them, he said to her, 'What could induce you to marry me?' 'Good heavens!' said Lady Byron, 'because I loved you.' 'No,' said he, 'you have a spice of Mother Eve, you married me because your Friends wished you not to do so. You refused me twice, & I will be revenged!' This is a fact, to be depended on.

Byron is a great loss to the Literature of the Age. He kept it always in excitement, with all the prerogatives of a man of genius – what is he about! – what has he done! – what is he going to do. With all his faults he was a fine creature.

May 27. I had a long conversation with Mr Lambton this morning, who candidly gave me no hopes. He spoke to Sir C. Long in the House last night, & Long said it was no use to raise hopes in me, for no *one* man would be entrusted with employment in the Art.

Mr Lambton said, 'In the case of commission, I have no hopes. In [the] case of the recent commission to Turner for the battle of Trafalgar, the Government were not satisfied. This has done great injury; we must feel our way first.' 'Yes, sir,' said I, 'if Genius could be raised like lettuces, it would be right to wait.' Lambton smiled – but he is sincere; he damps me, at least *tries to do so*.

August 15. These two months, having at last devoted myself to Portraits, I have enjoyed tranquillity, luxury, quiet, & Peace, and have maintained my family with respectability & credit. But, alas, what an absence of all original thought!

August 19. Called on Wilkie. The King had sat to him, which I was very happy to find. I imagined the awkwardness of his last visit had ruined his prospects in that quarter. Wilkie found himself unable to converse with the King – he remembered he was talking to a Monarch and became so nervous he could not converse! After two hours the King rose; Wilkie, in an agony of fear lest he had missed an opportunity that could never occur again, passed the evening in a perfect perspiration.

His portrait was not like. He was dissatisfied with himself, and with his conduct. The next time he went, he went early, and did a great deal before the King came in; at the end of his second sitting he was much pleased, and at the end of the third, he was pleased still more by the King's approbation.

I think, after all, this is a hit; the picture is a fine composition & Holyrood House will be a fine accompaniment.

August 29. Hazlitt's article in the last Edingburgh on Salvator is a disgrace to himself, to the Review. The misfortune is with him you can never get a genuine principle or an honest thought from Hazlitt. His passions & petty revenges so influence his thoughts and his opinions are entirely guided by them.

I am ashamed of Hazlitt, but he has turned out to me as Wordsworth predicted, and I have no body to blame but myself.

A man in misfortune is too tempting an object for his Friends to pass without insults. In 1820, with plenty of money and in high repute, Hazlitt would not have dared to have taken such a view, but now, without money or means & with prospects dimmed by ruin, Hazlitt thinks my principles a fair subject for attack.

September 18. I never read any thing like the King of France's death, or never read the death of any one that gave me so strongly the impression, as it was a passing scene to a happier World. He seemed to take it as the last act of Royalty, as if the moment it was over he would go down to his dressing room like an actor, put on his clothes, and come out a man, as a butterfly comes out from a crysalis. It was curious; if Catholicism produces such effects, I wish I were a Catholic.

October 6. I am entirely abroad in mind, occupied with a continuity of daily trifles; in the evening I have no abstract idea of expression or character to muse on till the next day. I leave off wearied and commence in disgust! I candidly confess I find my glorious Art a *bore*. I cannot with pleasure paint any individual head for the mere purpose of domestic gratification. In Portrait I lose that divine feeling of inspiration I always had in History. I feel as a common man, think as a common man, & execute as the very commonest. Alas, I have no object in life now but my Wife & children, & almost wish I had not them, that I might sit still & meditate on human Ambition and human grandeur, till I died! I really am heartily weary of life & all its enjoyments. I am not yet 40 and can tell of a Destiny melancholy & rapturous, severe, trying, & afflicting, bitter beyond all bitterness, afflicting beyond all affliction, cursed, not to be dwelt on. But I dare not write now. The melancholy demon has grappled my heart, & crushed its beatings, its turbulent beatings, in his black, bony, clammy, clenching fingers! I stop till an opening of reason dawns again on my blurred head!

October 7. Hard at work today on the Portrait. Arranged an Indian Shawl! Sublime occupation!

October 19. Sold Silenus for *half price!* Dear Mary & I melancholy the whole evening.

My mind certainly is not so active, I fear, as it used to be. Good heavens, with a great Historical Picture before my eyes, deductions were continually flowing into my brain, night & day. Now I go on in apathy, & I do not really think I have had ten new ideas or shall have them for months.

November 17. I have not thought on the Art before today for ages. Today I went to see the Raphael Tapestries, and all my old delightful feelings for Art crowded my mind with all its old associations of composition & drapery & expression, and all that is delightful & graceful & great.

Raphael is the only Painter I am never tired of – & am always unwilling to leave. As I looked round the room & saw this collection of designs, I could not help feeling my heart sink, knowing myself capable of producing designs like these for the honor of my Country, could I be but employed!

December 31. Now comes, as will ever come to the end of the World, as it has from the beginning, the conclusion, a passed year.

I have always reviewed every year as it closed. January, February, March, & April, my wants and necessities were horrible. In May a better Fortune seemed to dawn on me.

Kearsey (on the brink of Death) bought my Puck, which was the first symptom of better prospects. He gave me a family Piece; other commissions followed, and I have been kept pretty nearly in constant employment.

But devoting six months to Silenus after I came from Prison, without resources, involved me in Debt, out of which, notwithstanding all my employment and all my Fortune this season, I am not extricated. The education of the two Boys* & the expence of two infants are heavy indeed!

My domestic happiness is doubled; daily & hourly my sweetest Mary proves the justice of my choice. Dearest, dearest Creature, to thee I owe my life, & the sweetest moments in it! My boy Frank gives tokens of being gifted at 2 years old! God bless him! I have better prospects certainly than at the end of last year, though more in debt. I have worked less this year than last, & occasionally have had bitter fits of melancholy & idleness.

God spare me till my life will be of no avail to my sweetest Mary & Children. For the mercies of the year, O God, accept my gratitude. Amen with all my Soul. ½ past eleven in the forenoon.

1825

January 13. Suffered bitterly in mind. Went out & saw the historical attempt of a wretched Student. From them I banqueted on a fine Murillio, as fine an instance of tone as I ever saw. The softness of some of the heads were equal to Corregio. I gained greatly by studying.

I came home & looked at my own Portraits. There was firmness & decision, but not softness like Corregio or Murillio or Reynolds.

I sat up last night and enjoyed all the luxuries of solitude for two hours. The moment I am *alone* I seem to have all my old inspirations. Let them be delusions – never mind! they are rapturous! glorious! inspiring! I converse

*Haydon's stepsons: Mary's sons by her first marriage, Simon and Orlando Hyman.

with the Heroes of the World & pace my narrow – *now* narrow – room with Achillean strides, glorying.

February 3. Lambton called. I shewed him my sketches for a series of National subjects. He approved them, but said I might depend on it that the Government were *determined* that nothing of the sort should take place.

From Lambton only have I ever got the truth. He begged me not to have the least dependence on the promises of any man connected with Government.

February 17. To the great joy of my mind & relief of my heart, after weeks of agonizing torture into what to throw my talents, I began this day at ten o'clock or one minute after, a Cabinet Picture of Pharaoh dismissing Moses & Aaron at dead of night, on finding his first born dead at the Passover. Laus Deo!

February 24. Ought to have painted a Portrait. Looked at my historical Picture; thought I might as well set & arrange my drapery. I did so. There could be no harm in painting that bit! so I painted it. Then it looked so well there could be no harm in painting the other bit, and then the whole would be complete; so I did it, and dinner was announced before I was aware! Delightful art!

April 16. Fuzeli is dead! and in my opinion is an irreparable loss. Notwithstanding the apathy of the public latterly towards his works, Fuzeli had had his day. His Night mare was decidedly popular all over Europe. Fuzeli was paid 30£ for the Picture, and the Engraver cleared 600 by the print! His great delight was conception, not embodying his conceptions, and as soon as he rendered a conception intelligible to himself & others by any means, he flew off to a fresh one. The degeneration of style into which Fuzeli latterly fell could have been predicted from his very first work, and let it be a warning to all students who talk of the grand style when they ought to be drawing hard and correctly from Nature, and never venturing a step without her concurrence.

The Royal Academy may get a Keeper who may be a better instructor in handling the chalk, or inforcing the regulations of its Councils, but they will never get another who will have the power to invigorate the conceptions, enlarge the views, or inspire the ambition of the students, with such fastness, fire, and elevation.

How many delightful hours have I passed with him in one continued stream of quotation, conception, repartee, & humour. In his temper he was irritable & violent, but kind in an instant. In his person small, with a face of independent, unregulated fire.

His loss to the Academy is great, for there is no one to supply his place as a Lecturer, and in a few years so completely will Historical Painters be extinct, that no lectures will be given.

April 20. Let not a man seek for influence beyond his time! Fuzeli's Death has affected me deeply. I called at the Academy today. Fuzeli, whose voice used to make them all tremble, was silent! and the Porters and understrappers, strutting and talking of the *old Man!* I remember about 20 years ago, Lascelles Hoppner, Jackson, Wilkie, and myself were all making a great row in the hall of the Academy. I was standing with my back to the Academy stairs fighting them with my umbrella. Of a sudden they ran away. I turned round and saw Fuzeli's fiery face behind me. Out I scampered. The next day, quite ashamed of my boyish noise, I called on him. He received me with the greatest kindness, but said, 'don't make such a damn noise. I like fun myself, but I don't like to feel as if the ceiling was coming down.' Poor Hoppner is now insane! & Fuzeli dead.

May 21. What [a] time one always [has] in May in London. I always work harder in December. The regular small portion of day light keeps one on the alert. In May one gets uproarious with routs & parties, & Exhibitions, attacks, & criticisms, till one's head is in a whirl. So it is with me.

June 6. As I strolled for an hour in the Park today and distantly contemplated the string of fashion – how like ants!, I thought. There goes a little yellow looking box, and two little things with four legs & one little insect driving them, & one behind the box, and something, a living insect, behind inside, and these little boxes & insects constituted superiority!

No man can have a just estimation of the insignificance of his species, unless he has been up in an air balloon.

June 10. At Lord Grosvenor's. Never looked at a single picture, but gossipped, like an old Connoiseur. Sir George Beaumont said to a Friend, 'What a pity it is Haydon is not more employed.' It is, and what a pity it is, Sir George, that you employed me to paint a Picture, put me to 500 gs. expence, & then refused to take it. What a pity it is that you said you had no room for it. What a pity it is you took it two years after for 200gs. These are many of the pities, Sir George; I have no time for more now.

P.S. What a pity it is you specified a size to begin it on, & then wanted it smaller after I had began it six months. What a pity I was fool enough to trust you at all. This is the greatest pity.

August 13. I find the most favored Artists of the Great are those of *no education!* or those who *conceal* it. A man of rank came up to me & said, 'Do you know, Mr Haydon, I think Titian's grounds were so & so.' As long as I listened he appeared pleased, but this was putting a poker into a powder barrel. I exploded, & poured forth all I had obtained from experience & reading. He looked grave, – hummed, – talked of the weather, & took off his hat with a 'Good morning'! I can't think how Reynolds managed these things. Northcote says he always *appeared ignorant.*

October 23. Walked to Hampstead, after a harrassing week – the stillness of the meadows, the singing of the Birds – the cool freshness of the air did much to sooth my feelings, which were much wounded; – since I was in this road last, streets, in fact towns had risen and the beautiful fields at the beginning were disfigured by cart wheels, stinking of bricks and whitened by Lyme! – these wounds on solitude, purity, and nature are horrid.

October 30. Thank God, raised money enough for the exigencies of my dear Mary's expected confinement & my amounts. Laus Deo! & now to Work. God grant me health.

November 10. Idle. Called on Hazlitt, spent 3 hours with great pleasure. Began again at my Picture and finished Moses' left Foot.

November 12. Hard at work & finished his right.

November 13. Hard at work & completed my Principal figure Moses – the Leader of 600,000 rebellious Israelites!

December 1. My fit continues. I am all fits – fits of work, fits of Idleness, fits of reading, fits of walking, fits of Italian, fits of Greek, fits of Latin, fits of Religion. My dear Mary's lovely face is the only thing that has excited a fit that never varies.

December 2. I have read in my idle fit Sheridan's Life, by Moore.
Upon the whole it is [a] delightful book, but the excuse of an admirer.
Notwithstanding his passion for Miss Lindley, and his grief for his Father's death, who had ill used him, I question his having a good heart really.
His making love to Pamela, Madame Genlis' daughter, so soon after his lovely wife's death, renders one suspicious of the real depth of his passion.
His treatment of Storace's widow, the widow of one who had sacrificed his life to Sheridan's interests, ought not to have been omitted by Moore. Sheridan gave the House for a Benefit. The House was crowded of course. Sheridan went to the door keeper as manager & Friend, swept off all the receipts, and the Widow never got a shilling – so Prince Hoare told me, one of Steven Storace's intimate Friends.
No man with a good heart could have done this.
A Creditor whom Sheridan had perpetually avoided, met him at last, plump, coming out of St James's Palace into the Park from Pall Mall.

There was no possibility of avoiding him, but he never lost his presence of mind. 'Oh,' said Sheridan, 'that's a beautiful mare you are on.' 'D'ye think so?' 'Yes, indeed. How does she trot?' The Creditor, quite delighted, told him he should see, and immediately put her into full trotting pace. The instant he trotted off, Sheridan turned into Pall Mall again & was out of sight in a moment.

Moore's life of him wants courage. Society is his God. He cannot, like Johnson, tell all the truth and bid Society defiance.

December 8. I have not touched a brush or colour yet! The anxieties attendant on the confinement of a beautiful woman one loves to distraction are beyond all conception of those who are unmarried. Christ God! what a scene it is! The throttled yell! – the flushed clenched struggle! – the helpless yah, yah, yah, of the Infant the instant it tears its way into life! damnation! or eternal happiness! lacerate one's feelings beyond identification.

December 31. I may do a great deal in small Pictures and put forth grand conceptions, but still, the Dome of St. Paul's would be my glory! – and then would I raise my Country's name!

End of 1825.

THREE

1826–1831

1826

January 15. It is curious the mixture of apathy and anxiety with which I await the fate of my Picture. After all it is very little better than Dentatus, painted 18 years ago! I do think and ever shall think, considering that I was a youth from a Bookseller's shop, 3 years only from complete ignorance, when I began Dentatus, & four when I completed it, it is a remarkable instance of the effects of industry & Genius. How hard I must have worked, how deeply I must have thought in that short time, to come to such conclusions!

January 16, 17, and 18. Passed in amiable idleness & strolling about, looking into the National Gallery, &c., doing nothing, thinking less.

February 14. Had an interview with Sir Charles Long, on the subject of my Petition. He behaved very candidly, & told me he took a very different view of the subject to what I did. He said he had been long in the House of Commons, that there was nothing less known than Art, that when the Waterloo Monument was proposed, many different plans were sent in, that Lord Londonderry said the thing had better *be given up!!!* that all money voted by the House of Commons would be subject to supervision, and that the Directors, as independent Gentlemen, had determined, if the House voted the money, to *refuse* it. It was no use talking; he seemed to have a rooted aversion.

The fact is this. A Public Vote of Money will change the whole system of Art. It will take the power out of the hands of the Royal Academy, & British Gallery, and men who enjoy a monopoly do not easily relinquish its sweets.

April 1, 2, 3, and 4. Spent the day in excrutiating reflections what to do! with five children & surrounded with difficulties. The Royal Academy alone is open to me. Will it be inconsistent? No. The greatest part of the men now leading are my old fellow students. The Academy is not what it was when I attacked it. I consider it consciously modified, and why should

I keep a senseless hostility? Young men of talent have been admitted, & the whole state & condition are improved. So thinking, I resolved to send my Pictures there.

After the Pictures were gone then came the bitterness of reflection. Had I not violated a great principle? Had I not gone on my knees? God knows!

May 6. Dined at the Artists' Fund, & spent a pleasant evening. Robinson [Chancellor of the Exchequer] in the Chair.

It is curious & painful to see an elegant man begin most furiously a speech, the thoughts of which he is not certain of. The painful expression [of] his face, the violent action of his arms, the thumps he gives on the table, and then the lame periods, the rigmarole of 'I say, Sir – Gentlemen – When I reflect, I say, when I reflect, when I think, a moment, I say, Gentlemen, when I reflect, yes, when I reflect – I must say, I must be allowed to assert – and I am sure the Gentlemen present will permit me to do – Gentlemen, I knew, I thought, I foresaw I had only to ask permission of an Assembly of Men, a collection, a mass (I may say so) of talent, & Genius, alike distinguished. . . .'

May 14. This day, two and twenty years I left my Father's House for London! and it is curious that on this day Lord Egremont called & gave me a commission for Alexander! God grant me health & eyes, means & genius to make this my best work. Grant it, O God. Amen.

June 13. Got Alexander & Horse together well. He must look a Youth, or the gist of the thing is lost. At present he is like a long forked Horse Guardsman. How soon one could finish a Picture if one dashed at it like Rubens, careless of character.

June 20. Pumiced out my yesterday's head, & I hope succeeded in my new one.

June 23. Obliged to pawn my other lay figure, the female, for 5£; cost me 30; obliged. Borrowed a horse's head to paint the teeth & gums from, & had not 8/- to pay the man. However, I am in a good house, have my food, a sweet Wife, a sweet family, & good credit. I looked at Homer, at Tasso, at Shakespeare, but I kept them. I may do without a lay figure for a time, but not without old Homer. The truth is, I am fonder of books than any thing else on Earth. I have pawned my studies, my prints, my lay figures, but have kept my darling authors.

June 28. Westmacott called today – yesterday [I went] to see his horse in his statue of George III for the end of the long walk at Windsor. It shewed a great want [of knowledge] of the form of a horse, but in certain views it was grand and imposing. I hinted certain deficiencies, but I question if he was pleased. Still he thanked me.

July 3. At the Musaeum for Alexander. From his coins he wore ear rings & a necklace. Searched Diodorus Siculus for Bucephalus, nothing important.

July 5. Spent another delightful day, 5 hours, at the Musaeum. Searched Strabo, Aelian, and got considerable knowledge.

July 7. Being driven up in a corner, I applied to Lord Egremont. I told him my resources were exhausted, my ambition was to make Alexander my best Picture, and I only wanted tranquillity. I begged him to pardon my laying open my circumstances to him. I was warned of applying to him for money by others. It ruined Rossi with him, but Rossi, I suppose, applied in [the style] of a butcher.

Today I was at dinner. Oh, what anxiety dearest Mary & I suffered last night! 'It will succeed,' said she, 'or ruin you.' Had it offended him I should have had really great difficulties, but still I would have got through. Well, at dinner he called. I let him in with a beating heart. He walked up, liked Alexander very much indeed, and after looking some time he said, 'Why, what have you been about all your life?' 'Painting large pictures in hopes of the sympathy of the Public, my Lord.' 'That was imprudent,' said he. 'It was,' I replied (but I wish I could be as imprudent again, *thought* I). 'Well, I have brought you 100£,' said he. 'My Lord,' said I, 'that's salvation.' He smiled & put five 20ties on a chair. His manner was altogether mild & benevolent, and he had lost today that short sharp manner he has which he puts on, I am convinced, to keep people at a distance.

July 22. Worked from 8 to 7. Dozed for ½ hour between, from sudden dullness of brain, which went off. Succeeded completely. Tomorrow, God willing, at the knee & leg, to be sun burnt toned, rigid, muscular, warlike, and weather beaten! What a fine look it has to make the flesh the lowest part in colour, if done in tone & depth.

July 23. In an old life of Rubens, I read he made his great meal at night. He therefore suffered from indigestion. If you are careful of your diet, how much you can exert yourself; if you are guilty of the least irregularity, how soon you are fagged.

He used to rise at four, hear mass, & work till breakfast. He left off at five in the afternoon, & then rode on a black horse on the ramparts of Antwerp.

At his return he found an assembly of Friends for Supper, but all departed at XI, his hour of rest.

He used to keep wild beasts which he painted from; spoke 7 languages, & was visited by all strangers as the Wonder of Antwerp.

July 24. Out on cursed business.

July 25. I called on Sir Thomas [Lawrence] and I must say was amazingly struck by the beauty & force & grace of his women in his gallery. I think I can venture to say with truth that he is the only man since Vandyke who has detailed, without destroying, the beauty of a face! He is not mannered as he used to be, & a head of Lady Sutton's was really beautiful, pure in colour & expression, though, perhaps, a little *dollish*.

I did not say all I thought, because it might look like praising him to ingratiate myself.

Lawrence & Sir George Beaumont are the two most perfect Gentlemen I ever saw. At a large party once in a hotel [in] Jermyn Street, to breakfast with Sir Walter Scott, Sir George remained a long time with his empty cup waiting for tea. The conversation being lively, he was forgotten by Sir Walter, and I sat watching him, to observe how he would bear it. It was quite a study, to see how admirably Sir George, by anecdotes & laughing & listening kept every body from believing he was neglected. At last his cup caught Sir Walter's eye; he filled it, with apology, & Sir George took it, as if he had only then been thirsty. It was exquisitely done.

August 20. Sunday. Spent a heavenly day – quiet, diligent, & heavenly. No duns, no Lawyers' letters, no disturbance of any sort, but silent, peaceable, & holy in my feelings. My heart continually feeling grateful to God. I only say, if painting on a Sunday generates such feelings, and going to church & listening to a stupid Parson generates the contrary, which is most acceptable to God?

In the evening I walked into the fields. As we walked, dearest Mary & I, the moon rose, silvery & shining. Her lovely features shot out by its harmonious light, as if a silken gauze were spread over their beauty!! I talked to her as if for that moment only I had ever made love, and we returned, our affections heightened, and our mutual passion renewed. The love, the renewed love of those who have had children, is a million times more exquisite than the passion of innocence.

August 23. Out in the City on cursed money matters.

August 24. The same state – nothing and harrassed to Death.

August 26. I find I am not half so able to bear my difficulties when I devote my whole time to extrication, but if I mix painting & struggling, I get on a great deal better, and am quite adequate. Passed the day quietly & composing.

September 5. Saw elder Reinagle, a nice old fellow. He said he thought me infamously used, and wonder[ed] I had not gone mad or died. 'Where is your Solomon, Mr. Haydon?' 'Hung up in a Grocer's Shop!' 'Where your Jerusalem?' 'In a ware room [in] Holborn.' 'Where your Lazarus?' 'In an Upholsterer's Shop [in] Mount St.' 'And your Macbeth?' 'In

Chancery!' 'My God. Your Pharaoh?' 'In an attick pledged [to] my Employer.' 'And your Crucifixion?' 'In a hayloft.' '& Silenus?' 'Sold for half price.' Such was the conversation.

September 6. Out to raise money for water rates.

September 17. Walked into a delicious meadow, and sat down on an old stump behind some hay ricks, my back turned on the Edgware road. It was a beautiful seclusion; just after passing the Turnpike near West End lane, you turn down a lane which leads to the Harrow road; about a dozen yards on the left is a style, & close to the style hay ricks & a fallen stump. Here I sat and read Xenophon's treatise on riding & Cavalry exercise, in a French translation, which decidedly proves the Greeks did not shoe their Horses, as he gives instructions how to get the hoof so firm that it shall resist injury successfully.

September 16. As I was walking home from the City, I bought a copy of Burns' songs at a poor book stall shop in some bye street between Bloomsbury & St Giles. I went in, the price was 9. An interesting looking young woman was nursing a lovely Baby, clean washed & healthy. I put a shilling into its little fat hand; the Mother looked up with sparkling eyes. As I went away I wished it, little dear, success. This insignificant matter haunts me.

Hard at work today.

September 28. Hard at work on Darling's Portrait, without effect. In short, I do not think I have the least of the required talent that way. There never was such a damn thing as I made.

Darling is one of the staunchest of my Friends, and one whom of all others I should wish to oblige, but I fear it will not be in this way.

October 10. Began late but worked well till dinner.

My wedding day. Dearest Mary came down to dinner with a wreath of white satin bows entwined in her hair, and looking lovely looks, pregnant with sweetest remembrances. I pressed her to my soul & heart, & told her that my love had doubled since marriage. She was affected & kissed me.

October 20. Got in the Negro boy's head, and a very fine head it is. Poor little creature. He was a slave at Baltimore, and his present Master put an execution on his former master's property, and took him as part of it.

October 22. Perspectivizing all day. Lord Egremont called, and said, 'It will do. You may order a Frame.' He was uncommonly pleased. It gave me great pleasure. There is no pleasure so gratifying as having done justice to the benevolence of a liberal employer.

November 4. Left Town for Brighton, with my dear little family. The children got refreshed as they got into clear air.

November 7. Frank, the first time he saw the Sea, ran away screaming, 'It's coming, it's coming.' The first time, it must certainly look so.

November 12. Set off for Petworth, where I arrived at ½ past three. Lord Egremont's reception was frank & noble.

November 15. Sketched & studied all day. I dine with the finest Vandykes in the world! Lady Ann Carr, Countess of Bedford, is beyond every thing. I really never saw such a character as Lord Egremont! He has placed me in one of the most magnificent bed rooms I ever saw! It speaks more for what he thinks of my talents than any thing that ever happened to me! The bed curtains are difft. coloured velvets, let in on white satin. The walls green damask, sofas, easy chairs, carpet, & a beautiful view of the Park out of the high window.

What a destiny is mine! One year in the Bench, the companion of Demireps & Debtors – another, reposing on down & velvet, the guest of Rank & fashion & beauty! God in Heaven grant my Future may now be steady. At any rate, a Nobleman has taken me by the hand. Such is Lord Egremont. There is plenty, but not absurd profusion – good wines, but not extravagant waste. Every thing solid, liberal, rich, & English. At 74 he still shoots daily, comes home wet through, and is as active & looks as well as many men of 50.

November 18. I left Petworth today, & arrived safely at Brighton, where I found my dear children & dearest Mary well!

The expenditure of establishment at Petworth is 40,000 a year! His Lordship's income is 80,000. There were 5 men cooks, stables for 60 horses, 90 beds are made up, in short, the whole thing was munificent & Princely!

One day while I was lounging after dinner, surrounded by blazing wax lights, a fire that heated one's marrow, delicious wines, splendid Pictures, & Mrs King, a fine woman on my right, Lord Egremont looking venerable and noble, leaning on his hand, & the Lord & the centre of all this luxury, I began to think, 'can *he* be jealous of any thing or any body?' Just as I thought this I mentioned Cowdry Castle. 'Castle,' said Lord Egremont, 'what Castle! Cowdry is *no castle* – it was an old *Monastery!*' He was pettish & evidently disliked to have any thing like a *seat* to interfere with him! Such is human nature.

On the morning I left, I was waiting for the Coach, a man of the Town came up & asked if I was the *great* Painter. 'I do not know,' said I. 'But you painted the Entry into Jerusalem?' 'Yes, my Friend.' 'Ah, Sir, that was a Picture! What a Donkey!'

November 22. London dull after Petworth. Hard at work. I think Alexander the best, the best for effect & construction I have done.

November 30. Last day. 7 days only have I applied myself this month in consequence of various matters. But my Alexander is in fact concluded this day. And to a merciful Providence I gratefully render my thanks that I have been extricated with 5 children from ruin by the interference of Lord Egremont.

1827

February 9. Sir George [Beaumont] is dead. Poor Sir George! No man could write his character more ably than myself, but I defer it. He was one of the old school – one of the last of those links of the chain that united the Nobility & the Artists, first formed by Sir Joshua. I have spent many, many happy hours in his delightful Society. His loss, with all his faults, will not easily be supplied. He founded the National Gallery. Let him be crowned. Peace to him.

I fear I must take out & repaint the whole of Alexander. Lord Egremont was right; it is at present too much like a full grown, muscular man.

February 19. Hard at work. Repainted the head.

February 20. There are three things in this World I hope to see before I die – the Americans thrashed at Sea! my own debts paid, & Historical Painting encouraged by Government!

March 18. Spent 2 hours with Wm. Seguier. He told me as a singular coincidence, that three days before Sir George died, he wrote a letter to Lord Farnborough, and one whole side was devoted to me, that he thought me a man of great talents, &c. It is pleasant to find he went out of the world, with a smile and a good wish after all.

April 9. Sent Alexander to the Exhibition. I contrasted as I went down my feelings now and when I followed Dentatus, 1809, 17 years ago. Apathy now, *then* all nervous anxiety lest a dray horse should kick a hole; now indifferent if a house fell on it – not quite, but nearly.

May 13. Though the first Patrons of Art have been to see Lord Egremont's Alexander, which I laboured hard to make a Picture desirable to others! so that others might give me orders – but no – neither the Duke of Devonshire or Lords Londonderry or Lansdowne or Sir T. Baring, did more than praise.

May 18. Lord Egremont called, & behaved in the kindest manner; in fact, gave me another commission – for Eucles.

As he walked up stairs, he said, 'How do you find yourself? Have you anything to do?' 'Nothing, my Lord.' 'Why don't you paint Portraits?' 'My Lord, I am willing to paint anything for my family.' 'Only make 'em handsome,' said Lord Egremont.

May 28. Out all day on money matters. Mingled art as usual. Called in and saw Fuzeli's Pictures. There was a grandeur in Hercules & Pluto, a bawdiness in his women, and his men looked like surgical preparations who had burst, skinned as they were, out of the bottles in Surgeon's Hall.

May 30. Hard at work & nearly completed Eucles himself. It will be most pathetick in subject.

August 26. Went to the King's Bench to make sketches. I sketched the head of a smuggler. Never in my life did I see such a head! – air, wind, grog, risk, anxiety, sea, daring, & defiance, were cut into his handsome weather beaten head! 'After being at sea,' said I, 'does not this life hurt your health?' 'My health, sir? I keep up my health with grog. Eh, Bob?' turning round to a veteran crony. 'How many tumblers d'ye average?' 'Why, I think, sir, I may save *five and twenty!*'

September 14. At a quarter before six in the morning was born Frederick Haydon. Dearest Mary had a sharp & rapid agony.

September 17. I inherit from my Father a diseased appetite for Newspapers. It is extraordinary to what a pitch I long for the news of the day, knowing, as I do, the lies, & the folly & the humbug of the daily surmises of the Editors, but so it is, and as I get older, I find it encreases. Of all the trash I have read for 20 years, what do I retain? – not a syllable.

Frank said to me today at breakfast, 'How is it, Papa, I see things *I don't see?*' 'How d'ye mean, my dear?' 'Why, Papa, I see all sorts of things when I shut my eyes, and today as I was coming down stairs, I saw Baby falling over the stairs, though Baby was up in the nursery.'

This is imagination, and if he proves a Genius, it will be curious as an early proof of it.

September 18. Began a Portrait today, and I felt as if my hands & soul & Imagination & heart & being were numbed. How can I succeed under such impressions?

1828

March 1. I begin my new volume, not with the enthusiasm of my former ones. I have ceased to make great attempts, and have gradually sunk to fit my efforts to the taste of those on whom I depend. I have no orders, no Commissions. After all the Public sympathy of last year, I am still as much without employment as ever. The Exhibition of the Picture gets me a bare subsistence, and that is all.

What to do I am at a loss. My admission into the Academy is out of the Question. It has turned out as I predicted to Lord Egremont it would. I begin at last to long to go abroad, family and all.

March 26. My greatest weakness, I am sorry to say, is the expectations I

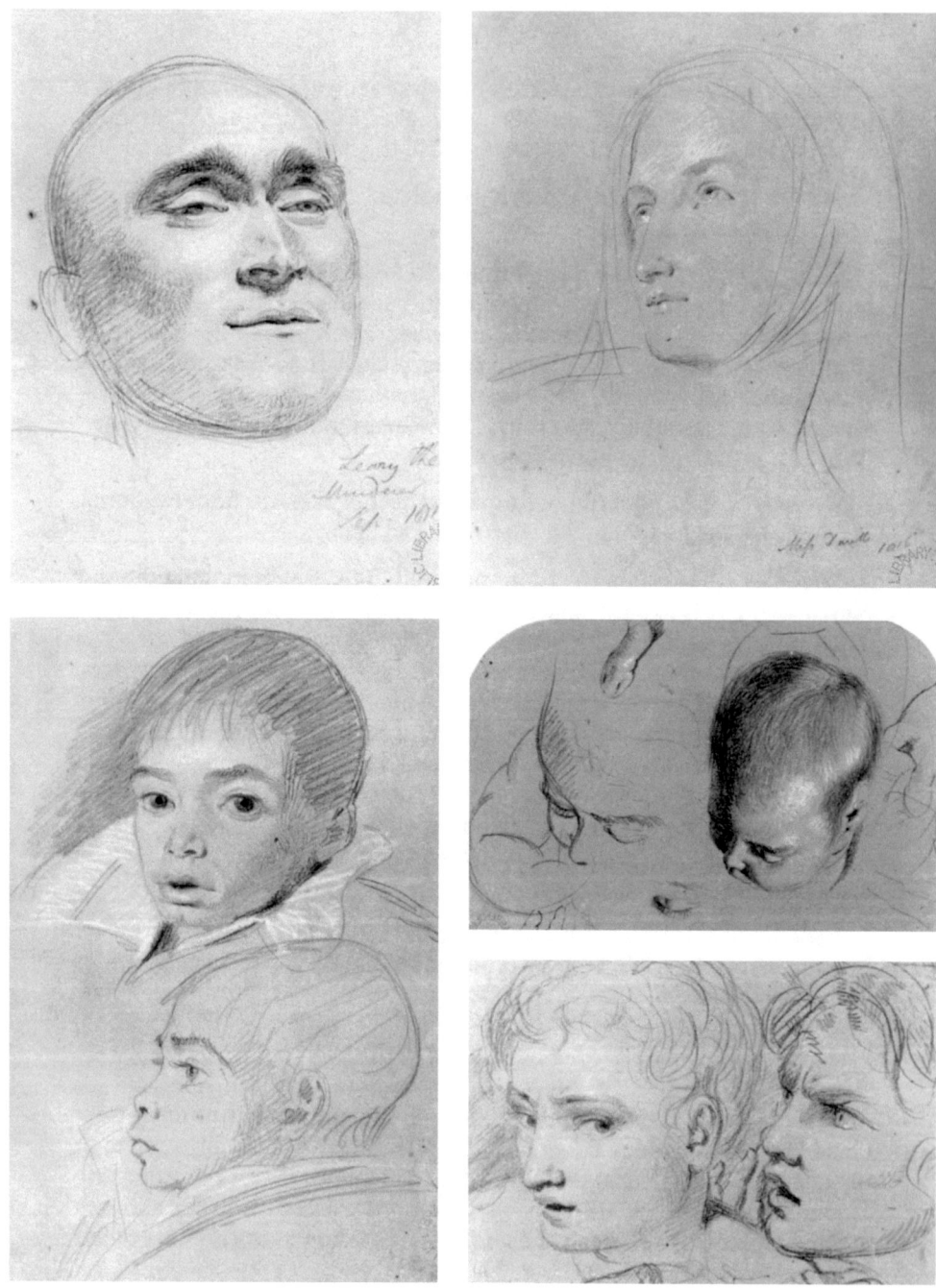

1, Sketch of a murderer, James Leary, 1813; 2, sketch of Miss Durville, 1816; 3, studies of a crippled boy; 4, two studies of a baby's head; 5, two studies of a child's head; 6, portrait study of a lady; 7, studies of physiognomy; 8, studies of eyes, 1816; 9, two sketches, *From Myself*; 10, study of a child's head

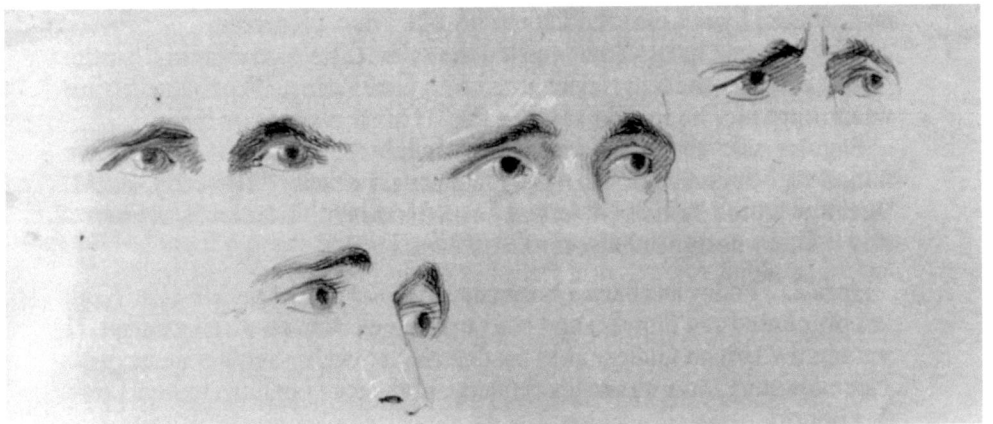

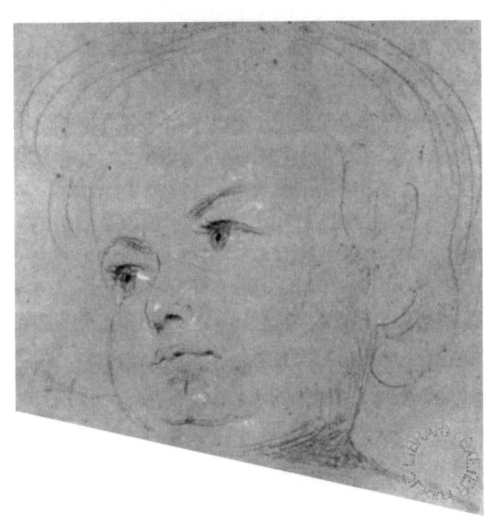

form of every Picture. I am then dissappointed, grow angry & foreboding, wander about, and return not to my pursuits till driven by conscience.

April 8. Sent in a Study of a Child's head to the Academy, and worked hard at copying an old head from a miniature. What an employment! After doing the Lazarus head! – to think at 42 years of age I am compelled to do this for bread!

April 18. This morning, to my unexpected surprize, the King, George IVth (whom God preserve), sent Seguier to say he would wish to see [my new picture] the Mock Election! For my part I am so used to be one day in a Prison, and the other in [a] Palace, that it scarcely moved me. God only grant this bit of Fortune may turn out profitable to my Creditors. Amen.

April 19. This morning I moved the Mock Election to St James' Palace. I rang the bell, and out came a respectable man, dressed in black silk stockings, &c. I was shewn into a back room, & the Picture moved in.

In a short time Livery Servants, Valets, & the devil knows who crowded around it. At XI Seguier came; the Picture was moved up into the State apartments. I went into the City to my old Friend Kearsey.

When I came back Seguier called me aside. The room was in a bustle. 'Well,' said he, 'the King is delighted with your Picture. When the Picture was brought in, he looked at it & said, "This is a very fine thing."'

Seguier said the King was highly delighted, & said, 'Come to me tomorrow.' Seguier said 'Can the King have it directly?' 'Directly,' said I. 'Meet me at the British Gallery at 12 on Monday!' 'That I will, my hero,' said I. What destinies hang on 12 on Monday!

April 21. Today has been a bright day in the annals of my life. The King has purchased my Picture, and paid my money [five hundred guineas]. I went to the British Gallery at ½ past eleven; at twelve Seguier came, with a face bursting, and was really rejoiced, and verily I believe to him I owe this honor!

To my Merciful Creator I bow & bend & beg that he will bless my next Picture of Chairing the Members, and that I may do nothing to incur his anger. Amen.

April 30. Began the High Sheriff's head, and succeeded. Sir Walter Scott called. I introduced him to the High Sheriff! Sir Walter kissed dear Frank's forehead and blessed him.

The great Art of the Portrait Painter is not so much the art of elevating the characteristics or expressions of his sitter, but the art of leaving out what is defective, purifying him, as it were, of the dross which encumbers the agreeable in his face, letting his best looks predominate.

May 19. My Portrait-day (High Sheriff's hands, finished them). By devoting a day to Portraits without interruption, I find my dislike waning. I then make it a study, and find it useful & delightful, & go to my Pictures the day after, improved by it. Worked hard.

May 30. Friday. Hard at work. Finished the High Sheriff. At the Opera, to see Otello – Pasta & Sontag – as fine acting in Desdemona as I have ever seen. Pasta's voice did not suit Otello's masculine tone – not as we imagine, but her action was fine indeed.

June 14. Idleness has restored me. Tomorrow at it again.

Feebly at work, but advanced. Buonaparte during the battle of Dresden, eat a tough leg of mutton. His digestion became deranged; and to his illness was attributed his subsequent misfortunes & loss of his Campaign. This it is. Lord Castlereagh eat buttered toast, which encreased his disease, & he cut his throat an hour afterwards! – and the crust of a gooseberry pye has impeded these last three days the thinking of a still more illustrious individual, B. R. Haydon!

July 6. Hard at work – 11 hours without fatigue. Advanced greatly.

July 9. The moment I quit my canvas, I get into all sorts of messes.

Whether it is the activity of my mind, or that trifles press more heavily on me when not occupied, I can't tell, but the Children seem to cry more than usual; the Postman knocks harder than ever; the dustman's bell makes more noise.

July 27. The principles & the practice of the Bible are like all principles and practice. The principles laid down are Divine, the Practice human.

God made a promise to Abraham, talked to him, shewed his glory! But Abraham was human, and when God left him, he was liable to human weaknesses & passions!

God selected Moses, talked to him daily, but this was no reason that Moses should not be liable to be governed by his passions & his failings.

In the Bible there are things I can't get over. The Sun's standing still is one; 'it is not written in the Book of Ashur,' says the Narrator, as if he leaned on the Book of Ashur, in case *he* (the Writer) was *doubted*. This makes it suspicious!

Then, says the doubter, *all or none.* I say no. *Here* are the great leading points to rest on. The Bible & Testament will undoubtedly render you *all* you could hope for, *if* you follow their directions in conduct. What d'ye wish more?

August 17. Sunday. I made Frank read prayers after I had sat my Palette, meaning to go to Work, but my heart got warmed with pious feelings, so I shaved, dressed, and went to Church.

I am glad I did. I felt a calm the whole day quite inexpressible, and though I have delayed my Picture a day, yet there is something in keeping your Sabbath according to the Wishes of your God.

September 1. Worked 2½ hours, and then went out on affairs. I have been ill this last week; after hard work one feels drawn out like an overstretched fiddle string, and as susceptible as if impaled.

I came down to lunch in a damp room, & caught cough & cold in five minutes. After 6 hours painting, you first feel delicately perspiring, and then the last two hours more, you do more than in the previous six, but confusion, dullness, langour succeed, and if I was to dine directly, I could not digest my meat. A walk restores one, but not till next day are you an adequate judge of what you have done.

September 28, 29 and 30. Hard at work and got all my Pictures well up at the Exhibition. Success to them!

October 1, 2, and 3. Finally arranged the Exhibition. Lord Egremont kindly lent me Alexander.

October 6. The Exhibition opened with great success thanks to my great Protector. Never was Picture more liked. Success to it.

October 13. Talfourd made us laugh excessively. Hazlitt was playing cards with a party at Charles Lamb's, when Lamb's Brother affirmed that Holbein's colouring was as fine as Vandyke's.

Hazlitt burst up & swore, and Lamb's Brother gave him a black eye. The Card table was overturned, & the room arose in confusion, to part the Combatants, when Hazlitt exclaimed to Talfourd, 'By God, Sir, you need not trouble yourself. I do not *mind a blow*, Sir; nothing affects me but *an abstract Idea!*'

October 17, 18, 19, and 20. Occupied. October is closing and I am ill. I always get ill between one picture and another.

November 24. Began Eucles & worked again, thank God, 2½.

November 26. Four hours today. Huzza!

1829

January 12. Concluded the additions to my Pamphlet, but up to this moment have not touched a brush.

January 14. Rubbed in Samson & Dalilah, a new Picture. Mr Strutt sent me 30£ more for my Drawings of the Chairing, which again rescued me.

The nipple should always be a little above the centre. In Rubens & common nature it is below, which gives a flabby, infirm look.

January 30. What an extraordinary man Wellington is [the Prime Minister]. The day I sent my letter his head must have been full, morning, noon, & night. Parliament opens on Thursday. The Catholic question was coming on. The Spitalfield weavers came in procession with a petition. There was a Council till six. The day before he was at Windsor. In addition to all this, consider the hundreds of letters & petitions & immediate duties, and yet he found time to answer himself my request with all the caution & presence of mind, as if lounging in his drawing room with nothing else to do!

January 31. At the Private day of Gallery. The Pamphlet has had a great effect. It has had one great effect of making every body acknowledge that nothing but a grant of money would do the thing. This is an immense deal.

February 9. The Duke's answer is, I fear, fatal for the present. Hard at work on Eucles, & settled the perspective.

February 14. Saw Agar Ellis by appointment, and told him all that had passed between the Duke and myself. Asked him if I had any chance by laying the plan regularly through the Secretaries before him. He said, 'Not in *the least*' – that last year the Directors of the Gallery applied to the Government for 3000, giving 3000 of their own money, to buy a piece of ground to extend the National Gallery. Lord Wellington *would not listen to it.*

Mr Agar Ellis begged me to continue my pamphlets every year, and whenever he saw a prospect he would make the motion requisite. The King is my only hope now, and perhaps he is afraid of the Duke, as every body seems to be.

February 22. Spent two hours with Wilkie and a very pleasant two hours indeed, looking over his Spanish Pictures.

We then of course got on the old subject – *my writing.* Wilkie said, 'It is not the most conducive to a man's interests to be *too right.*' (I thought this a good touch.) 'It is rather better,' said he, 'to let others imagine they are right & you wrong, if you want to get on in the World.'

April 14. Began Punch. Sketched in. God bless it with success & grant I may make it a moral Satire!

April 15. Finished one cursed Portrait; have only one more to touch, and then I shall be free. I have an exquisite gratification in painting Portraits wretchedly. I am rascal enough to take their money, & chuckle more.

April 24. Studied the Eucles once more. They find fault with the leg.

May 10. Read prayers at home – felt bitter remorse of conscience at my late neglect. I go on, day after day, like Johnson, in hypochondria, looking for hours like an idiot at my Picture, without the power to do one single thing. With my family it is dreadful. I am so often turned off my balance by pecuniary difficulty, that it is a perpetual struggle to get on the road again, and yet the only chance I have of getting out of difficulty is by hard work.

June 3 to 16. Fully occupied – in dissipation – Christening parties, Conversaziones – jaunts – dinings – drinkings, fatigues – long sleeps – and the dizzy dosings of ennui & pleasure. My God, what a life! This won't do. Next month is my month of trial. Creditors, Dividends & Lawyers' letters – By this day month, Eucles, thou must be complete.

Turner's Pictures always look as if painted by a Man who was born without hands, and having contrived to tie a brush to the hook at the end of his wooden stump, he managed by smudging, bungling, scrawling, twisting, & splashing, to convey to others a notion of his conceptions. His Pictures and his drawings have this look – they are the works of a savage, suddenly excited to do his best to convey to his fellows his intense impression of the scenery of Nature – without the slightest power in the World of giving the forms, he devotes himself solely to the effects & colour of what he sees.

On what metaphysical principles genius can be proved to exist in a Picture because every rational person mistakes an Elm tree for a Cabbage I have yet to learn.

It is a pleasure, it is a comfort, to find Academicians unanimous without evil intention, the thing, in fact, that most generally makes them so. The Landscape Painters stand up for Turner with an heroic adhesion, conscious if they don't what becomes of them.

June 18. Studied Vases – that is, lounged over them.

June 21. What are individual heads & small Pictures to me? – disgusting. I am adapted for a great national work, to illustrate a National triumph or a moral principle. My mind languishes in another attempt. It is the truth.

June 30. Hard at Work & got through my figures in Eucles. Nothing now to do but back ground & tone.

I cannot but feel pleasure in thus having got through this Picture of Eucles, after a great deal of trouble & misfortune.

I will now begin Xenophon and the Ten Thousand seeing the Sea from Mount Theches – this shall be my next Historical Picture to finish, with Punch, and I pray God bless its commencement, progression, & conclusion, Amen.

July 2. Perspectivising – and got my background ready for finishing. When perspective is done it is extremely delightful, but a cursed bore while doing.

July 3. At work – hard – & made sketches of Horses for Xenophon.

August 24. Went to Greenwich, and spent the day with my Friend, one of the purchasers of Solomon. Saw the Gallery they are making.

Never did any Gallery shew so compleatly the utter ignorance of the power, the public power of the art, as in the arrangement of this Gallery. Instead of making History the leading feature, adorned and assisted by leading Portraits of the Great & Illustrious only, it is a family collection of Portraits with names one never heard of – men who got commands through borough mongering, did nothing to deserve distinction, then or now.

September 25. Returned to Town after 10 days absence to vote for my Friend Capt. Lockyer, at Plymouth. Devonshire is a gem. I remember when a child I used to loiter behind my nurse to look & muse on the scenery of this enchanting place, & could not tell what there was to make my heart beat so. The fact is, the Scenery is so poetic it was impossible not to affect a Poetick mind. The deep shadow of umbrageous trees, the green emerald masses of Foliage, the crystal ripple of the limpid springs, were fit to excite emotions deep & passionate.

September 27, 28, and 29. I have felt peculiarly happy, as if life was a blessing, an exquisite one. This is all physical health & Devonshire air. I played fives today for four hours with my boy & beat him five games out of six.

My notion of a perfectly happy day is this. After a sound sleep to wake & find your cheek on the bosom of the Woman you love. Remembrances of the previous night flush her cheek; you press her rosy lip & pay the usual divine sacrifice to her beauty. After a dreamy delicious doze, you rise & pray from your heart.

You then breakfast, on chocolate & tea & chicken & tongue & eggs, take the bath after lounging over the Papers, paint four hours & succeed, & then ride with your lovely Mary by the sea shore or the winding copses of enchanting Devon. You then return, read two hours, & dine. After dinner, while sipping your wine, a glass or two of champagne, retire to coffee or tea, talk love on a satin sofa to the object of your devotion, and read to her, holding her lovely hand, touching her lovely person. The time of rest draws near, and her heart & your heart beat, in anticipation of another Sacrifice before rest. You then talk dozingly & encircled in each other's arms, sleep till day break!

October 18. I will not admit that any Portrait Painter, however eminent, is an adequate judge of the higher walk of Art.

A Man who has never seen the human figure but in an easy chair, must be shocked at the daring foreshortenings produced by the convulsions of passion.

November 7 to 11. Hard at work & harrassed. Punch nearly done, in spite. People are beginning to come to Town.

November 27. 'Why did not you bring Haydon among you?' said Lord —— to an Academician. 'Oh, my Lord, his *moral character!*'

My moral character – thus it is, after having been driven from all the ground they have taken for 20 years, this is their last. What I have done I know not. But what I have not done I know.

1830

January 1. The year has commenced. I am supersititious about omens & good luck. I called on my Friend Kearsey, and he paid me in advance on my Commissions for him & sent my dear Mary a fine goose. Of course this is good luck for a new year. It can't be otherwise.

January 9. Worked hard.

Lawrence is dead. To Portrait Painting a great loss. He was suited to the Age, & the Age to him. He flattered its vanities, pampered its weaknesses, and met its meretricious taste.

His men were all Gentlemen, with an air of fashion, and the dandyism of high life; his women were delicate, but not modest – beautiful, but not native. They seem to look to be looked at, and to languish for the sake of sympathy. They had not that air of virtue & rank which ever accompanied the women of Reynolds.

On the contrary every woman Sir Thomas painted appeared to display her lovely form for the sake of admiration. You were disposed, the moment you looked at them, to march up like a dandy, & offer your services, or twirl your [stick,] cock your hat, and say, 'Damme, will that do?' He will be dreadfully missed.

January 18. Arose before day light & walked to Town. The moon was up & the sky rosy and it really was a delicious bracing treat. I came home with a stride & a vigour, eat three mutton chops, and drank four cups of tea with a fury of jaw which would have done honor to Hercules.

Did less than nothing.

January 29. Lawrence's sudden death threw the Academy into the most bitter puzzle.

On Monday the Election [for President] took place, and on Monday morning out came the King's appointment of [Wilkie as] Sergeant Painter in the Gazette from Lord Chamberlain's office. The moment I read it I said, 'This will destroy Wilkie's chance of success,' and in the evening the Academicians rushed in as the time approached, fearful of some message from the King that it would be pleasing for his feelings if Wilkie were elected, that without regular ballotting they made every member write down the name of the man he wished. Wilkie had one or two votes – some tell me one & some the other – Beechey 6 – & Shee 18 – which was received with a hourra.

Shee is an Irishman of great plausibility, a chatting, speechyfying, colloquial, well informed, pleasant fellow, exceedingly waspish, conscious of no high power in Art, and very envious of those who have.

A man of such keen perception of what is gratifying to the envious is sure to be popular, and he will be the most popular President that the Artists have ever had; but the precedent established, viz., that high talent is not necessary to the highest rank in the Art, is one of the most fatal blows ever inflicted on the dignity of the Academy since it has been established.

February 2. Occupied with business preparatory to the Exhibition. Moved my Pictures in. God in Heaven protect us all & grant me success.

February 22. I never knew till last night that the Crown at the Coronation was not bought, but borrowed. Rundell [goldsmiths and jewelers to George IV] charged 7000 for the loan, and as some time elapsed before it was decided whether the crown should be bought or not, Rundell charged 3 or 4000 more for the interval.

Well, my private day was splendid. In the morning Seguier came up, with orders from the King to see the Pictures & if worth seeing *to bring them down.* The King said, 'On Saturday next, after the Exhibition closes, send down Punch by night, & he shall have it again on Monday by 7 in the morning.'

Nothing could be so good & considerate. But alas, he will think me a selfish fellow not to send the Picture direct. In God my Protector, my Saviour, indeed I can trust only in him. I am on the brink of ruin; Mary has lost her thousand pounds by the bankruptcy of her Attorney! and I have accepted bills for the month, but in him I trust who knoweth all hearts. Protect & save me, O God!

March 29. ½ past eight. I am this moment come into my Painting Room! – and the effect of Xenophon is absolutely *irresistible. Go on I will.*

O God, on my knees I humbly, humbly, humbly pray thee to enable me to go through it. Oh save me from Prison, on the confines of which I am hovering. I have no employment, no resources, a large family, & no hope! In thee alone I always trust. O God, bless my effort in this glorious conception. Amen. (By God's blessing I got through it, but was imprisoned & ruined first. It was raffled May 9, 1836, & won by the Duke of Bedford. So God listened to my Prayer but tried me first. BRH.)

April 4. Made drawings for Xenophon, but I actually tremble at the thought of concluding it, with my family & no encouragement. God guide me, for I hesitate.

April 5. Eucles was raffled for this day.

April 13. Out in the morning on the old story; called on a Lawyer, who had orders to proceed. He promised not to do so till he wrote; this was for

19 – my Coal Merchant. Came home very tired; lunched; sat to work. Dearest Mary sat, & before dinner I finished the female head in the Xenophon.

April 18. Sunday. Hard at work, and advanced well, head, neck, & arm of the principal figure. At any rate no one will deny I have shewn a characteristic of my glorious Countrymen, viz., Bottom. I fought to the last, and though floored, I have never been beaten & never will.

April 22. Finished a rascally Portrait, the last I have got – a poor, pale faced, skinny creature, who was biting his lips to make them look red, rubbing up his hair, and asking me if I did not think he had a good eye.

May 10. I am going out after a delicious muse on Xenophon. I completed yesterday the Back-ground, and it is extraordinary the improvement.

May 17, 18, and 19. Harrassed, and at last torn from my Family for £15.16. In Execution. Ah, what a sight! Mary tried for a long time to encourage me, and at last tears such as angels shed burst forth. 'Will you be taken from me?' 'Yes, my Love.' 'Can't I influence the man?' She went in, tears trickling over her cheeks; the man was touched, but could not yield.

May 30. King's Bench. Sir Robert Peel's kindness has relieved my mind greatly. [He sent BRH £10.] My miseries have been great indeed, but I feel a lifting of heart I can't get rid of – a sort of breaking in of light on my brain, like the influence of a superior spirit, like the secret support [of] a Deity!

O Lord, keep us all in health, and let me be restored to my dear Children before their dear Mother is confined. Enlighten my mind to conceive a petition which may advance the cause. On my knees I pray for thy blessing.

June 10. The English accuse the French of being vain. They are so, but it is public. They are vain of their Nation, they are vain of her monuments, her Art, her Science, her fame, while the English are more vain with less excuse, for the Vanity of the English is selfish, domestic, individual, confined.

A Mr Childers bought the tree against which Wellington stood at Waterloo, & has cut it up for timber to make presents of. He gave the Duke of Rutland enough for a chair. This is exclusively an illustration of the English disease. They can't let a thing remain for all to enjoy. They have no poetry, no national feeling; they must have it to themselves, they must cut it up for their fire sides, & shew it to their Christmas parties. Oh England, never were such a people. On every English chimney piece, you will see a bit of the real Pyramids, a bit of Stonehenge! a bit of the first cinder of the first fire Eve ever made, a bit of the very fig leaf which Adam first gave her. You can't admit the English into your gardens but they will strip your trees, cut their names on your statues, eat your fruit, & stuff their pockets with bits for their musaeums.

In short the ignorance, vanity, want of feeling, grossness, rudeness, consequence, & impotent impertinence of any given number of English when they are uncontrolled, is a matter of great & just complaint from Petersburgh to Lisbon.

As the conduct of Seguier to me in the whole affair of the King is an extraordinary instance of character, a narrative while I have leisure will perhaps hereafter be no uninteresting matter to my family & Friends.

William Seguier began to study the Art, but not having energy, he gave it up, turned Connoiseur, a much easier profession, and though without education or common knowledge, from sheer native tact, soon rose to confidential situations.

He is the most complicated mixture of good nature & spite, knowledge & ignorance, malice & simplicity, candour & intrigue, selfishness & generosity, pride & condescension, that his Friendship is a pang, and his enmity a fiendish dislike. Added to this, he is dissappointed because he failed himself. He is devoted to those who are dead, & dreads the success of the living.

Such are the gratifications, the vices, & the virtues of the man, who at this moment, on the whole, has more influence, more power, & more desire for it, than any individual Artist ever had, can ever have, or ever will.

His King does nothing without Mr Seguier's advice. At the B. Gallery he is keeper, hanger, judge, secretary, & factotum. At the National Gallery he is director, & every private collection is under his control, his management, & his protection, and the meaness of his nature renders him, though apparent Friend, the secret enemy of all modern Art.

With such convictions of this man's dispositions, to my utter astonishment, after a long absence, comes Mr Seguier to my house! I opened the door & in he walks. 'Have you any objection to let the King see your Mock Election?' 'Instantly,' said I! 'When?' said he. 'Tomorrow at XI,' said I.

All night I lay in anticipating agony & torture. Might not the King die? Might not the Aegyptian Hall catch fire? Good God! After what I had suffered, to be noticed by my Sovereign!

However, day broke as usual, the smoke came out of the chimnies, as it has ever done since chimnies were built, and up I got, nervous & anxious, and by eleven was in the Palace, with the Mock Election. Seguier soon made his appearance, and after a delay the Picture was taken up. The King was delighted, asked the price, gave him 525, and Seguier paid it me, as my Journal of the time, with all particulars, relates (1828).

I was astonished at all this. I hoped he was my real Friend after all, but

Mary positively asserted he had been ordered & could not help himself.

The Academicians were so enraged, they abused him whenever they met him, and Seguier, I have no doubt, determined, if any other opportunity occurred of a similar nature, to sacrifice me for the sake of again ingratiating himself with the Academicians and their Friends.

This being the state of the case, I finished the Chairing. No notice was taken of this Picture, and I was obliged to sell it for 300. I then concluded the Eucles & the Punch, after a great struggle brought the Exhibition of them to the very point, and about two hours before the Nobility came in on my private day, in walked Master Seguier. Immediately Seguier said, 'I have had this letter by Post, with orders from the King to see your Pictures of Eucles & Punch. Now,' said Seguier, 'I must see the King tomorrow, and if he should wish to have them down, what must I say?'

'Why,' I replied, 'say they shall be sent instantly.'

'If the King should keep them,' said he, 'it will ruin you with all this expence. I will tell him. He must not keep them *now*, & if he buys it, it can be said *purchased by his Majesty*.'

'It would not be fair to take them entirely away, but at the same time, if his Majesty should wish it, let it be done. I will take the consequences.'

On Sunday he went to Windsor. On Tuesday early I saw him. 'Well,' said he, 'the King has ordered Punch down on Saturday after your Exhibition closes, to remain with him all Sunday & return again time enough to open on Monday. I told the King *a week's receipts was an object to your family*.'

'My God, Seguier, how could you say such a thing!'

'Do you know,' said Seguier, 'he expected I had brought the Picture.'

'How could he,' said I. 'Why I did not tell you,' said he, 'I had orders to bring them down on Saturday.'

'Good God! You did not tell me that. Do not you know my gratitude to the King? What must he think of me? You have ruined me, Seguier. He will not buy Punch! You might as well have put a pistol to my head! What right had you to conceal his orders, to go down with excuses, as if from me, as if I authorized you, when I knew nothing of his wishes. Was there ever such treachery? My prospects in that quarter are blasted for ever.'

I went away cut to the soul, & left him looking embarrassed, joking & mortified.

One word from him would have made my fortune. He knew my dreadful danger, he knew Mrs Haydon had lost her 1000, he knew I was on the borders of ruin, and instead of holding out his hand & helping an old Friend, he withdrew his hand, and gave him a secret push that hurled him to the bottom.

All that week his restlessness was a curious object of speculation.

He evidently feared the King would buy it. He sent Sir Rob. Peel, he sent Watson Taylor, he sent all his rich Friends, to nibble in hopes they would buy it, and he kept urging me all the time to seize the first offer made.

At last the day came, and to see his anxiety that nobody should know where the Picture was going, his fidget, his envy, his jokes, his nervousness, I could not have believed it.

To cut an unpleasant subject short, the Punch went down, was taken to the King's bed chamber, & returned on Monday morning as promised.

On Monday I called on Seguier, and with a dry sarcasm & evident relish, he said, 'The King did not like your Picture.' My presence becoming, I saw, burthensome, I left him, & never will I speak to him to the day of my Death.

All my previous suspicions of this Villain are thus realized. Sir George & Lady Beaumont told me he it was who obstructed the sale of Jerusalem, that I might depend on it, he was my bitterest enemy. Thus after 26 years in intense devotion, I have been spurned without cause from the Royal Academy, ruined by the British Gallery, & now by the intrigues of a low bred Villain, a Slave, obstructed in the best prospects of the favor of my Sovereign.

June 17. Lord Stafford sent me ten pounds this morning, which has actually saved us from wants. Dear Mary! I trust in God I shall be home with her before the dear love is confined.

June 18. Why do not you leave the Country? Why, because I love it. I glory in its beef, its bottom, & its boxing. It is the duty of every Englishman of talent to stay & reform, to combat or destroy the prejudices of his obstinate countrymen. Their very virtues become their vices. The same invincible bottom which beat the French at Waterloo induces them to prepare to receive cavalry at every approaching innovation.

Thus it is, thus it ever will be. The English have the finest arms & the broadest chests of any nation in the world, and though by far the least looking men in Paris of all the Allies, took up more ground than ever the gigantic Russian Guards. This was entirely owing to the breadth of their shoulders.

June 19. Letter from Peel – kind & good. God bless him.

Whitehall
June 19, 1830
Sir,
From a communication I have had from the Treasury I am induced to hope that your wife and family will not be troubled on account of the arrears of Taxes due, and that time wld. be given you to liquidate those arrears by your own exertions.
I am, sir, your obedient servant,
Robert Peel.

Nothing could be kinder but a good commission, which would put it in my power to pay my arrears.

June 20. Passed the day in all the buz, blasphemy, hum, noise, & confusion of a Prison. Thoughtless creatures! My room came close to theirs. Such language! Such jokes! Good heavens. I had read prayers to myself in the morning, and prayed with the utmost sincerity for my dearest Mary & children, & to hear those poor fellows, utterly indifferent, as it were, was really distressing to one's feelings.

June 22. The next war will be the most terrific war ever fought! The great Nations of Europe are silently preparing for an attempt to crush us. Their visits to us after the last war ended, excited their jealousy, & they will never rest till they have made another desperate struggle.

But they will be beaten, & the glory & the language of England will be spread over the Earth. June 22, 1830. B. R. Haydon.

June 26. The King died this morning at 15 minutes past three.

Thus died as thorough bred an Englishman as ever existed in the Country. He admired her sports, gloried in her prejudices, had confidence in her bottom & spirit, & to him, & to him alone, is the destruction of Napoleon owing. I have lost in him my sincere Admirer, and had not his wishes been perpetually thwarted, he would have given me ample and adequate employment.

The people the King liked had all *a spice of vice* in their natures. This is true. There was a relishing sort of abandonment about them which marked them as a peculiar class, & one could judge of the King's nature by the nature of the companions he seemed to like.

The account of his Death is peculiarly touching. There must be something terrifically awful in the moment, physically considered. His lips grew livid, & he dropped his head on the Page's shoulder, & saying 'This is Death' died!

July 2. A Gentleman said to me, 'When you are in this place, you must get rid of all the *finer* feelings.' 'Pardon me,' said I, 'you must struggle hard to keep them. This is your only salvation.'

July 3 and 4. Read & wrote hard.

July 5. Dear Frank came. His little face seemed toned by misfortune! as if he had been prematurely thinking about something he could not make out. Sweet fellow! God protect him & grant him virtue and Genius.

July 13, 14, and 15. The Law of Arrest must have had its origin in savage times, when the novelty of money and the wish to gain it was of more consequence than the blood of Man. For how can any one reconcile on any principle of justice, greater power given to Society to secure the repayment of money, than to seize the murderer or the thief.

Supposing the same power was given to imprison a man on the simple oath of any other, even in Murder!! – could any thing be more repugnant to principles of justice?

July 19. Again put on my trial, and again honourably acquitted. At the conclusion the Chief Commissioner said, 'There has nothing passed this day which can reflect the slightest on your character.'

Throughout the whole of this Affliction, God has indeed been merciful and on my knees I bless thee that my dearest Mary has been preserved from premature labour. O God, have mercy & grant no delay may hinder my return to my family and my Art, and O God, Bless me with health & vigour to complete my Xenophon now began.

July 20. Returned to my family, & found all my dear children and their dear Mother quite well, & happy to see me. I fell on my knees & thanked God. Now to work like a Lion after a fast, as soon as I am settled. God bless my efforts.

July 21. Passed the day in a dull stupor, as if recovering from a blow. Studied the Xenophon, but quite abroad.

July 27. My worthy Landlord Newton, gave me a commission to finish Mercury & Argus for 20 gs. So I am set off. Darling gave me a commission to paint a head for 10gs. Oh, if I can keep out of debt & carry my great object!

July 28, 29, 30, and 31. Occupied in various ways, but recovered my spirits & health. My Grocer gave me a commission to paint his Portrait.

August 1. Again France is in Revolution & now perhaps will come that War Mr Canning predicted when he said the next war would be the War of opinion, and the most dreadful of all. Weak men always mistake the time of being decided; they concede when they ought to be firm, & are obstinate when they ought to concede. Because Louis 16 was blamed for not acting with more decision, Charles X, 30 years afterwards, begins by force, not taking into consideration the great difference of the people now & then.

The consequence will be, he will be dethroned, for they have all had a taste of the intelligence & Liberty of the Press, and the French Nation can no more exist without it, any more than the English.

August 8. Walked to Hampstead with dear Frank, and enjoyed the air & sweet scented meadows. Thought of the poor prisoners in the Bench, Bacon & others, who would have relished this sweet smell – what I have seen, and what I have suffered, always gives a touch of melancholy to my enjoyments.

August 10. Thank God! the French have settled their Government, and the Duke of Orleans is King! What a great point for Liberty over the whole Earth!

August 19. At ½ past five in the morning was born a fine boy, whom I think I shall call Benjamin Robert Haydon. God protect him and his dear Mother. Hard at work on Mercury, and greatly improved the background to Xenophon.

September 9. Began again Xenophon on the *saleable* size – size of Eucles. If they had not put me in Prison I should have nearly done it the size of life. April, May, June, July, August – all fine months for working and light. I have now September, October, November, December, January.

September 18. William Hazlitt is dead – a very formidable enemy to English Art, with the sophism of a metaphysician and the practical knowledge of a disappointed Artist, he added the malignity that ever accompanies failure.

Immoral in principle, treacherous in Friendship, yet he was a consistent, determined, heroic upholder of the rights of Nations. For this I honor him. He died poor, nor do I believe he would have sacrificed one iota of his political creed to have possessed millions. B. R. Haydon.

September 25. In spite of my affecting to despise Portrait, I am uneasy at my want of success. I went this morning to look at Pickersgill's, who has more tenderness of execution than any. I was much gratified. He is an old fellow student, and has a great deal of independence & noble feeling. I respect him excessively. My own Portraits looked hard & stiff.

October 2. Out the whole day on business. Heard from Lady Stafford, who kindly interested herself in getting Lord Stafford to assist me with £50 to get my eldest step son [Orlando] matriculated at Oxford, for which I am to paint a Picture. It is very good & kind of Lord Stafford.

October 12. I wrote the Duke, calling his attention to the report of Guizot, who had recommended the King to employ Historical painters to commemorate the late events. I contrasted the condition of Art here. I asked his Grace if he would suffer England to be inferior to France. This was his reply. I sent my letter at nine in the morning today; at two came his answer!

London, October 12th 1830.
    Sir,
    I have received Your Letter.
    It is certainly true that the British Public give but little encouragement to the Art of Historical Painting. The reason is obvious; there are no funds at the disposal of the Crown or its Ministers that are not voted by Parliament upon Estimate, and applied strictly to the purposes for which such funds are voted.
    No minister could go to parliament with a Proposition for a Vote for a Picture

to be painted and there can therefore be no such encouragement here as there is in other Countries for this Art.

I am much concerned that I cannot point out the mode in which this want of encouragement can be remedied.

I have the Honor to be, Sir, Your most obedient humble Servant,
Wellington.

October 25. Out, selling my Prints. Sold enough for maintenance for the week. Several people looked hard at me with a roll of Prints, but I feel more ashamed at borrowing money than in honestly thus selling my labours.

October 29. What an extraordinary, invisible sort of *stirring* are the impulses of genius. You first feel uneasy, you can't tell why. You look at your Picture, & think it will not do. You walk for air – your Picture haunts you. You can't sleep; up you get in a fever, when all of a sudden a great flash comes inside your head, as if a powder magazine had exploded without any noise. Then come ideas by millions – the difficulty is to choose. Xenophon is a hit. Every body says it will do. I am sure of it. O God, grant me life and health to complete this grand Work!

December 7. Worked lightly. Called on my dear Landlord Newton. Told him I could not proceed unless he forebore to press for rent till Xenophon was done. He consented. Huzza!

December 8. Sir Robert Peel called, and gave me a commission to paint Napoleon musing, the size of life.

I hope this visit will lead to good. My keeping my word to him to pay up my taxes has had no bad effect. God bless me through the Napoleon. Hard at work. 6 hours ½.

December 11. Out the whole day making studies from Napoleon's hat, with as much care as I would the anatomical construction of a limb. I know it now as well. The hat fitted me exactly, and my scull is, like Napoleon's, 22 inches in circumference. There was something terrific about its look, & it excited associations as powerful as the helmet of Alexander.

1831

January 1. Forgot even the beginning of a new, as well as the end of an old year. Out on business.

January 8. Hardish at work, but completed the Napoleon excepting glazing.

January 27, 28, and 29. All passed since 11th in a fit of ennui & self reproach, which my misfortunes & the remembrance of them sometimes generate.

March 8. Dreamt Michel Angelo came to me last night, in my Painting Room. I talked to him, & he shook hands with me. I took him to the small medallion over my chimney piece, and said, 'It's very like, but I do not think *your nose is so much broken as I had imagined*.' I thought it strange in my dream. I could not make it out how *he* came there. I thought he had a brown coat & complexion. All this I literally dreamt. In my dreams there is all great humour!

I certainly think something grand in my destiny is coming on, for all the spirits of the illustrious dead are hovering about me.

March 14. Out all day about money & rooms. I called on Sir Robert Peel & was admitted to his Library. I found him sitting in his magnificent Library reading, & very pale. He seemed harrassed. He is, I think, a nervous man. He promised to call to see his picture, Napoleon. In the afternoon he called, & was much pleased. But he had a cowed air. Why I know not. Politically he is, I daresay, harrassed about this reform bill, & his party wanting him perhaps to take the lead, and he is really unwilling to leave the sweets of private life for the turbulence & harrass of a public situation.

What would I give for such a library!

April 12. Wordsworth called after an absence of several years. I was *glad* to see him. He spoke of my Napoleon in high poetry of language, with his usual straight forward intensity of diction. We shook hands heartily. He spoke of Napoleon so highly that I told him to give me a Sonnet. If he would or could, he'd make the fortune of the Picture.

April 15. Wordsworth has promised a Sonnet.

April 21, 22, 23, 24, 25, and 26. All lost in politicks, heat, fury, discussion, & battling. Never was such a scene seen as in the House of Lords last Friday. Londonderry bent his fist at the Duke of Richmond! – and if it had not been for the Table would certainly have struck him.

April 27 and 28. There was an Illumination last night. The mob broke all the windows which had no lights. They began breaking the Duke's; but when the Butler came out & told them the Dutchess was lying dead in the house, they stopped. There is something affecting in the conqueror of Napoleon appealing, in pity to a People he had saved. What a change!

June 9. Mrs Siddons died this morning, the greatest, grandest Genius that ever was born! Peace to her immortal shade! She was good, & pious, and an affectionate Mother. Posterity can never properly estimate her power, any more than we can estimate Garrick's. Hail & farewell!

June 12. I received today Wordsworth's sonnet & fancied myself the greatest of men.

June 21. Thus ends half the year. Finished Napoleon – half finished another – 4 sketches – and advanced Xenophon. Horse nearly done. Instead of that detestable cart horse breed of Raphael and others, I have tried the blood Arab. It seems to give great satisfaction.

July 20. ¼ to nine. This moment I have conceived my Back-ground stronger than ever. I strode about the room imitating the blast of a trumpet, my cheeks full of Blood, and my heart beating with a sort of glowing heat. O, who would exchange these moments for a Throne!

Here is *my* Throne; let Kings bow to it. Now for my Palette! – & then, Canvas, look sharp.

August 1. Went to see the King's procession to open the London bridge, by particular desire, that is, of Master Frank, Alfred, Frederick, Harry, & Mary Haydon, not forgetting Mrs Mary Haydon the Elder. Well, I went, to the gallery of St Paul's, and after waiting about 5 hours, a little speck with a flag and another little speck with a flag, and another speck in which I saw ten white specks, and 6 red & yellow specks, came by, & immediately 200,000 specks uttered a shout I could just hear, and some specks waved handkerchiefs, & other specks raised hats, and this, they said, was the King, and directly a little round ball went up in the air and that, they said, was an air balloon, and then they all shouted, and Mrs Mary Haydon the Elder had a pain in her stomach, and Master Harry Haydon wanted to suck, and Master Alfred was hungry, and Master Frederick wanted to drink, and Miss Mary said she was faint, and Master Frank Haydon said, 'is this all?' – and Mr Haydon said he was very hot, and then they went down an infinite number of dark stairs and got into a coach & drove home, & each fell asleep and *this* was pleasure.

Now if Mr Haydon had gone to work with his Xenophon, neither Master or Mrs or Mr Haydon would have had a pain in their bellies and Mr Haydon's Back-ground would have been done, and his Conscience would have been quiet, & now he has spent 1.18.6 to get a pain in his belly, and has the pain without the money – *and this is pleasure.*

August 28. Out of Town to Ramsgate & Margate the whole week. Never did human creatures suck in the sea air with such rapture as I & my dear Mary & children. The beach at Ramsgate is superb. The steady blue sea, the glittering sail, the expansive & canopied sky, were treats that literally overpowered one's eyes & faculties, after being pent up in brick walls!

August 31. Thus ends August, and thus end the eight months – as unsatisfactorily passed as any eight since I began the Art. Peel's Picture, from anxiety to do better than well, was a dead loss, & though he gave me 130gs., 200 gs. would hardly have paid me.

The consequence is from appealing to him, I lost him. There is nothing will do with people of fashion but absolute submission. Whatever mistake you make, whatever caprice they have, whatever alteration they wish, *submit*; whatever loss you meet, *submit*. Never expostulate, never explain, never give them trouble. This, be assured, was Reynolds' way, and this must be his way who as an Artist wishes the acquaintance & Patronage of the great.

I am not adapted for the World. I could live for ever in my own. I want no other. But alas, with a large family, how often is my own World broken in on. I lose sight of it for days – illness, pleasure, worrit, the wants of a wife & 8 children, all take their turns of harrass, and make me weep when I lock myself into my painting room & gaze at my Xenophon! Why did I marry? – it was my ruin. It brought misery on a lovely creature, and brought other lovely creatures into the World, who would have been happier not born, but it saved my life & my health & certainly my intellects when trouble came. Yet it has cut up my habits.

September 23. My Jerusalem is purchased, and is going to America! Went to see it before it is embarked. In the room was a very fine head of a Pope, by Velasquez. As this opportunity for a lesson was not to be lost, I placed it immediately in the centre of my picture, & compared them heartily. The head by Velasquez was fresher, and there was evidently no yellow in it. In many of my heads the yellow predominated a little.

September 24. Out the whole day on money matters. I should have returned without a guinea, but for the kindness of my dear Friend, Talfourd, who lent me 5 Sov. I am nearly through Xenophon, but with not a shilling for the Winter, & my children literally in want of stockings for the cold. If I starve in my glorious Country, I'll thank God I starved no where else.

October 9. At work and improved the Xenophon still – but much excited about this Reform. What I fear is, that the people have been so trifled with that mere reform will not satisfy them – that they look beyond. The success of American independence has been the torch which has lighted the World for these last 50 years. It will now never cease blazing till Kings are over, & cheap Governments established. The Coronation of George IV may be considered the setting sun of that splendid imposition – Monarchy.

I wrote Lord Londonderry, & begged him to take care of his Corregios. God knows what the mob might do.

October 22. Under God's blessing my family are progressing well. The Eldest, Orlando, has an Exhibition in Hebrew, £26 a year, in addition to his Scholarship. The 2nd is a Mid, & liked & good. Frank is advancing in Classics under my own eye. Mary is [well] & the rest are all attended to & nothing neglected. Without making them Evangelical, I make them Religious. I read Prayers every Sunday.

Something extraordinary will happen with relation to Xenophon. I began it in the midst of anxieties & afflictions, under the most extraordinary impulses of such a nature that I felt as if some influence was in the room.

October 26. I called at the Palace today, but what a difference in the attendants! All George the IVth Servants were Gentlemen to the very Porters – well fed, gorgeous, gold laced rascals. Monarchy is setting. 100 years more I think there won't be a King in Europe. It is a pity. I like the splendid delusion. But why make it so expensive? – voting now 100,000 a year for the Queen, as if 5000 was not enough for any woman's splendour. Those things won't be born much longer.

October 28. A Glorious day! The King, William IVth, has consented to place his name at the head of my list for Xenophon. [Eighty raffle tickets at ten guineas each, were to be sold.] Huzza! God bless him.

Upon Reflection, I shall certainly vote for her Majesty having her 100,000, after this. What can a Queen do with less? – it is impossible. How short-sighted we are – I thought I felt peculiarly dull all day yesterday.

Drank his Majesty's health in a bumper, & success to Reform.

November 12. Hard at work. As time approaches for the meeting of Parliament people apprehend the decision of the Whigs. The bill will be thrown out, I have no doubt. God knows what will be the consequence.

What I complain of [is] the inflammation of mind this Reform bill has generated. I can fix on no reading but Reform meetings. I see the Lords' vote in the walls, from sheer imagination. I am sick of it, and wish for any conclusion that will be a conclusion – but the fact is, it will never conclude.

November 15. Both Parties are to blame – the Whigs Theory without Practice, & the Tories Purblind practice, which sees nothing beyond the routine of office regularity, without being alive to the advance of the age or the necessities of a people more informed.

The Times says Lord Grey's fall will be the worst since Adam's. It will be worse than Adam's; for Adam's there was every excuse.

Out of all this turmoil, the Whigs will resign & must, & in will come My Hero, Wellington, & carve through the whole to safety, benefitted by secession.

No one cares more for the People of England's voice than he. At Waterloo he said to the 95th, who had lost all their officers & were staggered, 'We must not be beat, 95. *What will they say in England?*'

November 18. This day my dear little child Fanny died, at ½ past one in the forenoon, aged 2 years, 8 months, & 12 days being born on March 6th, 1829.

Dear little Soul, she had water in the head, all the consequences of weakness & deranged digestion, and was one of those conceived creatures, born when the Mother has hardly strength from the effects of a previous confinement. Good God! She never spoke, or was not able to utter a syllable, & never walked.

Reader, whoever thou art, shrink not from Death with apprehension. Death was the greatest mercy an Almighty could grant.

November 20. I did nothing but look in the fire & muse.

November 23. Dearest Fanny was buried today! close to Mrs. Siddons, in a most retired and sweet spot, where I hope to have a vault for all of us. Two trees weep over the grave. It could not have been a more romantic & secluded spot.

Peace to her – little Soul, born weakly, but her weakness aggravated by improper treatment, always ill, in a large family, wanting repose & rest & never getting it. What a weakly child suffers from the healthy children! Good God! the teazing, the quizzing.

November 24. Began my family Picture, with dear Alfred's head, who is dying too. I went on painting and crying. It was, without affectation, the most touching thing on Earth. There he dozed, beautiful & sickly, his feet, his dear hands, his head, all dying, drooping, & decaying.

November 26. Hard at work on my family Picture. They shall see if I can paint Portraits, now my heart is in it.

Alfred is better today, but I have no hopes.

December 10.

My dear Sir,
The Letter, which you have had the kindness to address to me, has afforded me the greatest pleasure; for my Soul has been elevated for many Years by the contemplation of the important Pictures formerly sent to me, which occupy an honourable station in my house.

Most gladly will I add my name to the List of Subscribers to Your very valuable Painting, and I shall give directions to my Banker here to forward to You the Amount of my Ticket through the Hands of his Correspondents in London, Messrs. Coutts and Co.

Reserving to myself the Liberty at a future Period, for further Information as well about the Matter in Question and the Picture that is to be raffled for, as concerning other Objects of Art, I beg to conclude the present letter by recommanding [sic] myself to Your freindly [sic] remembrance.

W. Goethe.

Weimar, the 1 of Dec., 1831.

The annexed letter of Geothe's is an immortal honor – immortal indeed. Think of this great man saying his Soul is elevated by the Contemplation of the drawings of my Pupils from the Elgin Marbles – drawings which were the ridicule & the quiz of the whole body of Academicians, without the least exception!

December 22. Laid up in my eyes from studying Suetonius' Life of Caesar the greater part of the night – very interesting, but his Latin is not so delightful to me as Sallust's. My classical knowledge is so shallow I really ought not to give an opinion. But it appears far fetched & harsh in comparison.

FOUR

1832–1837

1832

January 1. How much I have to thank God for! I passed this first day in Peace & happiness. We had a good dinner, a good fire, & we crowded round it, & chatted innocently & happily. The children all well – eager, restless, longing to talk, flying from one thing to the other, & delighted with Pictures.

The only pain I felt was the thought of the many poor souls in cold & hunger.

In the morning I read Prayers. I find it a good method of correction to pray pointedly in the Prayers against any particular vice of the week. Thus, if a child swears, the next Sunday I pray against it, so of lying, quarrelling, &c., & it has cured them. They dread a falsehood, & correct each other.

January 16. Called on Wilkie & saw his Portrait of the King, which I like excessively. It is his best head.

We got into interesting conversation as we always do. I told him in talking of Lawrence that there were 3 things a Painter never got over: 1st, being a crayon Painter; 2nd, a coach Painter; & 3rd, a water colour Painter, all of which ruined his eye for Life. Lawrence, Martin, & Turner are evidences.

January 19. To give an idea of one's situation, on the morning [of the] 17 I was setting my palette & wondering how I should meet a bill of 12, my Butcher's! In came two Friends, one my dear Ed Smith. He looked over my small Pictures & seemed affected at the dying Boy. 'I should like that,' said he. 'Take it at 25gs., half down.' He agreed, & paid the money into Coutts to meet the bill. I went to work & finished the Boy's head before 3, happy & grateful.

January 27. Rubbed in Hope, a companion to the 'dying boy.'

March 27. I spent an hour last week with old Friend Sir T. Hammond, who amused me as usual. He told me an anecdote of the last King which shews the humbuggery of coronations. When the Bishops were kissing the King, & doing Homage, & the music was roaring, &c., &c., when the Bishop of Oxford approached to kiss the King, and did kiss him – the King said, *'Thankee, my dear.'* This is exactly like him.

April 23. I am perfectly convinced that if I could bring my mind to devote one whole year to a proper study of portrait, it would be of essential use to my history as long as I live. Then why do I not do it? It is a weakness and a disgrace to me.

I'll make no vows, but set quietly to work, and daily report progress. I have now an opportunity. A very pretty Spanish girl is going to sit. Lady Gower says she ought to be painted as a nun. Now I will make a regular trial, and this head shall be *my test*.

April 28. I have been again writing in Newspapers, which is wrong – it distracts & disturbs the invention. Yet I hardly see how I could avoid it. God knows what will become of me. If I was more diligent and not suffered my mind such discursive flights, I could surely keep from this continual necessity & pecuniary obligation.

At 46 I require great correction.

April 30. Thus ends April – a disgrace to my conscience – irritable, idle, disappointed. I have nothing to shew, think of, or talk of. I shall think of this Month with horror on my death bed.

May 9. I wrote dear Lord Gower my condition, & he sent me £25 directly. This will save me.

May 12. I lay awake from one till four in the morning, my heart beating violently about this Reform bill.

While these rotten boroughs exist no Englishman can call himself theoretically, as well as practically, free. We have nothing personally pressing on our liberty but the consciousness of this excrescence.

June 4. Worked at a Portrait not long, 3 hours. [On this day the Reform Bill was finally passed.]

June 9. Birmingham. Here I am after a day's journey, in which I was alternately baked, drenched, squeezed, cramped, & broiled. Atwood [Thomas Atwood, leader of the Reform Movement in Birmingham] sat today for his head, which is fine.]

June 10. Sunday. Went to Mr Hutton's meeting. He made a very powerful sermon. I after dined with him at his beautiful cottage, & found him a highly powerful & intellectual young man. His dinner was simple, & shewed narrow circumstances – two bottles of wine bought for the occasion, shaken & hot, a leg of mutton, home made tarts, & every thing denoting a limited income & principle.

Spent the evening with Jones, a leader. When the tax gatherer called he said to him. 'If you dare, Sir, to call again, I'll have you nailed by the ear to my door, with a placard on your breast saying who you are!'

June 22. Old Beddell, a republican, said to me as I sketched 'What's your name – Baker?' 'No, not Baker.' 'What then?' 'Haydon.' '*Haydon! I never heard of 'ee.'* This is Fame.

July 3. Grant I may bring this great work of New-hall hill [the meeting of the Unions in Birmingham to celebrate Reform] to a glorious conclusion; grant it may awake the national energies in favor of High Art; grant the moral effect of this great Picture, in keeping alive the remembrance of the people of their heroic & unadulterated conduct in the great political contest for Reform, may be intense & everlasting.

July 11. I spent the day at Guildhall, and the evening was, as Paddy would say, the most splendid day of my life. I breakfasted & dined with Committee, who treated me with the greatest distinction, and assigned me the place I had chosen, under Chatham's monument, to paint from.

I painted all the morning, & got in the room & window, amidst gas men & waiters & uproar, and by night, the instant the room filled, I dashed away. It was a lesson in colour I shall never forget. The Nobility treated me with great distinction. It was a splendid sight – a glorious triumph, & a curious fact in my curious life that I should be employed to paint it in the Hall.

July 17. Called on dear Lord Grey today with all my sketches. He was highly gratified. He gave me a Commission for it at 500 gs, and added,' 'You like your subject, I am sure.' 'Indeed, do I.'

Mr Wood was present when he asked me at what price. I replied 500 gs., so no mistake.

July 21. I went by appointment this morning. Lord Grey received me kindly, but wanted to get off, but I stuck to him. 'How long will you be?' 'Half an hour, my Lord.' 'May I read?' 'If your Lordship will hold your head high.' 'Where must I sit?' 'Opposite the window.' 'Ah!' said he, as if he thought it a great bore, took up his ministerial box, & came over. I sketched away like fire.

His Brother called & out he went & left me with ministerial boxes. I thought to myself now I may know (if I choose to be a Villain) something – not I – I kept my post like an honorable man, and went on chalking in the background. He darted in, but finding all right, sat down quietly. It was a very interesting hour, and I made an energetic sketch.

August 11. Sick of Pictures, Town, Nobility, King, Lords, & Commons, I set off by steamer to Broadstairs. Came in stewed by steam & broiled by sun. I fagged about till sick, & got lodgings for my dears, for a short breathe of sea air.

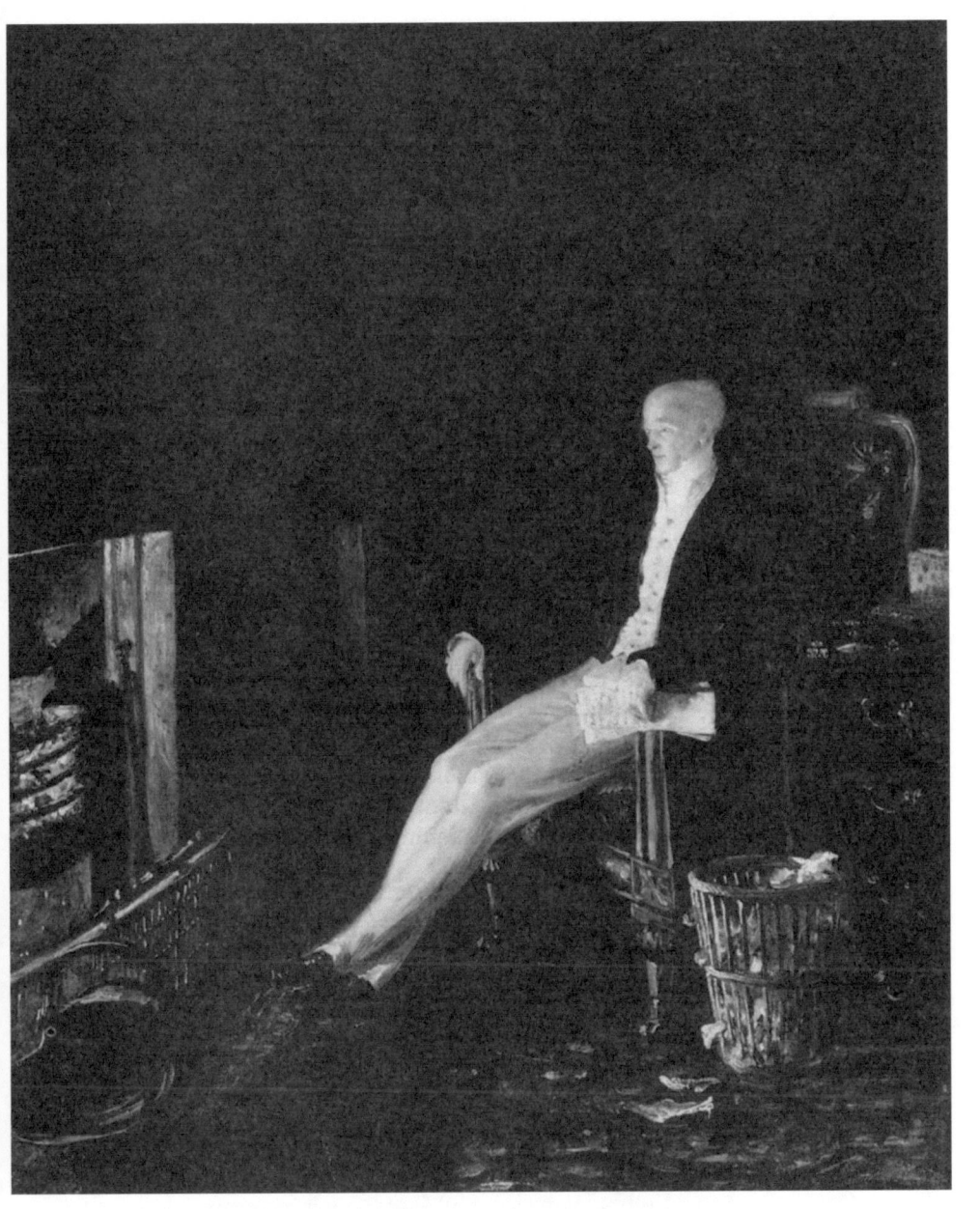

Lord Grey Musing, or *A Statesman at his Fireside*

Slept at an Inn in a small room, fried till morning, got up at ½ past five, took a delicious dip, & swam exulting like a Bull in June! eat a breakfast worthy of an Elephant, put off & joined the Ramsgate steamer, and was in Town again by ½ past four.

Today I am fatigued, & tomorrow I take all my dears down. It is 6 years since they have changed air, but for a day or two, God bless them, & I hope it will do them all good.

August 13. Ought I to spend 20 owing it as I do?

August 23. We have all been down to Broadstairs. The children vastly benefitted. Dear little Alfred, after the warm bath, said he had not had pains in his knees for two days! What ought to be my feelings to dear Lord Grey for advancing me half & enabling me to do this good to my dear children?

October 12. Lord Melbourne came, and a very pleasant morning we had. He relished my stories, and was extremely affable & amiable. He has a fine head, and looked refined and handsome. He asked about Hazlitt, Leigh Hunt, & Keats and Shelley, and seemed much amused at my anecdotes; in short, he seemed pleased with me as I am with him. I never had a pleasanter sitter – a delightful, easy, frank, unaffected, man of Fashion. Now if he is only pleased with his own head, it will do.

October 16. Lord Melbourne sat again today – a delightful two hours. He liked the head in the picture.

Lord Melbourne, in the course of talk, said he knew that Lord North often endeavoured to persuade the King not to continue the American War, but that the virulence of the old King's feelings obliged him.

October 18. Lord Althorp sat to me in Downing Street. He is not so conversational as Lord Melbourne, but the essence of good nature. I said, 'My Lord, for the first time in my life I scarcely slept when Lord Grey was out during the Bill – were you not deeply anxious?' 'I do not know,' said Lord Althorp, 'I am *never very anxious.*' This was a fine touch of character.

I afterwards called on Lord Palmerston, and was amazingly impressed by his good humoured elegance. He said he could no more sit than he could fly, but the first leisure hour he would not forget me.

His nose is small, forehead fine, & he is handsome. He was immersed in boxes, papers, & in a little snug study.

October 22. Lord Landsdowne sat, and I was much interested. His face is amiable in the extreme, his refinement, literature, & knowledge considerable, with great unaffectedness, and rather too much of a mild acquiescence rather than contest. He said he saw me at the dinner, and said, 'At least there is one present who is not eating & feasting.'

Lord Landsdowne articulates as clearly as an actor. I told him I thought the violent Tory principles inculcated into Lord Normanby probably made him a Whig. He laughed & said it might be. So violent were Lord Mulgrave's prejudices on that score, I had heard him deny Genius to Milton! 'That was rather a bold conclusion, ' said Lord Landsdowne.

October 24. Lord John Russell sat today. He is an interesting, mild, & determined creature. He thought Attwood not the man. I said, 'My Lord, to be Reformers now is the Fashion.' 'Yes,' said he. 'People find out now they have been Reformers but never thought of it.' He did not say much. There is a melancholy inflexibility of purpose about his head.

October 26. Went again to the Duke of Richmond's. The Dutchess came in to have a peep, & I think [she] did not think it handsome enough. They expect in an historical picture I am to perfume them like Lawrence. My object is nature & truth, for reference hereafter, and not Domestic Portrait.

The Duke did not seem at all in spirits. He seemed inclined to doze, and nothing but his good breeding stopped him.

November 2. Lord John Russell has just gone. Done sitting. He is highly pleased. The conversation was most interesting. He said he was an hour & ½ with Napoleon at Elba. He was abrupt; liked Lord Ebrington amazingly; said 'he is well informed, at least I think him so,' which was modest of Napoleon. 'His great mistake was marrying an Austrian princess,' said Lord John; 'he should have had a Russian.' He was perfectly conversational. I thought I would venture my own political lucubrations. 'My Lord,' said I, 'may I take the liberty to ask a question?' 'Yes.' 'Do not you think there is great danger, if caution is not used, that France may gradually get more powerful by an alliance with us, and ultimately endanger us again. 'If the Goverment should change,' said he, 'certainly, but not if the present Government remain.' This question made him think a little, & he repeated, 'In the Navy certainly.'

He was highly pleased with his Portrait, and put his autograph to the drawing, which gave me great pleasure.

November 3. Lord Goderich sat, and afterwards I went to Sir James Graham's. Lord Goderich began the instant he sat down. 'Well, we are to have a new Academy.'* 'Yes, my Lord.' 'How do you like the plan?' 'It is an honor to the Art certainly, but I fear its ultimate influence.' 'Fear! why?' 'Because by bringing the annual efforts of British Artists in comparison with the choicest works of the choicest ages, the inference will be too obvious, & the opinion of British Art sink. There is no hope for British Art

---

*Part of the present National Gallery, built between 1832 and 1838, was assigned to the Royal Academy, which occupied these quarters from 1837 to 1869, when it was moved to Burlington House.

but by a moderate and regular vote.' 'But how?' said he; 'we have no houses.' 'My Lord, there is the mistake. We do not want houses. We want public support for public objects in public buildings.'

We went over the old ground. 'Supposing a grant of money took place, how would you begin?' said he. 'At once; at the Great Room at the Admiralty! Take two great Pictures, of two of the most important epochs of English naval Glory. Adorn the other parts of the Room with smaller designs. Take two Portraits of two of the greatest Heroes & two Busts.' He shrugged his shoulders, and said, 'Well, Lords Grey & Althorp hold the purse strings. Propose it to them.'

November 7. Sir John Hobhouse sat. He said Lord Byron was not naturally melancholy, but a merry person, but that his melancholy was owing to his pecuniary difficulties, that he often wanted 50£, that he would have been arrested often, but that he was a peer. He agreed with me as to Lady Byron leaving him. He agreed with me that she was totally unfit for him, was a fool and an old maid by anticipation, that there was nothing between 'em but pecuniary necessity.

November 14. On the whole, public men shrink from discussion. They are so occupied with the fate of Nations, & their political relations, that *truth* even seems unworthy investigation. Metaphysical enquiry they detest. Matters of taste they skim. Religion they consider only as an engine of State; and I do not think much extension of knowledge on general principles is to be acquired by intercourse with them.

They are interesting from their rank & occupation; but a habit of having such mighty interests hanging on their decisions generates a contempt for abstract deduction, and an indisposition to enter into matters of Literature, Art, or morals.

November 18. After 40 years of struggle on the part of the Artists, at last the Government have consented, not to bestow employment & opportunity on Historical Painters, who have neither, but 25,000 to build a New Academy for people who have 40,000 in the funds, and to provide a better room for Mr Secretary or Mr Keeper.

My blood boils at this infamous job. I am meditating an attack.

November 19. Upon the whole I fear I am hardly a fair judge of any thing connected with the Academy, where my passions are concerned. The junction will either be a glorious triumph for British Art, or its decided ruin. If the Government back it up by a moderate vote, British Art will triumph; if they do not, it will be crushed!

November 20. Hard at work on Sir James Graham. I never, I think, passed a more interesting month. To be admitted, as I have been, on the most friendly terms to the secret recesses of Cabinet Ministers, & having the full command of them for an hour at a time, with no disturbance or interruption, is a very high distinction.

November 25. At Lord Althorp's again. By Degrees I got him on Art and the National Gallery, and the necessity of encouraging History by an annual vote.

He said an annual vote would be injurious, because it implied a necessity of *always* buying, when there might be nothing to buy. 'Sometimes,' said he, 'Pictures make a great dash & are forgotten. 50 years, I think, ought to pass before a Picture is bought.' '& the Picture rots in the mean time,' said I.

He seemed impressed with a notion something was wanting. This is the first step. I see Lord Grey this week, & I will be at him. God knows if any thing will come of it. They shall not be ignorant, and therefore all excuse is taken away.

December 15. A young Friend of mine, lately from Italy, examined the archives of the Convent where Corregio painted at Parma, & said he saw a great deal of *amber* had been used by him. Amber is a gum & very hard to dissolve. He dissolved it in oil of Spikenard, and he copied the celebrated Corregio, and after glazed this, with his amber varnish. He says it is as tough as treacle, and he got Corregio's look with nothing else.

December 17. Lord Headfort & Lord Auckland both sat.

Lord Headfort talked of Ireland. He said if the Union was repealed, Ireland must always be a province of America or France.

December 18. Advanced my Picture vastly. The rules of composition which originate in feeling are never violated without loss. Something ailed the Composition. I knew where but did not know how to ease it. The introduction of the Candlestick at the bottom has advanced the composition 3 months.

December 27. Twelve delicious hours in my painting room. Worked hard. I am sick of Sitters. I won't see another this fortnight. Levatt the Butler brought the gold things from the Mansion House today. I'll revel in plate, rich half tints against flesh, gold behind black coats, and glitter by the side of silvery cravats – now, Tintoretto, look sharp.

December 31. The last day of a year, perhaps the most celebrated of my life.

The immortality conferred on me by Lord Grey in giving me a Picture connected with Reform – the glory of that night at Guildhall – the return of Fortune, and the peace, happiness, & study I have enjoyed in consequence, are individually causes of my feeling deep gratitude to my merciful Creator. I regret it, for it is not high minded.

I have worked very hard today from nine to four, & seven to ½ past ten – 10½ hours – my eyes like iron.

There are two things I once hated – Portrait & perspective. This Picture has forced me to study them, and I will conclude by being capable of both.

It is now half past eleven. The conclusion is approaching of the most wonderful year in the History of England. Oh, how I glory that I contributed to the great result (however humbly) by my three letters to the Times [signed 'Radical Junior', Oct. 20 and Nov. 19, 1831, and 'Radical', March 27, 1832]. When my colours have faded, my canvas decayed, & my body mingled with the Earth, these glorious letters, the best thing I ever wrote, will obtain the enthusiasm of my Countrymen. I thank God I lived in such a time.

1833

January 19. Mr Hume sat again. He is a remarkable man, active minded, restless when he is sitting, conversational, and intelligent. He has promised to move a Committee of examination for the Academy. I hope he will. He is an extraordinary man certainly, has enlarged views & original ones, and in moral feeling of what is truly great, is in advance of his Contemporaries. He must be in the House like a bit of granite. He is quite the man.

January 23. Heard from Lady Brougham – successfully! The whole history of the Chancellor's consenting to sit is quite a capital bit. Every body said I should never get him. I therefore determined to paint him in as ugly as possible. This I did, looking spitishly at Lord Grey. The thing took, every body complained; I lamented with affected gravity my utter incapability to do him justice unless he sat, & last Wednesday came up Col. Grey. He was impressed with the Picture. Col. Grey said, 'At any rate, you have made the Chancellor monster enough.' 'What can I do? It must remain, if he does not sit', & tonight came Lady Brougham's letter, appointing Sunday!

It was a capital plan. Let a man be whom he may, he has a lurking wish not [to] be painted ugly, where there is a chance of his face reaching Posterity in a Picture likely to be celebrated.

January 26. Out all day. Had worked till I had not a guinea left. I drove in the City, & went to Fletcher, the Chairman, a fine, manly fellow, to tell him my wants, & to ask him for £5 to get through the night. He said he ought not, & I returned home in a state not to be described. When I came home the children had all been fighting, and no water had come to the cistern – Mary scolding, & I went into the Painting Room, and d—md all large Pictures, which always bring this evil on me.

The evening passed on, as it always does in a family where the Father has no money. There is either an over kindness, an over irritability, or an affected unconcern. I marched off to my landlord, Newton. Knowing he would relieve me, and anticipating success, I knocked. I heard the light steps of a girl; down went the candlestick, and the door opened! 'Mr. Newton at home?' said I, marching in, praying to God it might be so, though half fearing it might not, when I was suddenly stopped by, '*No, Sir,* he is gone to the play!' 'Damn the play,' thought I – 'this is the way. What business has he to be giggling at some stuff in the Pit, while I am in danger of having no money?' Away I tramped again, tired, croaking, grumbling, & muddy, and came home in a state of harass. 'Well, Sir, the man won't send the wood without the money!' was the first salutation! 'Sir, there is no water in the cistern, & has not been all day!' 'Why,' thought I, 'the very lead pipes begin to perceive their masters won't be paid for their trouble.' I sat down in a rage, pulling off my great coat. In came the Servant with a letter marked *private*, from Lord Grey! My heart jumped. I read it, & by degrees I recovered my good feelings, & went to bed at peace with my family & the World.

February 2. Worked hard. Duke of Cleveland called, & fixed Wednesday. Lady Say and Sele called, & finding I had not my Lord in, began to negotiate for his admission; assured me Lord Say & Sele was a thorough Reformer, & had been for years, asked my price, and instructed I should paint him *after.* All this is very pretty, but, I had better say, as a Woman said to a Member of Parliament when canvassing, 'leave your name & we'll enquire your character.'

Hard at work – the Chancellor at XI tomorrow; the Duke of Richmond 10 Monday; Duke of Cleveland Wednesday at one; Lord Ebrington Thursday at 12! What a destiny is mine! All this after being 3 times in a prison.

February 3. The Chancellor sat today. On his entrance he shook hands, and said, 'It is many years since I saw you, Mr Haydon.' *It is* many years, & nothing struck me more in Lord Brougham's appearance than his improved air, in manner & dress. I now had the most extraordinary man in Europe before me.

Depend on it, Brougham's is a nature that requires something to prey on. If Grey had kept him out, he would have shivered the administration to atoms.

February 5. Brougham on Sunday came in, his hair in apple pie order, and would any one believe what is true, when he thought I was at his mouth, his vulgar part, *he did the amiable,* wetted his lips to make them look red, & lessened the protuberance! Ah, Human Nature!

This is on a par with the dying man in the Hospital I sketched, who in a hollow voice asked if his night cap *was right!*

February 9. The Picture is solidly advancing. The line on Lord Grey's left is nearly full – Lord Chancellor, Dukes of Richmond, Cleveland, Lords Ebrington & Westminster have all sat this week.

February 11. Duke of Richmond sat. I asked the Duke if there was ever a moment in which he desponded at Waterloo. He said, '*Never.* For an instant some young officers might,' he said, 'when the Cavalry were on the hill & had got possession of the Artillery, but all *old* ones knew that Cavalry getting possession of Artillery was *nonsense.*'

February 12. Lord Westminster is a most amiable creature. He said Lord Essex was a most profitable Tenant. He moved about from house to house continually, and always left the house better than he found it. My children began to roar & make a noise. I rang the bell & desired less noise. He begged I would not, as he loved the noise of children.

February 20. Lord Morpeth sat. He has a fine forehead. We talked of Cobbett's speech on Taxation. He said it was tedious & unfair – & it was unfair certainly, for I deny the shilling to the poor is the 50 to the rich. If taxation went on in the ratio, the rich would be ruined, and what object in saving a Fortune if it is at last to be diminished by half when you have got it?

I said, 'The Irish Members seem great bores.' He replied they talked so fluently with so little thinking, which is in fact their great defect, 20 words to an Idea.

February 26. Lord Cavendish sat, and was ready to let me make use of his face – 3 parts of it, or half of it, & put him any where. Now, when I contrast this with some of the City Committee, who march up to the Picture & say, 'Put me *there*,' close to Lord Grey, it is really exquisite.

February 27. Dined with Mrs Norton to meet Lord Melbourne. Spent a delightful evening. Young D'Israeli was there, very affected in his dress, entertaining but [not] engrossing, too much affecting the tone of fashion, without the real consciousness that birth gives.

He talked much of the East, & seemed tinged with a disposition to palliate its infamous vices. I meant [to] have asked him if he preferred Aegypt, where Sodomy was *preferment*, to England, where it very properly was *Death*. Travellers in the East of the range of D'Israeli's intellect consider our severity of feeling as an unhappy prejudice on that point.

March 19. Sir Aug. Clifford sat again, and we indulged in regular gossip at Lady Lyndhurst's having 2000 a year left her by Lord Dudley. Poor Lord Dudley had a way of talking to himself loudly. While he was riding in his carriage with a Friend, he said, 'Shall I ask him to dine, or shan't I? He is not a pleasant fellow; he may offend.' The Friend, astonished, began to *think* loudly as well. 'Shall I dine with Lord Dudley, if he asks me or shan't I? He is a very odd man.' Lord Dudley, roused, burst out laughing; his Friend laughed too.

March 20. Lord Plunket sat, patiently & sensibly. Lady Howick & Miss Eden called after, and just as I was preparing to put in Lord Plunkett, up came an odd, independent looking man, fresh in colour, with great energy. He began, 'Sir, I have been a staunch Reformer 28 or 30 years. I dined here that day. Ought I not be here? I am a Magistrate, Sir Robt. Wheeler.' 'Sir,' said I, 'you have a head worthy of any dinner, but I fear my places *are taken*.'

March 23. Duke of Sussex sat amiably. I never saw any thing like it. He exceeds all my sitters for patience & quiet. There he sat smoking & talking. I felt quite easy, and sketched with more ease than I ever did before.

He is a very unaffected Royal Person. He smoked incessantly, told me his asthma was entirely gone, & that he had it from 11 to 36 years of age.

March 28. Lord Grey sat, but it was absolutely useless. Then he wrote a letter, then this & then that. I gave it up in my own mind, & went on as well as I could. Lady Grey came down, & her appearance of course softened his Lordship. He began to behave better; his expression became more pleasing, but still state affairs seemed to worry him. Sidney Smith came & began joking, & I went on sketching, but uselessly; I had been thrown off my balance. Lord Grey began in a bad humour, & put me in one.

I hate failure. Sidney Smith is enough to make any man fail; his heartless indifference to Art, and his awful looking face, now as he is getting older, there is always a mixture of pain in looking at a jesting Clergyman.

May 16. Mr Coke & Sir Ronald Ferguson sat. Mr Coke's head is the finest I ever saw. This is a genuine unsophisticated opinion. He told some beautiful anecdotes of Fox. He said the first time he came into Power he dined with him. He went on talking before the Servants. After they were gone some one said, 'Fox, how can you go on so before the Servants?' 'Why the Devil,' said Mr Fox, 'should not they know as much as myself?' This is a complete touch.

Mr Coke said he remembered a Fox killed in Cavendish Square, and that where Berkly Square now stood was an excellent place for snipes.

May 17. Dear Alfred died a little after seven – born December 8, 1825.

Poor dear Alfred! – the only child who had a passion for Art! – a beautiful head! His last words were, 'I should like to see Papa!' He laid his head on the pillow, and never spoke more. Mary the Girl ran down, I ran up half dressed. I am not certain if his understanding remained. He gave no sign of recognising me.

May 20. Alfred was buried. Dear Fanny's coffin was taken out, quite uninjured, & Alfred's put under. I cried when I saw them both put together, who had been together in life, & were now in Death inseparable.

The Clergyman read the Service impressively. I felt exceedingly obliged to him. He was a young man of innocent expression & sedate in air, named Gifford.

May 21. I feel much oppressed at the death of this dear little fellow. Sometimes I think he might have been saved; sometimes I think at the beginning he was left to nurses too much. Yet how could it be helped? Nothing essential was neglected; it always is the way in a brood – one or two are weak, & give in when strong ones would have *flourished*.

Mr Tom Duncombe sat yesterday, but I am very languid in the drawing. It is a painful struggle.

May 22. Mr Coke said This is the blessing of putting a Quaker [Charles Fox] in the House; the first proof he gives of his gratitude is to prohibit Cock-fights. Bye & bye we shall have a law obliging us to dress in brown, &
then fasts & public prayers to get God Almighty to put a stop to the rain bow.

June 10. Mr Coke called with Lady Augusta, 2 boys, a nurse, & a sweet Baby, a little girl. I had just finished very successfully Lord Tavistock.

The first thing the nurse did was to put down this dear little soul, close to Lord Tavistock's head, which in a very few minutes, while my back was turned, she demolished, covered her self with paint, and utterly destroyed a morning's labour! 'She has spoilt her pelisse,' said Lady Anne – never one word of sympathy for poor Lord Tavistock.

June 17. Being exceedingly exhausted I went out to take air.

While I was out, the Duke of Sussex called. This is always the way. He sat quietly by himself, looking at the Picture. Lady Duncannon called. The Duke left word he would call in two or three days, & give me a sitting. Now I have hardly been out at that time of day for several weeks, & the first day I do in comes H. R. Highness!

June 24. Monday. Dear Lady Seymour sat to me & made a successful first sitting. Sweet creature, beautiful creature! – quite irresistible. There she sat with her lovely face looking like polished ivory – her large eyes & exquisite mouth – a perfect Venus – enough to make any man an Idolater. Her simplicity is equal to her beauty.

Mrs Sheridan accompanied her, and was exceedingly spirituelle & witty. I passed a delightful morning, delightful indeed. These Ladies asked if Lord Holland was in. I said he objects because he was not there. *'Can't you put his head in a pie?'* There is nothing in it, it was the manner.

June 27. Sketched the Attorney General!

A few minutes after eleven at night was born Jane Georgia[na] Caroline Elizabeth Sarah Seymour Haydon.

July 12. Exceedingly ill from eating too many strawberries after I had painted them. Sir John Sebright called & chatted a great deal. I was too ill to paint him.

July 17. Was in the House of Lords early to hear dear Lord Grey open the Irish Church bill. He made an irrefutable speech. After he had done, he came over to me & spoke to me in the kindest manner before the whole House of Lords, whose eyes all followed him. It was a high distinction.

July 18 & 19. Attended this interesting debate closely, & with great advantage to the Picture.

The Duke spoke well & without hesitation. There is a manly honour about his air, and he enforces what he says with a bend of his head, striking his hand forcibly & as if convinced on the papers. He finished, and to my utter astonishment, up started like an artillery rocket Lord Melbourne! He began in a fury. His language flowed out like fire. He made such palpable hits that he floored the Duke of Wellington as if he had shot him, and it really was a high treat.

July 21. Hard at work on fruit. Mr Ellice sat. We talked of Lord Grey. Mr Ellice said that it was time for him to think of his course – an old man of 70 might drop off & leave the Country in a mess.

July 29. I was just beginning to work, when in rushed two Sheriff's Officers, saying they had an Execution against my person. This was an affair of 3 years standing. I had been security – paid half – the rascal had neglected to pay the other half, & they sued me. Away I was hurried, half bewildered. All my former agonies returned. After a day & night of torture, leaving my family & children bewildered, I recovered my faculties, after very nearly putting an end to myself during the night. I wrote Mr Ellice, whose head expressed such sympathy. He sent Mrs Haydon £50, [which] released me at once, and in a few hours [I] was as happy & hard at work again as ever.

August 12. Hard at work. Put in Charles Grey, & finished Mr Poyntz. He said he lived formerly with Sheridan a great deal. Once when he was dining with him at Somerset House, and they were all in high feather, in rushed the servant, & said, 'Sir, the house is on fire!' 'Bring another bottle of claret,' said Sheridan. 'It is not *my* house!'

I really begin to get sick of sitters, 97 heads, all portraits. I have not had a moment's rest for 9 months!

August 17. George Lamb sat. Lamb knew Actors & Actresses. He said Keen was exceedingly debauched. When he did not come home all night, his carriage used to drive about to all the brothels, to inquire if Mr Keen was *there!*

Here I am, who have never been debauched, at 47 stronger than at 27, actually, & Keen died before 47, worn out!

August 21. Lord Advocate is just gone after an hour's sitting, and a most delightful conversation. He knew Brougham from early years, & told me at one time for about 8 months he gave into all sorts of luxuries. He had a great notion of giving a grand dinner, and he said we had no notion like the Ancients of perfuming our rooms. He got all sorts of perfumes, passing through hot plates, so when they came in the suffocation was dreadful & they were obliged to open the windows.

September 2. Stewart Mackenzie sat – very amusing. He read letters about the Island of Lewis in the Hebrides, where they catch Lobsters. He said he had 15,000 subjects. When he first came there hardly any one could read, & there were no Bibles, & now not a child but could read it, and he had been obliged to send down a gross of spectacles for the old people who had learned to read.

October 10. Lord Palmerston sat. He said I had a great reputation for being the pleasantest Painter the Nobility ever sat to. This is a great point, and I must see what use I can make of it professionally. If they are as pleased with me as I am with them, *we shall do.*

November 27. Today I think I hit Lord Grey's air & expression. Gore sat. Gave me an exquisite account of the shooting at Holkam. The Duke is extremely near-sighted. At the end of the cover up sprung a hare. The Duke levelled, and Lord Spencer Churchill saw the muzzle of the Duke's gun right opposite his belly. Churchill made up his mind to be shot, lost his presence of mind, and instead of falling on his face, waited for his fate. The Duke's gun miss fired! – and his Lordship escaped!

The utter carelessness of Men of Fashion is astonishing! They talk of it as what must be expected.

December 23. Spent three hours with Charles Eastlake, & a very pleasant, argumentative conversation we had. He said he thought I should have born every indignity from the Academy rather than have endangered the great object I had in view. I said I found the great object I had in view could never be obtained while the great obstacle, their monopoly, remained in power. I did not proceed without deep meditation.

Eastlake spoke of his obligations to me with the greatest affection. He was my first pupil.

December 27. Mr Warburton sat. When he was leaving he asked for a slip of paper to present me with a draft on his Banker, which I refused, of course. No, no, my selection of heads is on a Reform principle. I have never received a sixpence for one.

As this Picture is closing up, my mind begins again to open on Historical subjects.

1834

January 1. O God, have mercy on us! Bless us through this year, as thou didst through the last. Bless my labours with success and Victory, that may establish my future. Grant these things, for Jesus Christ's sake. Amen.

January 14. While we were talking on Saturday to Sir W. Gordon, Lord Grey said, with the greatest simplicity of expression, 'What in God's name do you do with so many Sentries? What is the use of a Sentry in Downing St – at the end of the passage, why there's one, two by the Duke of York's column – what is the use of that? When the East Winds come *you'll have all the men laid up. That place is like a funnel.*'

January 23. I have now put down my name for the Professorship of Design at the London University. Shall I get it? No.

February 10. My health is beginning to be a little affected – my head got confused after 4 hours, and I did not recover, which I attribute to swallowing something at lunch which did not digest, so that blood came into my head. I did not recover all day, and have not yet. 18 months worry, getting 107 people to sit, writing myself – doing every thing myself, in fact – has tired me. If the thing was to do over again I should not be able to get them again. The enthusiasm is over for Reform in them – or dwindled.

February 15. Thinking Leigh Hunt was entitled to the distinction of a place in such a commemoration, I wrote a Friend of his. Hunt agreed to sit, and today he came; we had not seen each other for 12 years but once, and though quieter he seemed just as incarnately vain as ever! I repented putting him in because I will venture to predict he will think it arose not from my genuine & honest conviction of it being a merited compliment, but from a supposition that he is rising in the World, and that I think safe to court him.

February 18. Rubbed out Leigh Hunt, and the Company seemed relieved of an uncongenial face. It was very odd how Leigh Hunt's face looked. It was either above or below the company – at any rate it was not fit for it, and the composition is much improved by its expulsion. There is in Leigh Hunt an innate affectation which nobody can bear.

February 22. Saturday. A very interesting day. At 12 I went to O'Connell's, and certainly his appearance was very different from what it is in the House of Commons. It was on the whole hilarious & good

ABOVE Detail from *The Reform Banquet*: (*bottom row, left to right*) T. Duncombe Esq., Sir R. Ferguson MP, Josh. Hume MP, Sir John Hobhouse, Sir Francis Burdett MP; (*above left*) E. Bulwer MP (afterwards Bulwer Lytton); *(second from left at top)* Daniel O'Connell MP

OPPOSITE ABOVE Detail from *The Reform Banquet*: (*seated in a row, full faces, left to right*) Lord John Russell, Sir James Graham, Lord Melbourne, Earl Ripon; (*on his left*) Rt. Hon. E. J. Stanley MP (later Lord Stanley of Alderley), Rt. Hon. C. Grant MP, Lord Saye and Sele, *(hand on chin)* Viscount Morpeth MP

OPPOSITE BELOW Detail from *The Reform Banquet*: *(descending order, from right)* Lord Morpeth, Lord Duncannon, Lord Ebrington, Lord Tavistock

natured, but there was a cunning, low look. He has an eye like a weasel.

I was first shewn into his private room, which was a complete Irish pig stye – a shirt hanging by the fire, a hand glass tied to the window bolt, papers, hats, brushes, wet towels, & dirty shoes, gave intimation of dear Ireland!

After a few minutes O'Connell rolled in, in a morning dressing gown, a loose black handkerchief tied round his neck, God knows how, and held together nobody knows why, with a wig, & a foraging cap bordered with gold lace.

He sat down & I sketched him. We talked of *Repeal*. 'Do not you think, Sir,' I said, 'that Ireland, being the smaller, must always be subject to England, the larger island? If England loses her, France from Religion will predominate!' 'No,' said O'Connell, 'Repeal & Ireland from gratitude will be more devoted.'

A Gentleman came in, and was going away. I said, 'Do stay & keep Mr O'Connell talking.' 'Talking,' said he, 'Ha-ha. I should like to see the machine that could stop his talking,' at which O'Connell laughed heartily.

I have not used O'Connell fairly – to get into his house & then quiz his Irish habits. He is a fair subject if any body is, however.

March 16, 17, 18, 19, 20, 21 and 22. Occupied, glazing & toning. Lady Blessington sat. She seemed to complain of the Whigs bitterly. She told me many things.

The fact is the situation in which she lives with regard to D'Orsay is painful & suspicious. She, like all human beings who do wrong, have occasional depressions, and this day she seemed touched & in bad spirits.

April 14. 5 minutes before two, dear Harry died. God bless him.

The fate of this dear Child is dreadful. He was knocked down by accident in playing on his dear head, which shook his brain so that it produced effusion, and after a few days lingering he expired, sensible to the last.

I sat up on Saturday [April 12], & made him happy & comfortable. Mary took the next night, and he was screaming the greater part of the night. In the morning Death was evident, making rapid strides. His eyes were sunk & bewildered. He looked confused & glaring. He fell into a sweet sleep for an hour & ½, and awoke dying, looking with his dear & beautiful long lashed eyes as if he saw another World.

The Surgeon came & asked for sherry. I ran to get some. Mary said he had a slight convulsion – and then all was over!

This boy was my favourite child. His character was noble & talents great; he was as quick as lightening.

April 23. Began Cassandra. God bless me through it. Amen.

April 24. Advanced. Saw dear Lord Grey, & had a very interesting interview. He said, 'How does your Exhibition go on?' 'Badly, my Lord, I am losing money every day.' 'I am very sorry for it,' he said. I said, 'My Lord, the Middle Classes do not come.' Lord Grey mused with an air of excrutiating anxiety, and then said, 'The Picture is *not liked.*' I said, 'My Lord, it is not so; I have never painted a Picture more liked by the Artists or the Visitors.'

The fact is, the Government is not popular, and the Middle Classes give this Exhibition a political feeling.*

April 25. Hard at work, thank God, and well advanced Cassandra. I felt delightfully happy at the solitude & happiness of returning to my old habits of study.

April 30. The state of things is very alarming. The angry Tories are thirsting to revenge their defeat on the reform bill, & to *bleed* the people, as they say. The Whigs have not pleased the people by giving up the great principle of a right to interfere in Church property or the Great Church bill, and the people are disappointed because sirloin & Quarter loaves did not come through the roof after the bill passed – so there exist in all parties the *Elements of collision!*

May 12. Monday. Out the whole day on harrassing pecuniary matters.

It is really lamentable to see the effect of success and failure on people of Fashion.

Last year my door was beset; my house besieged; my room inundated. It was an absolute fight to get in to see me paint. Ah, that was the curiosity! Well, out came the Work – the public felt no curiosity – it failed, & since, except Lady Seymour, I have not seen *one*! yes, & Lady Blessington. My door is now deserted – no horses, no carriages.

May 19. Had a horrid night. My dear Mary went into violent Hystericks at my saying I thought she neglected Harry, relative to his hour of rest – it appeared as if I blamed her – which I did not. We both passed a melancholy evening, thinking of his dear little ways, his beautiful head, his extraordinary capacity. We have no cant – God's will be done.

June 1. Duke of Bedford looked at Cassandra but said nothing. He came again Saturday.

June 3. Dear Mary & I packing up her little favourite things – expecting ruin with creeping pace.

June 4. Began Cassandra, after it dried a month. Now for Executions, poverty, misery, insult and wretchedness.

I called on dear Lord Grey yesterday – waited – he was very busy. After a noise I heard a door slam, looked out, & saw him feebly & fatigued

---

*The Reform Banquet was exhibited at 26 St James's Street until August 29. [See 29 August.]

tottering along into his room. Some times you'll think he was going to die.

I worked under continual depressions hardly to be born. Mary is exasperated, what with nursing & harrass. I improved Cassandra.

June 7. Mary & I in agony of mind. My Italian Books were all gone, & some of my best Historical designs, to a Pawn Broker's. She packed up her best gown & the Children's & I drove away with what cost us £40, & got £4. Came home in exhausted spirits, & found 50 from the Duke of Sutherland, for a small commission – such is Life!

June 11. Took the Children into the Country, for a day of human pleasure. We drove to Frederick's School, anticipating all sorts of fun from his known humour. We found him *ill*. Then we drove on to go to Harrow & see where Byron sat & mused. It came on to rain, so we drove home & finished. So much for a day of pleasure.

June 15. My Cassandra, having dried six weeks, I really begin it this moment. O God, bless me through it. My difficulties are again accumulating, but let me, in my mature life, vanquish them as I vanquished those before. I prayed in my early youth that I might prove the Genius of an Englishman in 'High Art.' Under thy blessing I have done so. I now pray fervently & eagerly I may accomplish a system of reward for those who come after me.

I then opened the Bible, as I always do, to consult my fate, & I pitched (blinded) upon this – Isaiah, Chap. LIII, Verse 17, 'No weapon that is formed against thee shall prosper; and every tongue that shall rise against thee in judgement thou shalt condemn. This is the heritage of the Servants of the LORD: and their righteousness is of me, saith the LORD.'

June 19. Went to the opera with dear Mary. The King there & Queen too – a full house. L'Assedio di Corinto – Grisi – sang finely, but made faces which Catalani never did. La Sylphide followed – Taglioni exquisite.

The King looked well, Queen like an exasperated Tabby, with a mulberry face. As we were coming out Lord Grey's carriage stopped the way – & down hurried Lord Grey, looking old, and as if born down by the abuse of the press. Lady Georgiana & brother & sister were with him, but they all looked harrassed. What a situation it is for a Minister! – the butt of all parties.

June 28. Dined out in Russell Square and was much pained to hear Ministers so universally abused. Good God! – when I have seen the sacrifice of all personal comfort, the harrass, the diligence, the sleeplessness, & the anxiety, the perpetual struggle [of] Ministers to do conscientiously what is right, and to hear & witness such ingratitude – it is quite shocking.

July 10. There never was a Minister so basely calumniated. The basis of Lord Grey's character is amiability & affection. His fall before he has completed his measures is owing to nothing but the jarring elements he let in on opening the Reform doors.

Posterity alone will do him justice. Posterity alone will admire, separated from passion, his beautiful character, his consistency, & his moral courage in carrying Reform.

July 15. Spent a delightful evening at Mrs Leicester Stanhope's – acted charades – written and acted by that extraordinary creature for beauty & Genius, Caroline Norton. Her characters were inimitably acted. Mrs Stanhope, with her pretty oval head, played sweetly. I wish my dear Mary had been there.

I really prefer this private acting. There is none of the vulgarity of the profession. Every thing was delicately touched and done with a nature & simplicity delightful.

July 17. Duke of Sutherland paid 100 – a great blessing. 2 days more would have ruined me.

July 19. Advanced Cassandra beautifully. The great difficulty I have had to fall back into my old habits of study. I was in a perpetual fever for 19 months. I got so mixed up, my art was almost forgotten, though all this gave me an insight into the state of the nobility as to Art not to be obtained otherwise.

July 24. Spent the day with children at Worm[wood] Scrubbs, flying kites, &c., &c., – a delicious day.

August 1. Today I went to the Bench to see Lane. As I returned I called on Lord Grey & saw him. He looked well, but not as if in office – there is an inexpressible air of being out of office that can't be explained. I was delighted to see him free of that weak, harrassed look, as if worried. Lady Georgiana came in but there was no longer that look of public importance. They were essentially private.

August 18. Made a steam trip to Gravesend – dived, swam, bathed, & revelled, like a bull in June. Returned. Dined with Hill, M.P. for Hull.

August 29. Closed my Unfortunate Exhibition. Lost £230 by it. God knows if I shall recover this. God protect my dear children. If they should be stopped in their education it will be their ruin.

I undertook this Picture of the Reform Banquet for 525 gs.
I have lost 230.00   230
                                                            ─────
                                                            £295

Which reduces the price to 295. The City was to have had a copy, which it has not and never will have. But for the Commission of the Duke of Sutherland I should have been crushed.

August 30. Went into the City in great misery, having raised 1.10. by pledging valuable studies. Fletcher, the Chairman of the City [committee], gave me ten pounds for some sketch he is to call & select. This relieved my mind. I called on my Creditor, & saw the attorney's clerk, a humane & worthy young man, who seemed shocked [at a man] of my Fame begging mercy for my family. He promised no execution till he heard, and I came home comparatively happy from this promise. Cassandra this whole week untouched – from sheer harrass.

September 2. In the City all the morning. While I was waiting for a Friend the new Post Office flashed in my mind as adapted for Agamemnon's Palace. I bought a sixpenny book, & borrowed a pencil of the shopman, & made a sketch; when I came home I rubbed in a new Background, and it is a great addition.

September 3. Today after a week of misery, came 100 from the Duke, & 20 from Hill, M.P. for Hull, so that here I am again up in the sky. I drew 4 hours with delight, & got all my figures ready from the naked.

These anxieties are proper correctives! Continued prosperity would make us impudent, voluptuous, & ungrateful.

September 4. Called [on] dear Lord Melbourne – was very glad to see him & he me. We had a regular set-to about Art. I went on purpose. I said for 25 years I have been at all the Lords of the Treasury without effect. The 1st Lord who has courage to establish a system of public support for High Art will be remembered with gratitude by the English People. He said, 'What d'ye want?' 'A vote of 2000 a year.' 'Ah,' said Lord Melbourne, shaking his head and looking with his arch eyes, 'God help the Minister that mingles with art.' 'Why, my Lord?' 'I'll get the whole Academy on my back!' 'I have had them on mine, not a Minister & a Nobleman, & here I am! You say the Government is poor; you voted 10,000 for the Poles, & 20,000 for the Euphrates.' 'I was against 10,000 for Poles. These things only bring over more refugees,' said Lord Melbourne. 'What about the Euphrates? Why, my Lord, to try if it be navigable, & all the World knows it is not.'

September 15, 16, and 17. At Hampton for air. Dearest Mary came, & we passed a sunny day in a retired spot. She looked as bewitching, as graceful, as lovely, & as devoted as that delicious afternoon in a lovely meadow [when] I first told her I loved [her]. She said she was perfectly happy, & so was I.

October 8. Worked hard. Directly after the Duke's letter came, with its enclosed cheque, an Execution for the Taxes. I made the man sit for

Cassandra's hand & put on a persian bracelet. Lazarus' head was painted just after an arrest; Eucles finished from a man in possession; the beautiful face in Xenophon in the afternoon of a morning of begging mercy of Lawyers; & now Cassandra's head was finished in agony not to be described & her hand completed from a broker's man.

October 19. Called on Lord Melbourne, and after a little while was admitted. I went up and he was very happy to see me indeed.

He looked round with his arch face and said, 'What now?' as much as to say, 'What the devil are you come about – Art I suppose!' 'Now, my Lord,' said I, 'Do you admit the necessity of State support?' 'I do not,' said he. 'Why?' said I. 'Because,' said he, 'there is private patronage enough to do all that is requisite.' *'That I deny,'* I replied, at which he said, 'Ha! ha!'

He then went to the glass, & began to comb his hair. I went on: 'My Lord, that's a false view; private patronage has raised the School in all the departments where it could do service, but High Art cannot be advanced by private patronage.' 'But it is not the policy of this Country to interfere,' said he. 'Why?' 'Because it is not necessary,' said he. 'You say so, but I'll prove the contrary.' 'Well, let's hear,' said Lord Melbourne, 'where has it ever flourished?' 'In Greece, Aegypt, Italy.' 'How? by individual Patronage?' 'No, my Lord, *alone* by the support of the State.' 'Has it flourished in any Country without it?' 'No. How can your Lordship expect it in this?' He did not reply.

'Now, my Lord, A new House [of Lords] must be built. Painting, Sculpture, & Architecture must be combined. Here's an opportunity that never can occur again. For God's sake, Lord Melbourne, do not let this slip; for the sake of Art, for your own sake – only assure me it is not hopeless.' Lord Melbourne looked up with his fine eye, looked into me, and said, *'It is not.'*

At present there will be only a temporary building till Parliament meets. There's time enough.

October 20. Out to battle with Lawyers; pawned all my Birmingham studies for £5, and my lay figure for 4£. This was a great help. I was able to pay off balances. I have received 120 a week ago; it is all gone!

If the Duke had not been so kind, God only knows what I should have done.

November 2. Awoke at four, my mind filled with such a stream of thought as kept me alert till I got up. I directly poured them out in a petition to Lord Melbourne. I carried down the petition to Lord Melbourne & sent it up. I leave it to its fate.

November 9. Sent down in the morning to know if Lord Melbourne could see me. He sent back word 'at one.' At one I called, & saw him. The following dialogue ensued, 'Well, my Lord, have you seen my petition to you?' 'I have.' 'Well, what do you say to it?' He affected to be occupied, & to read a letter. I said, 'What answer does your Lordship give?' 'Why, we do not mean to have Pictures. We mean to have a building with all the simplicity of the Ancients.' 'Well, my Lord, what public building of the Ancients will you point out without Pictures?' – I was going on talking eagerly with my hand up. At the moment the door opened and in started Lord Brougham. He held out his two fingers & said, 'How do you do, Mr Haydon?' Lord Melbourne, evidently embarrassed at such a contempt of all that was due to a Nobleman in his own House, looked really quite awkward. I was astonished and stood still, Lord Melbourne looked at me, & said, 'I wish you a good morning.'

I bowed to both, and when I came out I said to the Butler, 'He is just come at the wrong moment.' The Butler looked frightened, as if he would have it for letting him up. In fact, there was something in the air of all the House, as I came down – curious.

November 15. By Heaven, Lord Melbourne is out! Did I not say last Sunday there was something in Brougham's air? I think the King wrong. Lord Melbourne was a Man to manage parties, it appears to me, and a crisis.

I called on Lord Melbourne in Downing St. at four. He sent out word he was very busy but would be happy to see me another day.

November 18. Spent the whole day in Lord Grey's room, Downing St., sketching every article for the Picture of Musing by the Fire. Lord Melbourne returned no more. Lord Grey's furniture was moving. The Duke takes possession tomorrow.

December 17. Hard at work on Greek pavements in Cassandra. Very much advanced.

December 20. Very hard at work.

December 24. Worked at a Wheel. Xmas time. The Children came roaring down, for me to go out. I was as much inclined as they, for the Picture was nearly all but done – so out we went, and spent a pleasant 3 hours, wandering, peeping into Print shops, seeing sights, stuffing at Farrance's, loitering in promenades, longing to buy all we saw, & see more than we could, & came home with the appetite of Tigers for our feeding time. Dearest Mary with us looking like the eldest daughter.

December 31. 9 o'clock morning. Painting Room.

Last day of 1834! Thank God I have got up to it! & Cassandra is done except two trifles, which I hope to accomplish before night.

O God, on my knees I bless thee for the mercies that my children are advanced in knowledge, that I have through all my difficulties the means of advancing their education.

Benjamin Robert Haydon in 1828 by Georgiana Zornlin

Restore my dearest Mary to health & happiness. She is now anxious & not well. Have mercy on us, and let our love encrease. Tomorrow I begin a new Picture, with the New Year. I feel more vigorous, more confiding, more elastic than I have felt for years. O Lord, let me this day twelvemonth be able to kneel to thee in Victory & gratitude. Amen.

1835

January 1. I knelt down as I entered my Painting room, took the Bible to read the destiny of the year, and opened by fair chance at once to Verse 4, Chap. XXXV of Isaiah, saying:

4. Say to them that are of a fearful heart, Be strong, fear not; behold, your God will come with a vengeance, even God with a recompence; he will come & save you.

5. Then the eyes of the blind shall be opened, and the ears of the deaf shall be unstopped.

I got up grateful, elastic, braced for every trouble on Earth. Is this Vanity, is this superstition? No! It is the Whisper of the Great & Awful Being.

January 2. Going to begin Achilles this Instant. Success! – under God's blessing. Amen.

February 1. Called on Lord Melbourne. He was lounging over the Edinburgh Review. He began instantly, 'Why here are a set of fellows too who want public money for Scientific purposes, as well as you for Painting; they are a set of ragamuffins.' 'That is the way,' said I; 'nobody has any right to public money but those who are brought up to Politicks. You never look upon us as equals, but any scamp who trades in politicks is looked on as a companion for my Lord.'

'That is not true,' said he. 'I say it is,' said I – and he then roared with laughter, and rubbed his hands!

I take more liberties with Lord Melbourne than any man he knows – 'Lord Melbourne, will ye make me a promise?' 'What is that?' 'Pass your word to get a vote of money for Art, if you get Premier again!' Not a word.

February 3. At the Duke's, and sketched his cloak he wore at Waterloo, the coat, plain hat, &c. Tomorrow they are [to be] sent to me. The contrast of his house with Lord Grey's was extraordinary. I was shewn into a waiting parlour full of pistols, muskets. All about Lord Grey was antimilitary, while every thing martial seems to be the character of the Duke.

February 5. This history of this affair is quite an event. I wrote the Duke to sit. He declined. I wrote for his clothes. No reply. Supposing his occupation prevented it, I wrote Colin, his valet, taking him to be the medium of communication with the Duke for his clothes. Colin asked the Steward.

The Steward begged me to call. I did so, and selected what I wanted, telling him I had written the Duke. The clothes were sent, and I, considering this could not be done without the Duke's knowledge, in writing the Duke to say I wished to shew him the Picture, thanked him for his *noble conduct* in sending his sword, &c. As he knew nothing of it, there was devil to pay.

I really enjoyed seeing in my Painting Room the tin hat case of Field Marshall Duke of Wellington, the sword of Waterloo, and the frock coat, such as he wore at the battle!! Now I shall destroy the Picture & have nothing more to do with the thing.

February 12. Worked hard. At the first dawn of morning had a flash of an Imperial Guard musing at Waterloo, as a fitter companion for Napoleon. Finished it *over the Duke!* This is the first time an Imperial Guard extinguished the Duke. The Picture will be a curiosity. The line of the Duke's sword can be traced across the trousers of the Guard. His right arm is *actually the Duke's blue coat!* Ha! Ha! B. R. Haydon.

February 25. Exceedingly depressed in spirits from great want of money. Idled, read, moped, slept. Went to a party in the evening. Met Mrs Leicester Stanhope, who had had a tooth drawn, went to a ball, danced till five, & was now out again with an inflammation in her gum! This is what I call *bottom*. In fact people of Fashion have ten times the spirit of the low bred.

March 7. Finished the Duke of Sutherland's Napoleon. Called on Hamilton, who advised me to send a copy of the Petition to the Duke of Wellington, which I did.

I am most anxious about this matter, because it really is the climax of my efforts, to accomplish this great National object. If the Committee, Lords or Commons, if the Duke takes it up, it will go on. God only knows. The misery is the Art is considered but as an embellishment – a sort of gilding! – nothing more.

March 9. No answer. Went into the city for money. Came back disappointed. Rubbed in a grand subject – Orestes hesitating to murder Clytemnestra – ghost of Agamemnon.

March 14, 15, 16, 17, and 18. Hard at work, and completed my little Picture of A Statesman musing after a Day's Fag.

Cassandra much liked. One of the papers said the '*Veteran* Haydon.' This is the first knell towards the grave. Bye & bye, '*Old Haydon;*' then '*Poor old Haydon.*'

March 28. Took my dear Giorgy to Sir Charles Clarke [physician]. I am reduced to 1.15., with a dear infant ill, & bills to meet next week to the amount of 50. Began again Achilles, which I wish I had never left for trifles.

April 1. Began Achilles really, & got in a capital head. God bless the commencement, progress & conclusion, Amen.

I had 1.15 Saturday to pay 50. *I trusted.* Cutler Ferguson sent to me Sunday, 10.10 – I sold a share in Xenephon for 12.10 then I saved myself from immediate ruin, wrote a petition for Lord Morpeth & am now home, after racing to Lawyers for mercy for a day.

April 8. Perhaps in the whole history of infamous corruption, the conduct of the Times newspaper is unrivalled! The bronze impertinence of their beastly turn-coating is not to be thought of without rage. Today I dashed the paper down & will give it up. After having heaped on Lord Grey every term of abuse, & helped to drive him from office, today they talked of his being above subjecting himself to the Scurrillity of the Parties!

April 20. Lord Melbourne in again! huzza! – if only for the pleasure of making the King take him. I wish him success.

April 22 and 23. Finished Achilles.

April 25. Worked half a day, on 'John Bull.'

May 1. Hard at work and nearly completed the 'We are a ruined Nation' – being obliged to put in a couple of portraits spoils it, but to such hard uses does necessity drive one. Lord Grey's help today has secured me from immediate ruin.

June 13 and 14. Exceedingly grieved at the loss of Giorgy, my dearest child, & Mary was nervous & agitated. So many traits turn up when a little dear is gone, which you hear nothing about before. I have no employment. My Landlord allows me to pay off my debt to him by Achilles & allows me 5.5. a week for 5 months to do it in.

June 16. Out the whole day with my dear Children, to Red Hill, & Mary to rub off our melancholy – the sweet hay air was delicious. We rolled in the hay and felt renovated beyond belief.

June 21. Longest day – now we decline to winter. The death of my dear Giorgy has given me a shock. I have lost a fortnight in musing sorrow & disgust at life.

July 11. Yesterday was a grand Review in Hyde Park, the King there. How my dear Harry would have gloried! How his frame shook at a trumpet, how gloried in the thunder of cannon! How his little heroic soul filled at hearing Homer read! He would have been a Hero! – had he lived till 20, and been blown to pieces on a forlorn hope.

July 14. Tuesday. Hard at work. Wrote the Duke of Devonshire, Lord Morpeth, & Hulme for help to pay my rates & Taxes.

Not a sixpence from either, *I'll bet*. I'll bet any money if I was to write the Duke of Wellington & ask him to help me to pay my taxes & rates to vote for Lord Melbourne, he would send me a cheque!

August 15. [On August] 26 I lecture at the Mechanics Institute. It is quite an experiment – God support me. I shall get through as to matter – but self possession in face of a multitude is different from self possession in a study.

August 22. Finished Achilles, thanks to God!

At ½ past nine my dearest Mary presented me a boy. Shall I call the dog B. R. Haydon? [He died May 16, 1836.]

August 24. Hard at work & made a sketch of Christ raising the Widow's Son.

August 29. Such was my necessity last Saturday I was obliged to take down all my drawings in the parlour, while Mary was actually in labour pains, & raise money. But I shall carry my great object – glorious creature, she will suffer any thing rather than I should fail.

August 31. In the evening I called on a Creditor, who had been robbed, & he began crying & saying his faculties *would go*. I told him he wanted a blue pill & sea air & left him in better spirits – think of a debtor being obliged to keep up the spirits of a Creditor!

September 5. This evening, at *last*, I lectured at the Mechanic's Institution. After all my humiliations, it was at first a little nervous affair. The audience paid me keen & intense attention, and ultimately were enthusiastic. I laid down principles which must reform English Art, & I had an audience who gloriously comprehended them.

September 26. The Agony of my necessities are really dreadful. For this year I have principally supported myself by the help of my landlord, & by pawning everything of any value I have left, until at last it is come to my clothes! I literally today sent out my dinner suit, which cost £10, & got 2.15. on it for tonight's necessities. Oh, it is dreadful, beyond expression. I could not go to dearest Mary & ask her for little Jewelleries – but I am now, if invited to dinner, without a dress to dine in!

I finished the feet of the Widow's Son capitally, & if I can complete the hand left, I shall have done the Picture – but these wants press hard indeed.

September 28. Threatened on all sides. Wrote Lord Spencer & Mr Harman, in a state not to be understood. I improved the Picture, and not having a shilling sent a pair of my spectacles, & got 5/– for the day.

September 29. Tuesday. Sent the T[ea] urn off the Table, & got 10/ for the Day. In God I trust.

October 2. Harrassed. Awoke at 2 with heated consciousness of approaching ruin. The Children expect something, & are nervous. What an instinct there is in a house. The Creditors met last night. All that came granted me time.

October 9. Worked deliciously, as I was resolved to paint, let what would happen. This ruined me in 1823.

October 10. My wedding day! Worked hard & finished the Mother. This week ended so far well – nearly all my Creditors have agreed to my terms. But still there are some who harrass.

October 13. Called on Lord Melbourne & had an hour's interview. 'Is there any prospect, my Lord, of the House of Lords being ornamented by Pictures?' 'No,' he thundered out. 'What is the use of painting a Room of *deliberation?*' 'Ah,' said I, 'Maintain me for the time & settle a small pension to keep me from the Work House!' He looked up with real feeling. 'Let me,' said I, 'in a week bring you one side – as I would do it.' He *consented!* – & we parted most amiably. God knows what will come of it.

October 17. Saturday. Worked very hard, & delightfully. Made a Sketch of one side of the House of Lords, as I propose to adorn it – viz., with a series of subjects to illustrate the principles of the best Government.

October 28. Wednesday. Worked hardish. Put in a Negro.

On Sunday I sent down by Lord Melbourne's desire the Sketch of one side of the House of Lords, containing Pictures to illustrate the best Government for man. He saw it, and seemed more nettled than pleased I had proved its feasibility. After musing some time he said, 'It certainly does [express] what you mean, but I will have nothing to do with it.'

October 30. God protect us! – Amen! A successful day – sold some Prints which relieved our actual wants, & nearly finished the Figure, though being so dark it may want supervision.

November 6. Up to this moment I have not actually painted. Why? Harass, anxiety, want of money, loss of time, in being obliged to trudge about, & sell my own Prints – at 50 years old nearly, and after 31 years of intense devotion to the Arts. It is hard, but God's will be done!

November 7. Out the whole day to sell Prints; had the greatest fun & enjoyed it excessively.

November 10. Hard at work and put in a fine head.

November 15. Read prayers to my dear Children, & wrote my 3rd Lecture out. After, called on Lady Blessington.

December 5. An Academician said the Sun of Art had set in this Country – the Silly Creature – it has never risen! The Comets, Reynolds, Hogarth, Wilson, Gainsborough, were blazing but irregular lights; we have never had a steady effulgence of an established Sun, revolving on unerring principles and shining with regular effulgence.

December 6. Read Prayers. Passed the day in blessed peace, my dear Mary looking Angelic. Remodelled & arranged my second Lecture.

December 7. Harrassed to Death – all day, & threatened with Execution. Mary sacrificed her jewellery & shawl. I hope to prevent it.

December 15. Had a glorious conception of Macbeth at the Staircase. I think his Figure the finest I ever invented – it flashed like lightening on my brain.

December 28. Began to glaze Achilles, & got on gloriously! – with simple margylp made of my own drying oil & Brown's mastick. It would be better if I made my own mastick, which every artist is bound to do. My drying oil is from a flemish receipt given me by Mrs Hoppner.

December 31. The last day of 1835! Another last day! On reviewing the year, though I have suffered bitter anxieties, I have cause for the deepest gratitude to my Great Creator in raising me up such a Friend as my dear Landlord who has employed me to paint the Widow's Son & Achilles, paying me 5 guineas weekly, to the amount of 100 gs. each, & then striking off 400 gs. each from the gross debt.

I have painted this year a small Picture of the Duke musing & an Imperial guard musing, 'Discovery of Achilles,' 6 feet by 4. 8, 'Raising the Widow's son' (same size). I hope they will be successful.

1836

January 9. Completed the rubbing in of the Picture, & made two sketches of Lion & Man, and had the following kind letter from the Duke of Bedford: [A letter from the Duke of Bedford is attached to the diary. He enclosed £5, concerning which Haydon noted, 'The 5 was a real blessing. I took my dress coat out of pawn to lecture at the Mechanics' In. B. R. Haydon.']

January 12. Compressed the lecture – & faddled – read – roasted myself by the fire – half dozed – owing to the frosty weather.

January 13. Read my second lecture – at the Mechanics' Institute – with great applause, on the bones, and introduced the naked Figure.

I told them all if they did not get rid of any feeling of indelicacy in seeing the naked form, & did not relish its abstract beauty, Taste for grand art would never be rooted among them. This was received with applause, & I broke the ice for ever. I always said the middle classes were sound, & I am sure of it. Good God, this morning, when all my Friends are congratulating me, in walks an Execution for 50.

I wrote to Lord Melbourne, Peel, Duke of Bedford. Lord Melbourne sent me directly a cheque for 70. (Peel never answered.) This was kind hearted. He told me I must not think it hard, but decidedly he could not repeat it.

February 17, 18, and 19. Worked & harrass.

The R. A.s complain I do not go on in a *Gentlemanly quiet way.* Exactly so. When I got into a Prison nothing would have pleased them more if I had *died* in a quiet *gentlemanly* way.

March 2. Harder at work. Lord Audley has given me a handsome commission. God bless its commencement, its progression, & conclusion. Amen. The Black Prince thanking the Lord Audley for his Valor after the battle [of Poitiers] – subject chosen. This will bring me into English history, which I have long wished for.

March 5. Lord Audley called & sat. Settled the size & every thing. All now afloat, thanks to God! God bless the beginning, progression, & conclusion of Lord Audley's commission. Amen.

What have I not gone through – these papers testify! Let any man of feeling reflect that on the loss of a beautiful infant, we were obliged to pawn our winter things to bury her!

March 9. Lord Audley said, 'Money is at your command.' He talked of making my daughter presents, but I shall not allow [this], and if he does any thing out of the way in point of liberality for me, I will write to his Eldest Son, for I do think he is eccentric.

He praised my daughter (who is beautiful), and said, 'If Bill likes her, & she will marry him, I will give him 50,000!' He told stories capitally well, & laughed heartily, & then stopped, & laughed, & looked serious. His manners were peculiar and made me melancholy. He said our meeting was providential, and I should never want. He got excessively tipsey with little wine – I sent for a Coach & sent him home.

March 10. Lord Audley called; was highly pleased, & left me £85. He was highly pleased & talked no more of Bill & 50,000. He saw my little dear, who said, 'Lord Audley is different today.' I did not tell her, but the fact was he was *sober* – all the difference.

March 21. Hard at work and advanced rapidly. Pictures that used to take me years, I now do in months; those which *now* take me months, I hope soon will only take me days.

March 30. Lectured at Mechanics on Composition; tried them on the Academy, & succeeded. The Committee were in a funk.

In the Committee afterwards they said, 'Your enthusiasm carried them on, or they would not have born it.' No. It was their understandings carried them on. They have an instinct against oppression.

April 17. Sunday. As I passed the Haymarket a large dog stopped close to Frank & I & howled most dreadfully. A Cab Man said, 'Sir, that means somebody's death!' I stood studying the expression, which was very fine. Perhaps the dog had lost his Carriage!

May 3. Finished my lecture.

May 4. Delivered it & concluded the series triumphantly! Frank and dear Mary were there, & when she came in with her beautiful face, they gave her a round of applause.

May 9. The great object of my anxieties for 5 years, the raffle for Xenophon, took place at last & the Picture was won by the Duke of Bedford. [The total received was £840.]

The raffle was highly exciting. The audience was curiously mixed, some from the City, some from the West End. After I had thanked the company, I had forgotten to propose thanks for the Duke; one of the subscribers rushed over & said, 'For God's sake, don't forget the Duke,' in a whisper. I turned round so quietly & without a change, diplomatically did 'em – as if the most experienced! Sir Gore Ouseley said, 'I second the motion,' & it ended most happily.

On Saturday night I was attacked with influenza; lay in bed all day Sunday & perspired with some violent medicine; got up sensitive of the wind & afraid of a large room without a fire; & creeping down St. James St. saw a fire in a crumpet shop. I asked leave to sit by it; in I crept & sat down & got quite warm. By the time the hour came I was ready for any thing, and though very ill got through with my knees sinking.

How little the World know the real nature of appearances! Here was I just out of a sick bed! – doing the happy with a pain in my limbs that made me writhe.

May 16. My dear infant died at ½ past 8 – pretty dear – Newton, aged 8 months & 3 weeks.

This is the way the Almighty reminds us of his power in the midst of the most brilliant moments of Life.

May 25. All my Children are born healthy & strong. They become weak, but are never born so. While in the womb, where their nourishment is certain, they do well; when they come into the World, they seem to stop advancing. For the loss of my dear Harry I blamed the medical man. Now [Dr] Darling attends, the Child dies the same.

Worked and made great alterations in the composition.

June 4 and 5. I called on Lord Melbourne, but he wouldn't see me. He was ashamed. His Valet stroked his chin, just as Servants do when they are awkward. I am glad to see these symptoms of feeling.

June 10. Lord Willoughby D'Eresby sat, and a delightful hour I had. He said he knew Tom Sheridan intimately. One night he had got excessively tipsey, & the Ladies were rather annoyed. At Breakfast the next morning, the door opened, & he stood before them *in a sheet!*

June 13. Hard at work! – on Lord Willoughby! He was very amiable and sat in martyrdom, to serve me. We talked on entertaining matters. I told him several things I ought in delicacy not to have done – but while painting one chats away to amuse one's sitter, & forgets the scandal that pours out. It is wrong, and it pained me afterwards. I'll not do it again.

June 24 and 25. Worked & advanced.
I called in yesterday at the Committee of Arts. Martin was examined. Howard was there. Good God! What a singular bit of retributive justice. He was on the hanging Committee that used me so ill, 1809. Good God! How he looked! How altered! How humbled!

June 28. O God, thou knowest this has been my great object, for 26 years. Bless my examination! Grant it may be clear, effective, & *just.* Grant nothing may happen to render me confused, or in any way to injure the value of my evidence. Grant the result of this Committee's labours may be a final & effectual blow to the imposture of Academies all over Europe.
7 o'clock, evening. I was examined & the result was glorious. Accept my gratitude, O God. Amen.

July 16. Justice, indeed, triumphed! Shee, the President, was examined, & Ewart in the Chair.
Shee went on verbiaging away, & Ewart repeatedly begging him to be concise.
At last began his examination. 'Do you think Academies beneficial or no?' 'Extremely beneficial.' 'Do you think the Academy is conducted with that feeling for justice, &c.?' 'Certainly.' 'Do you think it just that 600 Artists should be kept out on Varnishing days?' 'Certainly. This is one of the privileges of the Academy.'
'Do you think 40 enough?' 'Certainly. I know no man of great Genius out of the Academy.' So it went on – blind to all genuine principle, all he saw was the Academy & its members – and he thought Landscape painters [able] to teach the Figure. He then again abused me for saying the Academy was founded in the *basest intrigue!* & mentioned Reynolds, Chambers, West, & Paul Sandby, as men whose characters were a security, when four more old intriguing Rascals never lived!
Was not the whole scene a scene of retribution? The very men, the very

hangers – Shee, Phillips, & Howard – who 29 years ago, used me so infamously in hanging Dentatus in the dark – by which all my prospects were blasted for ever – at which Lord Mulgrave so complained – were now at the bar before me like Culprits under examination.

July 18. Idle, & lectured at the Milton, a delightful Theatre – cool. I felt like a Lion & read like one.

July 19. Attended the Committee and the impression Shee had made was decidedly unfavourable to his cause.

July 23. Wrote Peel & proposed to him to endow a Professorship of Painting at Oxford.

July 25. Lord Audley has completely deceived me about his resources; after telling me he was the *richest* Peer, it turns out he is the *poorest!* I fear his honour & his character.

August 27. Called at the Russell Institution, & saw Xenophon well lighted & up, with the following inscription:

'Xenophon's first sight of the Sea, in the retreat with the 10,000 – painted by Haydon & presented to the Russell Institution by John, Duke of Bedford. 1836.'

This is very grand.

Lord Audley has written me to say he can do no more for me at *present*. It is extraordinary how instantly being left again, my mind leaped to its wonted energy.

September 9. At breakfast with the dear Children. A timid tingle of the bell made us all look anxiously. A whisper in the hall, and then the Ser[van]t entered with, '*Mr Smith*, Sir, wishes to see you.' I went out & was taken in Execution. After lingering two days at Davis' Lock up House, Red Lion Square, on the 12th I was moved again to that blessed refuge to the miserable, – the Bench.

Newton, my Landlord, offered to pay me out. I refused, & proceeded to prepare for the Court directly.

What a fight it is – it is wonderful how my health is preserved and my dear Mary's too.

September 12. Committed to Bench.

September 13, 14, 15, 16, 17, 18 (Sunday), *19, 20, 21, 22, 23, 24, 25,* (Sunday), *26* – my Angel came, *27, 28, 29 and 30.* Passed in Prison!

October 1. Almighty God bless me through this Month, and my dear family. Amen.

October 7, 8, 9, and 10. Anniversary of my wedding day. My sweetest

Angel came, & we passed in Prison the happiest & most delightful anniversary of the Wedding Day we ever passed. She looked just as beautiful as ever, & I kissed her often. Then I did the Wedding night – & I swear with more fury.

God in Heaven, save us in health to proceed again & secure a competence for old Age, & marry our dear Children honourably & well.

October 26. Read Cobbett's History of the Reformation through with fury & eagerness. It is [as] usual full of all his power of mind & full of all his exaggerations, wilful suppressions, & gross omissions.

There is no doubt that the poor generally were better off before the Reformation, & that it has been the sole cause of the poor laws, but has not a race sprung up as compensation, the keen, acute minded Merchants. Perhaps the people fed better when they were Catholics, but were they so free in mind or so pure in practice? The Monks filled their bellies at the expense of their freedom of conviction. Would they have read Cobbett?

October 30. Dearest Love came in nervous dejection, and left me today affected like herself. This is one of those occasional variations in the feelings of those who love with all their hearts. Sweet Angel!

November 10. Read Moore's Byron.

Read Byron's Journal late. I delight in Byron – his sincerity, his true searching into humbug.

Oh, how I sympathize with all he says of parties – the nothingness, the chatter, the loss of time. Ah, would I had known thee!

November 14. My Angel came & I enjoyed Rapture belonging to Heaven! How I eat her up! – devoured her, crushed her! – how I was convulsed! – quite a convulsion lasting a moment longer – insanity would have resulted. Oh, the love!

Lord William Paget came in Prisoner, & brought a beautiful innocent boy with him! There he was watching his Papa, up at eleven o'clock, when the dear ought to have been sleeping & in bed. I watched him with the feeling of a Father. There was something peculiarly innocent in the look of the boy with his white collar.

November 16. Last night, poor Paget set all the Prisoners agape. One must go out of his room, for my Lord wanted 3 beds; another was applied to for one thing, & some for another. This morning the *bill* was presented at usual, for all Bills are paid here daily. His Lordship looked astonished, said a bill was a nuisance, and as soon as his *Friend came* again he would leave £5 with the Landlord, & when it is out he must tell him.

The positive evidence that *he*, my Lord, had no money was palpable.

It is extraordinary how a Man from such a family could come into a Gaol without money. You read of Lord Anglesey dining in Court at Paris, and here is one of his Sons in the Bench! It is degrading!

November 17. I went up to Court today, & was treated with the greatest humanity. Commissioner Law seemed by his face to have the greatest sympathy. He seemed *feeling* all over. He never asked me a single question, and the whole Court hastened my discharge with the rapidity of lightening.

O God, accept my gratitude for all thy manifest mercies during my imprisonment; great they have indeed been.

November 29. Set my palette today, the first time these 11 Weeks & 3 days! Good God! – I relished the oil, could have tasted the Color, rubbed my cheeks with the brushes, & kissed the Palette! Ah, could I be let loose in the House of Lords!

December 1. God bless me with the rational means of existence throughout this Month – also with health & vigour of body & mind – and keep me free from Sin of every description. Amen.

Wrote & worked & advanced Saragossa.

December 5 and 6. At work. Advanced Saragossa & Macbeth small.

December 9 and 10. Worked & advanced well Falstaff & Saragossa.

December 15. Today the Woman who lights my fire was looking at Falstaff, & she said, looking at him, 'What a charming looking old Gentleman.'

This is precisely the thing & will be the effect on the public.

December 22. Called on Wilkie after a long absence. He seemed much annoyed at my saying in my evidence that he had been frightened at being seen with me in the Streets after my attack on the Academy. I told him it was *true*, which he did not deny, because it was.

December 25. Christmas day – for the first time I did not read prayers, meditate on the Birth of Christ as I used to do. I was the whole day occupied in writing my lecture on the Mural Paintings of the Greeks. God forgive me. Amen.

December 31. Last day of 1836 – I have lost more time in this year than in any before during my Life from 18 years old. I began several Pictures, & have finished none. I have never had so many *began* Pictures at once in all my Life.

1837

January 9. Monday. Met Ewart yesterday in the Streets. He told me all was going wrong with the school of design. The Council has resolved that the *Figure* should not be the basis of the education; 2nd, that every Student who entered the school of design should be obliged to *sign a declaration* not to practise either as Historical Painter! – Portrait Painter! – or Landscape Painter!

January 18. Poor Lord Audley is dead! He was more the dupe of Villains than a Villain himself. He died of apoplexy on 14th Instant.

January 25. This is my birth day! – born 1786 – 51 years old today! I find after 33 years struggle the State of Art certainly in better prospect, the Academy completely exposed, the People getting more enlightened, a School of Design began, and more than hope the House of Lords will be adorned! with Pictures.

February 18. Hard at work & completed Sampson, God be thanked! – after all hindrances & obstructions. How grateful I am! What a singular destiny attends my historical Pictures! The Crucifixion just rubbed in, was seized, I ruined, & is still, after 14 years, in the same condition.

May 11. Left Leicester after giving my last lecture last night, to a brilliant audience and receiving a vote of thanks – and arrived safely into my dear Mary's arms at ½ past 8.

Exactly two months after my departure – 11th March – how much I have to thank God for! My tour has been a complete triumph! – beginning with the Edingburgh dinner & ending with the vote at Leicester. How grateful I am to God, that all the dangers of travel I have escaped, by sea & land, find my dear Children well, & my Wife faithful, in our health, & benefitted, & money in my pocket.

May 16, 17, 18, 19, and 20. Left Town for Manchester & arrived in 19 hours – 186 miles, allowing one hour for meals & changing, which is 18.

June 1, 2, 3, 4, and 5. Lecturing till I am sick. I am not happy in Manchester. The association of those hideous mill prisons for Children destroys my enjoyments in Society. The people are quite insensible to it, but how they can go on as they do in all their luxurious enjoyments with huge factories overhanging the sky is most extraordinary.

June 17 and 18. This was imagination. I have examined since large factories – 2000 in one room, & found the Children healthy, strong & the room well aired and wholesome. B. R. Haydon.

June 24. Returned to my dearest Mary – after 5 weeks' absence – and the greatest success in Manchester.

July 9. Felt degraded in my own estimation in condescending to ask the Duchess of Sutherland to interfere with the Queen to appoint me her Historical Painter. If it succeed, what will become of my Liberty? I do it for dear Mary's sake, as her health is feeble.

July 24. Passed a harrassed & anxious night. My dearest Mary still ill, but slept well – 10 children, suckling them all, and my troubles in addition with the imprisonments, have shaken a constitution not strong – God in Heaven protect her & bring her through it.

August 4 and 5. Got on today well – & this morning felt again my old interest and glorious feeling in looking at a large Picture. I think I will give it all the interest of a *fight* – storming & fight – with a beautiful woman leading. God bless me through it, and grant I may bring the Heroine of Saragossa to a glorious and triumphant conclusion.

August 7. Made an oil study for my heroine. She must be a Spanish beauty. After all my success this year I have returned to my winter studies with only 3 sovereigns left.

August 8. Went to the National Gallery, & studied the head of the Virgin in the Murillo. As to *impasto* nothing can be finer – it was a treat. What is want, affliction, imprisonment, the rack, for an hour of such enjoyment! I felt the taste of the colour on the tip of my tongue!

August 9. Never disregard what your enemies say. They may be severe, they may be prejudiced, they may be determined to see but in one road, but *still* that road they see clearly.

They sneer at my success in lecturing, & say, 'it is a pity he does not paint more.' Of course it is a great pity, considering my deficiencies. That is a sneer that I can & will profit by.

August 14. Sketched Spanish Costume & arranged the dresses.

Hayter is a Clever Man – has painted the Duchess & the Princess in their retirement, & paid them that attention which I omitted to pay. I think it right the Queen has appointed him, though my Lazarus entitles me to the highest honours of Art.

August 17. Sir Joshua says if a negro painted Venus he would paint her thick lips, short nose, wooly hair, & black skin. He would – but would [it] be right? God made man in his own image. Was God black skinned, wooly haired, thick lipped, & short nosed? Why not? He cannot be. Why? Because intellectual power is the great distinction of Man, because Negroes have never yet established their right to be intellectual. It is more likely that when the Bible says, 'God made man in his own image,' the Bible meant the image in which God created the White Man, & Adam was his White Man, with all his characteristics & the image of his Creator.

September 8. This day year I was taken from my dear family – to a lock up house & then a Prison – and yesterday I received a Commission from Liverpool for 400 gs. Such is the turn of Fortune's wheel – such the blessings & punishments by which the Father of us all corrects & rewards.

September 15. Seized with a furor to write my lecture on Beauty and did it.

Half the Month is gone. Falstaff is done, the Sketch for Liverpool done, Saragossa, quite ready to do, and Poictiers nearly done.

I am waiting for another reply & to fly at my Canvas.

I am engaged for 20 gs. & 30 gs. – 50 before Xmas lecturing.

October 5. Left Town at 8; arrived ¼ to 7 at Birmingham; left it by Train, and arrived at Liverpool at 12 at night.

Received most kindly by Mr & Mrs Lowndes. Members of Committee [of Liverpool Blind Asylum, who had commissioned Christ Blessing Little Children] dined Friday & Saturday. All treated with great kindness & distinction.

October 29. At present I stand higher in the opinion of my Countrymen than ever. The Enthusiasm following my lectures is extraordinary; the crowds encrease and I verily believe will go on encreasing. We shall see. I have received a Commission from a public body. I have maintained my family in comfort since March, and I trust in God I shall be spared in health & strength of Body & mind.

October 30. Yesterday Her Majesty sat to Sir David Wilkie for her state Portrait. Today her Majesty sat to Mr Hayter. On Friday Her Majesty sat to Pistrucci. On Saturday Her Majesty knighted Mr Newton, Miniature Painter. On Sunday her Majesty went to Church with Sir Augustus Calcott, the landscape Painter. On Monday Her Majesty sat to Mr Tomkins, the Black Chalk drawer. On Tuesday Her Majesty sat to Jenkins, the lead pencil outline designer. On Wednesday Her Majesty knighted Smith, Tomkins, & Jenkins.

November 13. At the British museum to collect materials for a concise History of Art.

November 14. Lord Egremont is dead! – a great loss to all, especially Artists. He was an extraordinary man – manly, straight forward, tender hearted, a noble Patron, an attached Friend, & an affectionate & indulgent
Parent. He was one of those left of the old School, who considered a great Artist as fit Society for any Men, and at his table, as at Sir George Beaumont's, Lord Mulgrave's, or Sir Robt. Peel's, Painter & Sculptor, Poets & Ministers & Soldiers [were found].

November 20. Saw the Queen pass the gallery to the Lords. Her appearance was singular. Her large eyes, open nostril, closed mouth, small form, grave demeanour, & intellectual look, had something awful & peculiar.

She looked like a creature of which there was only one species, & this was a specimen, covered with diamonds, fed on Gold, & sleeping on satin & drinking nectar!

November 22. At the B. Musaeum all day – hard writing for my History of Art.

December 19. Began my history 22nd of last month & have got to the Carracci, & through.

December 31. The last day of 1837 – O God, accept my gratitude for it. The cause of Art is advancing among the people. I am incessantly employed lecturing, and received with applause. A shrewd Government would back this and turn it to advantage.

FIVE

1838–1842

1838

January 25. Manchester. Up to this very day I have neglected my journal. I left Town, and arrived after a rapid Journey by Train from Birmingham, here, & was received with the same enthusiasm as before. Today my Birth-day, when I complete my 52nd year, A meeting took place in the Committee Room of the Mechanics, to consider the propriety of founding a school of design. I read my proposition, which was received with cheers – finally an active Committee was formed to take the proposition into serious consideration preparatory to calling a public meeting.

January 28. Dined out with a very fine fellow, Darbyshire & met Heywood (Banker), Fairbairn (Engineer), & others. Liked Fairbairn much – a good iron, Steam Engine head – 'I can't get through novels,' said he. It shewed his good sense. He has risen from a foundery-labourer to Master of as great a Manufactory as any in the world.

January 29. Lectured at R[oyal] I[nstitution] & Mechanics'. Audiences stuffed. Laid the [subject of a] School of Design before them. Enthusiastically received. Committee met today. All goes right. Monied Men must not be bullied. Great effort to keep the Mechanics temperate.

February 1 and 2. Closed last night – with an enormous audience.
Dined at Fairbairn's Engineer, after passing the morning at his vast Engine Work. Boilers for 400 Horse power Engines – Iron melting by fire, that would have made the Devils look astonished! – roaring like Thunder – dark with brightness, red with heat, & liquid like lava!

February 21. Set off for town, where I arrived after having accomplished all I had left Town to do – a School of Design, & the excitement of the people.

March 18. Went to Church, but prosperity, though it makes me grateful, does not cause me such perpetual Religious musings. I am sorry to say my piety is never so intense as when in a prison, and my gratitude never so alive as when just escaped!

March 30. Called in on old Sir Thomas Hammond, whom I had not seen for a year – an old Courtier & Friend of George IVth. He was getting infirm but looked well. There he sat with a white cap on his head, like a manufacturer.

April 9. Expected to hear from Liverpool, but did not – on the 8th I was promised my money – but this is the way with Committees. I promised Landlord & Collector of rates & Taxes, & have broken my word with all of them. I feel lowered again.

April 28. Such is my life – Aujourd'hui j'ai reçu cent guinées sterling, hier au soir actuellement sans quatre schellings! Telle est ma vie! – un jour au sommet, pendant le jour suivant au bout de besoin et misère!

Grace au Dieu pour sa bonté! ce matin. ½ past *one*. Was there ever any thing like it? This moment j'ai reçu de Liverpool l'autre £50! Cent cinquante cinq livres dans un jour – apres la plus grande necessité. Grace au Dieu encore.

May 27. Walked & looked at the grand entrance to the Rail way [the stone entrance at Euston-grove]. It is extraordinary how decidedly the public have adapted Greek Architecture. Its simplicity, I take it, is suitable to English decision.

June 8. Painted in a head. Is it equal to Titian or Reynolds, Vandyke or Rubens? *No* – disgrace that it is not. My mind is teeming with improvement, and something will come of it. The first symptom is disgust at what I do.

Lectured. Hard day's work.

June 15. The great tendency of the Whigs has always [been] not to uphold the glorious supremacy of England, but so to dim it as to prevent its offending France. Even when I shewed Lord Melbourne the plan for adorning the H. of Lords & had made one subject, 'le dernier charette' at the Revolution, his reply was, 'I will have nothing to do with it. *It will offend France.*'

I will venture to predict before the Whigs leave office, England in influence will be reduced to a Second rate power.

These are the Whigs to the bone & marrow – with a Bankrupt Income! an entangled Foreign Diplomacy, an insulted Country, an irritated population, an apprehensive Church, a starving poor, proposing laws they can't carry, & passing them after enduring Tory castration, eating their own words, swallowing their own Vomit, and allowing their noses to be rubbed in their own filth, as they do to dogs when they dung a drawing Room.

The above is written in a passion, but it is true to the Bone.

June 22. Hard at work. Met Lord Melbourne. He turned into the Home Office as if he said, 'Damme, here's *Haydon*,' which I know he did.

June 27. Out in the morning to call on Mr Winstanley about the Liverpool Picture. Came home & worked half a day.

The people with this Coronation are crazy. I hope it will be fine for little Vicky's sake – little ugly, round faced hussey.

June 28. It was a finish day. The procession was very grand, say they who *saw it*. *I*, who only saw the three Horse guard feathers, three Hammercloths, and the top of her Majesty's State Coach, thought it a shabby affair, & was astonished at the apathy, hardly any cheers, except when Marshall Soult passed.

July 5. Towards dark I took an anxious look & found my Picture in a Complete mess. I reset my palette & set to work. I filled up, dashed out, & recomposed, and this morning to my infinite joy, I found it will do *once more*, & better than ever.

'The national pride of France is embarqued on the Conquest of Algiers,' said Palmerston for not further interfering with Algiers. What a reason for an English Statesman! What dereliction of principle, what horror of Revolution, what blasphemy in religion!

Would Chatham have said this? Would Pitt? Would Wellington? Would Peel?

July 9. At the Review, and grand sight it was. Soult was there. The Guards formed squares like Waterloo, which I hope gave Soult *reminiscence* & be d—d to him.

Studied some exquisite effects of Smoke for my Saragossa – the beautiful softness against the dark feathers & caps, the flash – *dark*, fiery, yet *light* – shall be made use of, with great effect, in that Picture, I hope.

What struck me, as an old *reviewer*, was the amazing improvement since I was a boy in quickness of motion. When the whole was in square, the line was reformed – Cavalry in the seat – in 2 minutes. No Troops could make better use of the ground, or file off in so narrow a space with less Confusion.

It was a magnificent sight. The day was splendid. The Queen & suite were glittering and gorgeous, and it was impossible for a Foreigner not to be struck with the proficient & uniform character of the Splendour from the Sovereign to the people.

July 10. The Russians have taken Teheran. What will Palmerston say? The national pride of Russia is concerned in the Capture!

July 13. Hard at work.

'We have looked again at the letter of B.R.H. and have decided not to publish it. The fierce & malignant spirit which pervades it would offend every right minded reader and the effect would be injurious to the cause which the writer means to serve.' July 13, 1838. Times. To Correspondents.

You are a beauty, you are.

July 25. A meeting for Nelson's Monument today. Meant to attend but could not.

July 29. Sunday. When I go into my Painting room, in health & Spirits, after all the necessary blessings of physical existence, when I see my Picture well advanced, I feel so grateful to God I shout out an exulting hymn of enthusiasm & acknowledgement!

July 30. Painted right out 7 hours, & finished the Soldier.

The whole of the background figures are managed more like a great Artist sure of his hand than any I have ever done. (God be thanked, with all my heart.)

August 25. Worked hard – in a nervous agony – the knee & leg were weak of Christ. Altered, did not effectually do it, but by dark saw the *Error*, and tomorrow I will put it *right*. Drapery will always look awkward if it be not 'the vehicle of the limb it invests.'

There is no shirking this great principle. I worked the whole day as if I was bewildering the Centre of the Picture, nearly done as it was. But a Voice said '*You* KNOW it's wrong.' When the *people* know it as well as you, *they'll* find it out, & you'll be dead, so you had better not shirk it.

August 31. I have got fairly through my Picture, ['Christ Blessing Little Children'] for which mercy I offer God my grateful thanks. I began 8 of October, went out of Town in January, recommenced in April, & got through it in August – fair hard work it has taken me 6 months.

September 1. Went to Gravesend with my family for a day of relief & pleasure. First we all got into an Omnibus & were jolted & suffocated [to] the Bank. Second the Steamer at the Bridge had just gone. Third we had to wait amongst Porters & Packages ¾ of an hour for the next. 4th we got on board the sunny side in a cabin, close to the Boiler, & were alternately baked by the sun & broiled by the steam pipe. Fifth we got to Gravesend tired & *hungry*. 6th we walked to a romantic *love* lane, which was a garden straight walk with dirty wooden seats, and sundry evidences that people in Gravesend had good digestions & sound peristaltic motion. 7th we ordered Roast Beef for Dinner, and my dear Mary kept her appetite to enjoy a hearty meal, when the Landlord put down lamb she *hated* & so did I. 8th we had rum as hot as aqua-fortis, & then old port as weak as children pap. We all got aboard with indigestion. I fell asleep on Deck & got a pain in my head, and we got home tired, grumbling, ill humoured, had tea, & crept to bed.

Today I am heated, discontented, & indignant, & it will take 24 hours more to recover in. For this *earthly* happiness I paid 2. 12. 6. – enough to feed us for a week! – so much for pleasure.

September 2. Sunday. Read prayers & studied Newton's Prophecy with real pleasure. No geological theory can overturn the awful reality of the existence of the Jews as a Nation without a Country in spite of their repeated destruction as a people. 'I will not make an end of thee.'

September 7. Moved the Picture to the Gallery by the Duke of Sutherland's leave. It was enormous the extraordinary Effect of a full sized room – exactly what I had arranged in the Sketch. I placed my Picture by one of the finest Vandyke's and Murillo's in the World. What a lesson; the Grey tone of Murillo's background was blue black. I sent away immediately for blue black, seeing the superiority over my own; before one my back ground was done, & at 40 feet such an improvement is not to be described.

September 16. Sunday. I bless God with all my heart that I have paid my rent, rates, laid in my coals for Winter & have enjoyed health, happiness, & freedom from debt ever since this Commission.

September 19. Wrote all day – it was so dark – a fair copy of my lecture on Beauty. Could not glaze or paint.

September 21. Glazed and finished my Sampson & Dalilah. Nothing comes so near the Colour of manly flesh as light Red & White & Black for half tints, glazed with Bt. Sienna. Sampson's flesh is that, & it's capital. Finished my Lecture.

September 24. What is the use of talking of the 800,000,000 of debt? It is the price we paid for keeping our independence and should be considered so, & not a bit too dear. My politicks are the Energy of Cromwell, the Nationality of Nelson, & the Fierceness of Blake.

September 26, 27, 28, and 29. All passed in gossipping & shewing my Picture, puffing & being puffed.

Last night as I sat musing whether I should put forth my Soul in designs for this Nelson Monument, my old Voice whispered, 'Here is at last the very moment you have sought for. Will you miss it?' 'No,' I inwardly said, and felt a glowing & glorious aspiration!

October 1. Took out my Canvas & began on [a] Sketch of Nelson Monument – Britannia bringing Nelson to Mars for Nursing. O God, bless me through it.

October 5,6, and 7. Nearly finished the Sketch. Duke of Sutherland called. He said they were on their journey to Italy, & were going to Winsdor to take leave tomorrow. All I hope is he won't spend his money on Foreign Art.

October 30. Set off for Manchester, where I staid for two days & Nov. 1st, arrived safely at Leeds, where I was heartily welcomed. The Liverpool men are speculatory & spirited; the Leeds men, steady & persevering; & the Manchester, industrious & wealthy.

November 17. I conclude my lectures tonight – 12 nights in succession. Thank God I have had the strength. I should like to have left Leeds with a Commission; it would have been a triumph, but I trust in God I shall not be deserted.

November 19. Left dear old steady Leeds at XI. Got to Manchester and dined. Set off by train & came like mad in the hour to Liverpool. Had a letter from my darling Mary, sweet Soul, which charmed my heart & Soul.

December 5. Lowndes came the other night & proposed to me to paint a grand Historical Picture of the Duke. The very thing I have been thinking of for these 2 years. How extraordinary!

December 9. Sunday. Passed over to Woodside in a Steamer, into a pretty church, & heard a very good extempore Sermon by a man called Knox. He agreed that the ultimate burning of the World did not infer its annihilation, but a purifying to prepare it for the Kingdom of Christ. It was very well done.

December 14 and 15. Dined out, & gave my last lecture to a crowded and elegant audience. The success of these lectures at Liverpool, and the success of the Asylum Picture, [and] the Victory of a public commission, are really so glorious, that no gratitude to God can be great enough. I prayed sincerely for a successful end of this labour, and it has ended successful.

December 16. Left glorious Liverpool by train & arrived home to my darling, whom I found as lovely as ever. There is real enjoyment in a pure, voluptuous embrace of a lovely wife that no libertine can enjoy or ever did.

December 19. Chalked in the Duke. ½ an hour at work on sketch. Unpacked colours, palette, Brushes, Books, & arranged every thing for work. God bless me again in my Painting room! Amen!

December 22. On Saturday began the Duke & Copenhagen [the horse which Wellington rode at Waterloo] at 53 minutes past 9 A.M. First touch of color 56 minutes past 9 A.M. Huzza & Success. Now it's afloat – Huzza! & one cheer more – Huzza!

December 31. The last day of 1838 – a year of competence & work &

prosperity, comparatively. The people are more alive to Art than ever. Every where have I been received with enthusiasm, and the importance of High Art is no longer a matter of doubt with them.

Thus ends 1838. Could I hope that every year would be equally Blessed by Employment & competence, every wish would be gratified. May I deserve it. Amen!

1839

January 2. Worked hard. Got the Duke's position settled. Horse not right yet – more like a Camelopard [giraffe] than a blood Horse – so far.

January 9. Worked like a new one, & altered the whole position of Duke & Horse. Better than all the rest.

January 17. Worked very hard at Nelson's Monument.

January 30. Sent in the Design, which is as likely to succeed as any thing else I ever did for a Committee, but I trust in God it may do good.

March 4. Arrived safely in Town, thank God.

March 5, 6, 7, and 8. Did nothing yet, but business. Found my dear love any thing but well.

Up to March 14th. Occupied in busy stuff about the Nelson Memorial. Saw Sir George Cockburne. Had a long argument. He stuck to the Column, but was open to conviction. I told him height alone would not do; breadth was as essential.

March 17. Sunday. Called on Wilkie, & found him with several Pictures, not one of which is worth the fiddle in the fiddler's hand, of the Blind fiddler. It is melancholy such a decay of power. Such a Queen! Kneller, Hudson, Ramsay would have disowned it!

March 23. Lord Lansdowne sat again today. He had the gout in his feet, and came out on crutches. He dozed several times and seemed in much pain. He was very amiable, and I amused him about the Americans – much – stories I heard in Liverpool. He said it was curious that a settlement called *Liberia*, [founded] by them, was a nest of Slave dealers.

March 25. Left Town with my dear innocent Boy Frank, for Manchester, by Train. Arrived in little more than 10 hours. Took lodgings in 99 Mill Street, and was much interested at his (Frank's) utter ignorance & inexperience, and though I have educated him, Religiously & Classically, I almost fear the Vice of a manufacturing Town. It is a complete sacrifice, though his passion for engineering is invincible.

It is his own choice & God bless him for it.

April 21. Hull. My lectures at Newcastle on Tyne were received every night with encreasing enthusiasm, till the last night was crowned with a Victorious cheer. Newcastle has encreased in splendour of look & architectural decoration more than any Town in Europe.

There is a spirit among them, which will ripen into most effective advance in Design.

May 4, 5, 6, and 7. Lectured at Warrington. Enthusiasm just the same.

I returned to the arms of my dearest love & my glorious Art yesterday, by Train, after a most successful tour. On Monday I went to Liverpool, settled every thing with my Committee about the Duke, flew off to Manchester, saw Frank, paid up his arrears, dashed off to Warrington, & was home to tea. Good Heavens, what superb travelling – 73 miles in two hours & 40 minutes, for that was all the time it took.

May 25. I wrote the Duke & here is *his* answer. I suppose there was an indelicacy, as a candidate, of writing him as a Member.

London, May 24, 1839.

The Duke of Wellington presents his Compliments to Mr Haydon.

The Duke *is a Member* of the Committee for the Execution of the plan for erecting a Monument to the memory of the late Lord Nelson. He is not the *Committee*, not the *Secretary* of the Committee; and above all, not the *Corresponding Secretary*.

May 30. Advanced the Duke. It is really now ready for Completion, but I want my horse accoutrements — clothes, hat, & sword.

June 6. Moved all my books upstairs to a small Room out of my Painting Room, as they seduced me to read at wrong times. I felt pain at the separation, but it is right. I can now retire & read & write after due labour; but I miss my Books, and felt melancholy all day.

June 9. Sunday. Took dear Mary & went to the Chapel Royal to hear Dr Hook, who made a most admirable lecture on the antiquity of the Book of Prayer. He said, 'It is not *in Religion* as it is in *Science* – nothing new can now be added.'

The Queen came, looked calm & collected. I met her large Eyes several Times. I wonder if she remembered me! I thought her intellectual & not feminine, not amorous, not likely to marry.

June 10. Worked, & certainly with more abstracted devotion to my Art than when my books were near; I have stuck at it all day, and in the evening walked up into my Book room. There they were, silent, yet speaking! teeming with thoughts, bursting with Sublimity. I walked about in extasy, but read nothing, dwelt on what I had read, & was content.

June 12. Worked gloriously hard. I pulled my Picture about, changed my lights, lifted up & lifted down without the least fatigue, & worked outright till dark.

Whilst I was hard at work, just as I used to be, who should call, after a long absence, but David Wilkie, looking old & feeble.

His total failure this year seems to have shaken him a little, & the total neglect of the Court has brought him more to the feelings of former times. He did not like to be reminded that it was 30 years ago since we were in Devonshire. He shrunk from his age. I never do, and it is not absurdity to say I feel stronger, after 9 hours' solid painting yesterday, than I did at 27 years of age.

June 22. The Nelson monument is decided, & not in my favour.

Westmacott told Hamilton my design was the only reasonable one. The public, [when] admitted, decidedly approved, and had it been left to the public, I think I should have had a strong support. So ends my Nelson affair.

June 30. [The following letter is attached to the diary:]

London, June 27, 1839.

The Duke of Wellington presents his compts. to Mr Haydon. He hopes he will have some cessation of note writing about Pictures.

The Duke knows nothing about the picture which Mr Haydon proposes to paint.

At all events, the Duke must decline to lend to any body his Cloathes, Arms, and equipments.

This is all very fine, my dear Dukey, but luckily when I had his cloaths by accident 4 years ago, I painted six views of his cocked hat, measured his coat & sash, drew his boots & spurs – so, my Dukey, I am in the Windward,
at any rate.

July 5. Five days are now gone and I have not touched a brush but once. I overworked & deranged myself; my digestion got low & exhausted. I have recovered by leaving off & pretending to bustle as if I was full of importance.

July 6. Called on Lord Fitzroy, & asked him if the Duke wore belt inside or outside. He replied inside, if he had to throw off his coat often – in the Peninsular Campaign & Waterloo. His Sash he wore – 3 or 9 balls in front; his pantaloons blue knit, his straps hooked and eyed, under his foot. It was treating Lord Fitzroy almost like a Valet, but his good nature excused it. Every time you meet a Waterloo Hero pump him. In a few years they will all be gone, Duke & the rest.

July 12. Ordered a pair of trowsers of the Duke's Taylor, exactly like his own, but to fit *me*; so that I shall, as *on dit*, kill two birds with one Stone – wear'em & paint'em. So, my Dukey, I *do* you in spite of ye.

July 29. Never in the World was the insecurity of wealth or the vanity of Fame or earthly glory [manifested] so entirely as the calamities that overwhelmed Titian on his death bed. As he lay in the Plague, Thieves entered the House, stole before his Eyes his gold & jewels, his finest designs, and left the House.

August 16. Thirty pounds having unexpectedly come in, I determined to start for Waterloo. My dear Mary, who is a Heroine, agreed to endure my rapidity of journey, so we packed off, and got on board the Ostend packet by 7 o'clock on the 7th Inst., and after the usual miseries of a wet, stormy passage, got into Ostend at 9.

We were delighted with Brussels, & on the 10 went to the Field of Waterloo. I examined Hougoumont, recognised the locale of the last charge of the Guards, & made my sketch from Picton's position.

We went to Antwerp, & were amazingly impressed with Rubens' great works – the Elevation of the Cross, Descent, & Crucifixion.

August 21. The sight of Rubens' House – the quiet seclusion of his Summer house – the Silence of Antwerp – the golden Splendour of its Altars – the power of its Pictures, affected me deeply! I think I will Settle there. I begin to feel a yearning for the Continent, with all its risks of War.

August 27. Was at the House the last day of the Session and had a glorious study of the Duke. After I had watched him all the evening, when the House was up I darted round to catch him. He recognised me with his eye & large lid & bowed & smiled, so that we are a degree nearer. At a distance he was very old; *near* he looked younger & fresher.

August 30. The age of miracles has not ceased! I worked today, & the sitting he gave me in the House of Lords was splendid the other night. Every body says, 'It is the Duke's character.' Oh, I trust it!

September 6. Walked 21 miles.

September 9. Began the Duke's back-ground after days of severe meditation. Painted 6½, then wrote letters of advice about Art & lectures. Felt the good effects of my walk.

September 10. Out in the morning on business. Came home. Got in remainder of the sky. Darked part – Dark ashes; Middle part, medium as it approaches Sun, lightest ashes. The Tint is truly exquisite – not an atom of varnish, only linseed oil.

October 8. [The following letter is attached to the diary:]

Walmer Castle, October 9, 1839.
The Duke of Wellington presents His compts. to Mr Haydon.
If Mr Haydon will be so kind as to come to Walmer Castle when ever it may suit

Napoleon, 1829 and opposite *The Duke of Wellington*, 1839, both painted on a window shutter at Chatsworth

him, the Duke will have it in His Power to sit to him for a Picture for certain Gentlemen at Liverpool.

B. R. Haydon, Esq., No. 4 Burwood Place, Connaught Terrace.

October 10 and 11. Left town by Steam for Ramsgate. Got in at ½ past 6, dined, & set off in a chaise for Walmer, where I got safely in hard rain. A great bell was rung on my arrival; and after taking tea & dressing, I was ushered into the Drawing room, where sat his Grace with Sir Astley Cooper, Mr Arbuthnot, & Mr Booth, who had served with his Grace in Spain. His Grace welcomed me heartily, asked how I came down, & fell again into general conversation.

The Duke said, when he came through Paris, 1814, Md. de Stael had a grand party to meet him. Pradt was there. In conversation he said, 'Europe owes her Salvation to *one man.*' 'But before Pradt gave *me time to look foolish,*' said the Duke of Wellington, 'Pradt put his hand on his own breast, & said, *"C'est moi."* (Capital.)

The Duke talked of the want of fuel in Spain, that the troops suffered, and that whole houses, so many to a Division, were pulled down regularly & paid for to get fuel. He found Bivouacing was not suitable to the English character. I said, 'Your Grace, the French always bivouac.' 'Yes,' he replied, 'because French, Spanish, & all other nations lie anywhere. It is their habit. They have no homes.' (Beautiful.)

I came to my room, & said, 'God bless your Grace.' I saw him go into his. Good God, when I got to bed I could not sleep – here I am tete-à-tete with the greatest Man on Earth, & the noblest – the Conqueror of Napoleon – sitting with him, talking to him, sleeping near him. His mind is unimpaired; his conversation powerful, humorous, witty, argumentative, sound, moral.

October 12. Saturday. At ten the next day we breakfasted – the Duke, Sir Astley, Mr Booth, & myself. He put me on his right. 'Which will ye have, black tea or green?' 'Black, your Grace.' 'Bring black.' Black was brought, and I eat a hearty breakfast. In the midst 6 dear healthy, noisy children were brought to the windows. 'Let them in,' said the Duke, & in they came, and rushed over to him, saying, 'How d'ye do, Duke? how d'ye do, Duke?' One boy, young Gray roared, 'I want some tea, Duke.' 'You shall have it, if you will promise not to *slop it* over me, as you did yesterday.' Toast & tea were then in demand. Three got one side and three got the other, & he hugged 'em all. After breakfast I saw the Duke romping with the whole of them, and one of them gave his Grace a devil of a thump. The Duke said, 'I'll catch ye! – ha! ha! I've got ye!' at which they all ran away.

He then told me to choose my room & get the light in order, and after hunting he would sit. I did so, & about two he gave me an hour & ½. I hit his grand, upright, manly expression. At first I was a little agitated, but I hit his features, and all went off. His colour was fresh. All the Portraits are too pale.

October 13. Sunday. After breakfast Mr Arbuthnot told me to go to the village Church and ask for the Duke's pew. I walked, and was shewn into a large pew near the pulpit. A few minutes after the Service had begun the Duke & Mr Arbuthnot came up – no pomp, no servants in livery with a pile of Books. The Duke came into the presence of his Maker without cant, without affectation, a simple human being.

I really do think that Arthur Wellington, in the Village Church of Walmer this day, was more interesting to me than at the last charge of the Guards, or in all the Glory & paraphernalia of his entry into Paris. I would not have missed seeing him.

The Duke after dinner retired, & we all followed him. He then yawned, & said, 'I'll give you an early sitting tomorrow, at 9.' I wished his Grace good night, & went to bed. At ½ past 5 I was up, set my palette, & got all ready, & went to work to get the head in from the drawing – by night. The door opened, & in he walked, looking extremely worn – his skin drawn tight over his face; his eye was watery & aged; his head nodded a little. I put the chair; down he sat – & was altered from Saturday. It affected me. He looked at his watch three times, & at ten he got up, & said, 'It's *ten.*' I opened the door, and he went out. He had been impatient all the time. At Breakfast he brightened at the sight of the Children, and suddenly looking up at me, said, 'D'ye want another sitting?' 'If you please, your Grace.' He replied, 'Very well; after hunting, I'll come.' At lunch I was called in. The Duke, Ct. Bruno, & myself lunched away. The Duke asked me to have chicken but I liked chop. At 3 he came in to sit. He was fresher, but the feebleness of the morning still affected my heart. It is evident at times he is beginning to sink, though the sea air at Walmer keeps him up, and he is better than he was.

November 23. Hard at work again & improved the Duke, as I should go on doing to the last. There is no unalloyed pleasure but in the Painting Room! – here I feel like a God!

Wrote the Duke a frank letter, telling his Grace he went too long without his food. I said I observed it at Walmer, and that from 10 to ½ past 7, 9 hours & ½, was too long without intervening sustenance. I begged him to consider the value of his Life.

November 28 and 29. Finished my lecture for Leeds on the History of the Arts.

I think this Taste of the Queen for Historical Portraits in Composition is an advance in Taste.

November 30. Last day of November. The Duke is fairly done, and I return thanks to God for enabling me to carry it through gloriously. I began it, & prayed for its success as I always do, and therefore I am grateful.

1840

January 1. O God, accept my deep gratitude for thy merciful preservation of me to the beginning of a new year, for the sake of my dear Family & dearest Mary.

I leave Leeds tomorrow, and the taste & love of Art is certainly improved since my visit. The hospitality & kindness of the Inhabitants have been great, and on the whole the Visit has been prosperous.

January 29. The difficulty I have to resume my brush is laughable; it is ridiculous; it is shameful; it is abominable. Yet I march about, look at all my Pictures, sure of my Commissions, put my hands in my pockets, talk to myself, curse my being obliged to lecture for family's sake, then write an attack on the Whigs, long to be at the Academy, & then get wretched at not painting. I shall have a burst, & away will go Evil Spirits.

February 10. It is to me as a Briton dreadful to think of the Laziness, the Apathy; the indifference of Lord Melbourne is dreadful; we are losing our rank, decidedly. In the Mediterranean it is impossible to keep up our influence. If we act independently the French, the Russian, and Mehemet's fleets may act, and who is to prevent them?

We are certainly check-mated. The growth of such fleets should have been watched and prevented.

With Lord Grey's twaddle & Lord Melbourne's apathy & Lord Palmerston's Dandyism, we are in a promising way.

February 13. Every Minister of England should base His whole proceedings on the instinctive Ambition of France. In Dancing & Cookery they have conquered the World, and they believe, from the moment of perception to the last gasp of existence, their conquest of the World in all other matters is only delayed & obstructed by England.

February 26. Started for Oxford – a day dream of my youth.

February 27. Received by Vice Chancellor, Dr Shuttleworth and Wardens with every kindness. Leave was granted to lecture in the Radcliffe great room, which could not be done without meeting of Trustees. Dr Shuttleworth then sent me to the Ashmolean, where I begin on Tuesday [March 3]. God grant me success. I make no charge. I admit all members *free.*

March 1. Dined with Dr Shuttleworth (en famille) at New College, & spent a delightful time.

We got on the Duke, and he said He had one singular trait – he was mean in money matters, & that he actually suffered himself to be sued for the amount of his silk gown before he paid the money. It was near an Execution. The Warden said the trouble they had to get the money was dreadful – it was years. Perhaps this may account for his indisposition to lend his Cloathes to Artists.

March 3. I began today at The Ashmolean Museum, & had *complete Success*. All are alive to common sense & Nature – the refined Scholar & the humble Mechanic. It was beautiful. And, Oh God, how grateful ought I to be, to be permitted the distinction of thus being the first to break down the Barrier which has kept Art begging at the Universities to be heard.

March 11. Dined at Maudlin with an old Fellow Grantham, who smelt of brandy at 12 o'clock in the day – rather unclassical.

March 13. Last Lecture of the 6. Audience quadrupled. I came to try a new ground. It was neck or nothing, and all Classes rushed to hear me till the Mania became extraordinary.

March 14. Arrived home full of enthusiasm, & expecting to find my dear Mary to hang about my neck – when I found her *out!* not calculating I should be home till dinner. I then walked into Town after untrapping. When I returned *she* was *home*, & was hurt *I* did not *wait* so, this begat mutual allusions which were any thing but loving & happy. So much for Anticipations of human happiness! Oh Dear – perhaps this necessary bit of evil was a proper check on my Vanity. I endeavoured to take it as such.

March 29. Sunday. Went to Church with my dear old Landlord, Newton. He has been to me & my family an everlasting Friend, a pivot to work on, a friend to rest on, such as I believe no other human being ever had before.

I thanked God for it with all my heart. He does not look so well as he ought. If I lose him I shall lose a Man indeed.

April 15. 'The King's College' Council has appointed a professor of Fine Art – Huzza! This is a great point, and must be attributed to the influence of my success at Oxford.

April 16. Lectured at Islington, with great success. Worked hard – I am not satisfied with my mode of painting a head – not at all. It is not the system of a practised Artist, but I *will* conquer it. I see character so soon, I *dash* at it before my surface & color are impastoed enough, & get the expression before my preparation is ready to receive it, and then don't like to meddle.

May 26. Finished my Romeo & Juliet, & now my Employer (a Hull dealer) won't pay me my balance £45, till I deliver the work, & I won't deliver it till I get my balance. How unlike the Nobility.

June 1. Went to see Bewick's copies from Michel Angelo. I had not seen my old Pupil for 17 years! His mind seemed quite gone.

The old Dutchess of Lante had kept him, & he appeared as if Italian Women had drained & destroyed him. He appears as Wilkie does, totalling & weak. The Italian Climate seems to have ruined their brain.

June 29. Lucretia Mott, the leader of the Delegate Women from America, sat. [For the Anti-Slavery Convention.] I found her out to have infidel notions, & resolved at once (narrow-minded or not) not to give her the prominent place I intended first. I will reserve that for a beautiful believer in the Divinity of Christ.

Scobell called. I said, 'I shall place you, & the Negro together.' Now an abolitionist on thorough principle would have gloried in being so placed. This was the touch stone. He sophisticated immediately on the greater propriety of placing the Negro in the distance, as it would have much greater effect.

Now *I*, who have never troubled myself in this Cause, gloried in the Imagination of placing *the Negro* close by his *Emancipator*. No – the Emancipator shrunk. I'll do it though.

July 1. God bless me & my Labors through this Month. Amen!

July 11. Hard at work & well advanced. The Americans are intruding & inquisitive. I have great trouble to parry them. I perfectly agree that such a number of honest heads were never seen before. So said the Dutchess of Sutherland, and so say I.

I have not missed a day since 12th of June. God be blessed.

July 19. Sunday. Went into the City to see a poor relation as a matter of Conscience. Found her better. Left her 5/- for the present moment. I set her up in business when I could ill afford it – £25. She sold the goods, lived on the whole produce, & never thought of the net profit only. She has been a trouble, Heaven knows, but not only 7 times but 77, says our Divine Master.

July 30. Worked not hard. I was tired with Lecturing last night.

Poor Lord Durham is dead! – a victim to mortified ambition, bad liver, bad temper, & the intrigues of his enemies! His temper was perfectly uncontroulable, and at times he behaved like a brute to the gentlest Woman in the World, yet loving her sincerely.

August 8. Worked hard – completed 10 heads this week. I think the neck of the Picture is broken. I began 24 of June.

32 heads are done – 7 days over for rubbing in & getting the Picture in order. But my dear love is attacked in her womb, & lies helpless & suffering. It keeps me in awe in the midst of success! Thy will be done! Amen.

August 9. Sunday. Though no Man can blame Lord Palmerston after what has passed, for signing a treaty with Russia, Austria, & Prussia, yet what a mess the Whigs bring Countries, Quarters, Individuals, Persons, principles, & Institutions into, from want of experience & want of moral courage.

Who did not foresee that the policy of the Whigs with France must alter if Britain wished to keep her supremacy in the World? Who did not predict that Austria & not France was the natural & ancient ally of Britain?

Depend on it, the British people will find the present peaceable, talented, prudent, & politic King of France a more dangerous enemy than Napoleon, because he has the cunning of a diplomatist without the frankness of a Soldier, because he has lived long amongst us, & knows the principles of our superiority & the elements of our greatness, & is aware how to outwit, to rival, & to lower our pride.

Nothing could have [been] more calculated to sap the influence of Britain than this Man's diplomacy from the instant he outwitted La Fayette and got possession of the Throne.

It would not be just to say the Whigs were not sincere; they were sincere, but they were deluded; they were led away by the Vanity of doing something different from the Tories, and in cultivating the Friendship of France, they believed it originated with themselves, when secretly they were the merest tools of Talleyrand.

When the Duke left office, there were no symptoms in France of a desire to add to their navy or pretend for a moment to rival ours, but the Instant Louis Phillipe got to the Throne, a tendency in that direction was visible, and one cannot help admiring the skill with which the work began, so as to blind us to any suspicion of our Neighbours.

Perceiving the extraordinary apathy of his Friends, Louis pushed his Navy with skilful promptitude. He put into it one of his own sons to raise the morale & dignity of the profession, which had sunk to the lowest depth. It became from that hour no longer a disgrace to be a French Naval officer, and the wealthy & high born no longer withheld their sons. Wherever Merchant vessels sailed, Ships of War accompanied them; quarrels were picked with disorganised & feeble Nations, less as an excuse for injuring our commerce than giving practical experience to their fleets.

In spite of all the Treaties in the World, whenever it may best serve France or Russia, War *will come*, and let the British people be assured it will be a war for National existence.

The Engines of War are more destructive than ever known. Steamers render Invasion no longer problematical, and with all pretences of Russia, nothing would gratify her more than the Mortification of Britain, or delight the French so much as billeting a Regiment on the Duke of Devonshire, or 6 Grenadiers on every householder in the Strand!

Let us get rid of the folly of living on former repute. A sincere Friendship between England & France is utterly impossible – France, gay, blasphemous, volatile, bloody, bawdy, amiable, & unprincipled, instinctively military, can never unite with a Nation, solid, virtuous, commercial, religious, philosophical, unmilitary, & money getting, which has to France ever been a rebuke & a mortification.

All Frenchmen are intriguers & Soldiers, and all Russians diplomatists & liars, and the only way to render nugatory their mutual efforts is to shew you are ready with a broad side for both.

August 15. Buxton sat and I never saw such childish vanity & weakness. He brought a Clerk to dictate letters to, and appointed 2 American Delegates to hold forth to him on the advantages of the Colonization Society in America. The Man so bedimmed my brain, a bad head was the consequence, and what with his (Buxton's) dictating letters, signing, correcting, & talking, I passed literally a most distracting morning, & told him so.

August 22. Excessively & gloriously hard at work. Finished a head, hand, & figure in two days.

Nothing astonishes me so much as my rapidity with this Picture. It is truly the result of all my previous fagging – for years.

September 4. Hard at work, & heard from dear Wordsworth, with a glorious Sonnet on the Duke & Copenhagen. It is very fine, so God bless him.

October 1. What one admires so much in Christianity is the *good sense* of the founder. You find no metaphysical arguments about the *origin* of Evil, no reproaches about its existence, but Evil is taken for *granted* – & the *remedy* laid down. Oh, it's wonderful. My heart warms!

Worked hard, very hard, & accomplished a great deal.

October 8. Idle the whole day, & was miserable. My Chimney & the room were swept, much against my inclination. All was dust & mess, & nothing ready till too late to see.

November 11. Dr Lushington sat, and a very pleasant sitting it was. He thought the Speech of Louis peaceable, that so many intermarriages had taken place, so much commercial intercourse, that the two Nations had been so completely interwoven that he believed all the respectable part of both Nations wished Peace & that the other Nations of Europe were equally disposed to wish so.

I said, 'Sir, remember Venice. She was so long in Peace & relied so long on the forbearance of her Neighbours that when War came, they yielded from inanition.' He agreed.

He told me he had been at Eton with Lord Melbourne, and that all the great public Schools were going down, especially Westminster, and he said as Lord Durham had before to me, he would *never send a boy to any – such was the Vice* – & abomination. He told me he never would fag, & got continually beaten.

But still I am for public Schools – see what a race they produce as Statesman, Generals, Admirals, &c. Boys should be brought up with each other; Vices are always rooted, and they should be inured to resist, by early precaution. I know I saved my boys by early precautions.

I explained the fatal consequence of the school vice – they went dreading it & as much aware of it, as Men. It was an experiment, & it succeeded.

November 12. My dearest Mary seriously ill. Worked hardish.

November 13. Rubbed in a Napoleon for Sir John Hanmer, & worked at the Slavery Picture. Their bringing me 31 heads more after arranging 103, is rather a joke, but if they like, they shall have heads all over, like a peacock's tail.

December 31. The last day of 1840 – a year to me of great blessings with bitter sorrow, because my sweet & lovely Mary, with her Noble heart & tender nature & devoted love, has sunk in health & been prostrate.

My pecuniary resources this year from Constant employment have been great. How grateful we ought to be that in such sorrow we have not wanted.

With respect to the prospects of Art, the people are certainly advancing. My lectures continue as much as ever exciting. Fresh engagements pour in, and wherever I go the same enthusiasm is excited.

I have lectured on the naked Model in London, Edingburgh, & Manchester, & lately had wrestlers to struggle before 1500 people at Liverpool, with immense approbation. 50 years ago such things were not credible.

For all thy Mercies, Gracious God, this passing year, 1840, accept my gratitude. Amen with all my soul, Amen. Amen.

1841

January 2. Arrived at Sheffield – by coach, and was more tired with this paltry 40 miles than the 1260 miles I have travelled by rail. But I saw the Country, which is peculiarly Scotch & Romantic after Staley bridge.

January 4. Heavy snow. The air is sharp & cutting at Sheffield. No wonder they are celebrated for knives. Lectured, but the audience the dullest I ever knew.

January 9. Lectured – so bitter cold the Ladies put their muffs under their feet.

January 16. Spun home in 9½ hours from Sheffield. For all the Mercies of God during my preservation from Death for 2 Months in eternal risk, I am grateful!

But found my dear Mary *very ill.*

January 25. My birth day! 55 years old! O God, this day I recommence my great work. Bless me through it, in spite of all obstructions! Restore my dearest love & let us descend to the Grave together.

January 27. Put in 3 heads. Worked moderately – 3 hours!

January 28. Put in 3 more – moderato – 4 hours.

February 1. Out all day on business connected with the Great Picture. My dearest love out of danger.

February 9. Sketched O'Connell. We talked of the Catholics & Protestants. He said, 'If you apply to a Man's *reason*, you only apply to *half* of him, & the *smallest* half.'

He said the Puseyites had adopted the great proportion of the Catholic doctrines (I did not know). He said the Whigs would go out, but the Queen would not let them.

There is in O'Connell a keen, lynx look, and great good nature, but cunning & trick[y]. 'You English,' said he, 'don't know what is going on in Ireland. Repeal will triumph.'

O'Connell swore the Duke was wounded in his bum in Spain. It is not true. He replied, 'One of his Aide-camps told me so.' This was a bit of O'Connell's spite, but seeing I didn't relish it, he ceased.

February 22. Worked in the midst of great domestic harrass. My dearest Mary is now broken down in health, and yesterday as I myself washed her pale face & hands, for she would let no one else touch her, as I looked at her beautiful, shrunk face, the tears trickled over my cheeks, and seeing me crying she wept bitterly herself. But she will weather it & I support her; under it there is nothing I would not do for her, to make her happy.

March 4. My Eyes fatigued & strained. I could hardly see, so I rested & walked out. In dear London amusement is never wanting. I went into the City & walked home.

March 14. Called on Hammond. Just as I was coming away, who should drive by but the Bishop of Chichester. I was going to hear him. He drew up & was very happy to see me, and I told him I was going to Queen St. Chappel to hear him; he begged me to mount, which I did. He made an Excellent Sermon & said what I had said to Shelley once – there is no evidence of any Hospitals in Greece or Rome, till Xtianity had influenced the Empire about Justinian's Time. His voice is gentle, but the poor listened to him, & it was a Sermon fit for all Classes & spared none. He came back in his way to Wandsworth & saw my Picture, & they were all gratified. I must say People are much pleased. They say it is so natural.

April 14. Shee said to the Trustees of British Gallery when they were discussing whether they should buy an oil Picture of Raphael's or not, 'They had better spend their 3600 at the Royal Academy Exhibition, & for his part he never saw any Picture by any old Master that could assist him.' Rogers muttered to Sir Charles Bagot (who told the story) '*I believe him.*' (et Ego.)

April 24. Saturday. I have now completed really my last head this day. The Picture is, in fact, except toning done.

April 27. The Moment a great Canvas goes from my home I dread to look at my Painting room. When a great Canvas is up I feel sheltered, though I have not one farthing in my Pocket. Extraordinary is habit! Grant me, O God, *a long life*! The more Pictures I paint, the more worthy my mind will be of another World!

April 28. Ordered another Canvas 12 by 10.

May 24. If there be dissolution, what shall I do? The Whigs have not done *all* I wish, but they have done a great deal. Will Peel do as much? I fear not. Whigs granted me a Committee. They have formed a Central School as I advised in my evidence. They have begun branch Schools, as I recommended. Ought I not to be grateful & pleased? I did. I will write Sir Robert & ask him point blank, 'Will you continue to support the School of Design? Will you continue the support of the Spital-Fields & other Branch Schools, & will you sanction another attempt to get the Royal Academy amenable to public interposition?'

He will write, 'Sir Robert Peel's Compt. to Mr Haydon, & he declines to give an answer, on a public principle.' If he do, I vote against him. B. R. Haydon.

June 13. Sunday. Read prayers & prayed for the soul of my dear old Friend David Wilkie. Amen.

Poor dear Wilkie, with all thy heartless timidities of character – with thy shrinking, cowardly want of resolution, looking as if thou had sneaked through Life pursued by the ghosts of 40 Academicians – thy great Genius, our early Friendship, our long attachment through 36 years, thy touching Death & Romantic burial, brought thy loss bitterly to my heart!

June 19. Like Johnson's hypochondriasm, there I sit, sluggish, staring, idle, gaping, with not one Idea. Several times do these journals record this Condition of Brain.

It goes off always after connection with Women. But now my wife is ill, & my fidelity keeps me correct. I think I suffer by becoming cloudy & thick.

June 20. Went to Church, & heard an admirable Sermon from the Bishop of London. He said when one went to the top of a Stately Cathedral, which crowned this superb Metropolis, when one looked down & saw it lying in Sunny Splendour at one's feet with its Towers & Columns & Palaces, could any Christian forget the belt of misery & Vice and wretchedness which surrounded its beauty!

This was amazingly touching. I was affected deeply, & could not help wondering this had never occurred to me!

July 2. Called on Hamilton, who gave me a letter to Barry. [Charles Barry, architect of the Houses of Parliament.] He said Eastlake had been examined, and that I had no chance of being employed to adorn either House.

That if I had gone 20 years ago to Italy, it would have made all the difference.

Where did Shakespeare go? – What absurdity!

July 9. God bless my labours through this day!

It may be laid down 'that self destruction is the physical mode of relieving a diseased brain,' because the first impression on a brain diseased, or diseased for a Time, is the necessity of this horrid crime. There is no doubt of it.

July 10. Bless & protect me. My Eyes strained.

Saw Barry Thursday. Aim to see him today, & he promised me Sections & plans of the Houses of Lords & Commons. We talked of it. He said whether any thing were done or no, he would leave the Hall & House of Lords, so that they would be in a mess if Painting was not introduced.

July 11. New Houses of Parliament. Extent specially appropriated for painting:

Westminster Hall. 546 feet long, 16 feet high.
St Stephen's Hall. 192 feet long, 15 feet high.
Central Hall. 4 Compartments, each 28 feet long, 16 feet high.
Public Corridors. 376 feet long, 12 feet high.
Royal Gallery. 320 feet long, 15 feet high.
Queen's Robing Room. 108 feet by 12 feet high.

July 17. Worked hard. I think my next Pictures will be better in every way. My dear Art was never more intensely in my brain, thank God.

July 24. Out the whole day on business.

The difference of the drying of oil in Italy & England is owing to Climate. Oil in Italy, like oil in a hot summer in England, gets clammy in the middle of the day; hence that gemmy surface & preservation in old Pictures. In England oil required longer time; gum is added, which gives the feel but splits in time. At the British gallery are three pictures, a large one in the middle & two small ones, by Canaletto. The small ones have been painted in England & are both cracked, the large one, painted in Italy, is perfectly sound.

August 1. Went to Church & heard a very good sermon – from Ephesians, 'be careful for nothing,' & I did not receive the Sacrament as I intended because I could [not] keep myself in sufficient purity & calmness.

August 2. Worked well. Advanced the Picture of Mary of Scots, well.

August 11. Wrote on adorning the House of Lords.

English Art never stood higher than at the end of the War. Foreigners were astonished at our condition, & they might well be. The reason was, blockading kept the rich from running over the Continent; our energies were compressed & devoted to ourselves, & we flourished accordingly. Wilkie was in his Zenith, so was Lawrence, so was Flaxman, so were our Water Colour Painters, & so was I, for my Solomon was an English Triumph, & Landseer was beginning to bud.

August 16. Got my first lesson in Fresco from Latilla, a good natured fellow. I saw him put in a head, & now I fear not.

August 19. Prepared for my own attempt, which God bless. Latilla's cracked from being in too great a hurry to begin & not giving the Lime time to mature.

August 20. I began Fresco today, and I have succeeded & taken off all apprehension as to the process. I'll take to it.

September 3. I have been compelled to sell the copy right of the Duke to fit out my boys – one for the Navy, & the other for Cambridge. To be sure it is hard. I took several Months about the Picture, when a Portrait Painter would have taken one. I went to Waterloo to be correct, which the Portrait Man never would have undertaken. It has been 1 year & ½ engraving, and I can only get two hundred pounds for the result!

And the publisher will make thousands. But then is the repute nothing? But I have thrown away a trump that might have been a property for Life.

September 22. It may be laid down as an axiom that in the proportion Fresco looks well when just done, it will look ill when dry. I have not tried yet to glaze as a Fresco head approaches drying, & this may remedy the evils of drying.

October 3. Travelled all night – to Sheffield, to lecture tomorrow.

I predict & foresee the result of the decoration of *our* Palace of Westminster. Hayter will be the Man, & if Sir Robert does not make a firm stand, the Art will be ruined.

Lectured at Sheffield, with great Success. A School of Design is beginning.

December 6. Came down by Train – with McDonnell, the Catholic Radical of 1832 – to Birmingham. 'Do you believe we are instantly in existence after Death?' 'Certainly.' 'Why?' 'From what Christ said to the Thief on the Cross – from Dives & Lazarus.' 'Why did Christ cry out on the Cross as if dissappointed of the aid he seemed to expect?' 'To be a consolation to the Disciples. If *he* complained, when they suffered they might do so without crime. It was bond of sympathy.' This was the best answer I have ever had.

December 31. Last day of 1841. I have had great prosperity & constant employment. The health of my dear love is much improved. I have planted one boy in the Service, who promises well, & has obtained the approbation of his Officers & Captain. I have got the other to Cambridge, who has got through his first term. I have paid for all with my own earnings – for all which blessings I thank God, for the well being of human creatures who depend on ye, & have been brought into the world by ye, is after all the most important duty of Man.

On reviewing 1841, I think I have less to repent of than any previous year of my previous Life.

1842

January 1. I have always been right in my perception of the motives of others, and if I acted & not talked, or been too fond to prove to others, my sagacity, my acuteness would have advanced my interests.

January 13. In the Press, now, I have hardly a Friend, except the Chronicle & Spectator. I have only to shew a work to set the whole Press in an uproar of abuse. The last picture I exhibited was the Sampson. All the sound principles of its composition, its colour, its story, its drawing, its light & shadow were utterly unseen, & the Picture held up as an abortion not to be tolerated.

January 17. My soul begins to yearn for something else. My attempt in Fresco has opened my eyes so completely to a power I knew nothing of, that all Art here palls on my senses. Great & merciful Creator, spare me till I have realized what I now foresee I can do! Amen.

I am without Employment. Save me from Difficulty, & my family from distress. Bless my boys, my daughter, my dear Mary.

January 20. I am very discontented all of a sudden, & cannot tell why. It is the agony of ungratified Ambition – that is the reason. I could execute now a series of fresco foreshortenings with terrific power. Why don't ye? No money!

January 26. The mysterious influence under which I always begin a great work, is hardly to be credited, under all circumstances of necessity. Here was I with hardly money for the week – with commissions deferred – seized at day break with an irresistible impulse – a whisper audible, loud, startling, – to begin a great work [Alexander and the Lion]. The Canvas was lying at the Colourman's to be kept till paid for. I could not pay. I wrote him & offered a bill at 6 months. He consented; the Canvas comes home, & after prayer, ardent & Sincere, I fly at it, & get the whole in, capitally arranged, in two days, about 12 hours' work.

May 22. Wordsworth called today, and we went to Church together. We sat among publicans & sinners, and I was much interested in seeing his Venerable white head close to a Servant in livery, and on the same level.

The Servant in livery fell asleep, & so did Wordsworth. I jogged him at the Gospel, & he opened his eyes and read well. A Preacher preached when we expected another, so it was a dissappointment. We afterwards walked to Rogers' across the Park.

As Wordsworth & I crossed the Park, we said 'Scott, Wilkie, Keats, Hazlitt, Beaumont, Jackson, Charles Lamb are all gone – we only are left.' He said 'How old are you?' '56,' I replied. 'How old are you?' '73,' he said; 'in my 73rd year. I was born [in] 1770.' '& I in 1786.' 'You may have many years before you.' 'I trust I have – & you, too, I hope. Titian was 99.'

May 25. O God, save me from harrass. I have not had a single Commission for 6 years from the Aristocracy. 2 little things from Sir John Hammer & one from Rogers – 30gs. each – 90gs. in 6 years! 15 Guineas a year! Magnificent Patronage. But I have lived to see State support begin, God be thanked.

May 27. Went to Spital Fields ball last night – a splendid sight – though Albert always pains me. He looks like a cowed & kept pet, frightened to sit, frightened to stand. The Queen last night evidently treated him as if they had previously disputed. The Queen looked red, intellectual, & fiery.

May 30. Spent the day at Woolwich. My dear Boy 1st in Mathematics, 7th in Classics. Dear Frank – this is a fine beginning. I am grateful to God.

June 1. Dined last night at Talfourd's, who is one of the best hearted men on Earth, with Wordsworth. Talfourd is fond of wine & we had a great deal of fun!

I went for the Poet in a nice fly & dashing Coachman. The Venerable Poet looked grave & half took me to task for my extravagance, so I sent the Cab away when we were landed, & we both strolled home tired & lost our way till a Dandy from a party with a cigar in his mouth put us in the right one. Wordsworth's last Vol. has not succeeded & he seems rather low.

June 16. Wordsworth breakfasted early with me, & we had a good sitting. He was remarkably well, & in better spirits, & we had a good set to.

His knowledge of Art is extraordinary in technical knowledge. He detects hands like a Connoiseur or Artist, & we spent a very pleasant morning. We talked again of our old Friends, and to ascertain his real height I measured him, & found him, to my wonder, 8 heads high, or 5 ft. 9.

June 17. In going down to Bolton St., I saw a fine fellow on horseback, with a white hat, lounging up South Audley St., & who should this be but Lord Melbourne? As he passed he smiled & bowed & looked gracious. I never saw him look so well, brown, Sunny, & good humoured. How many associations did this view of him bring up! Ah Melbourne, what fun we have had!

June 21. Went to Windsor Castle – a fine gloomy, old Gothic palace, but I was dissappointed with the inside.

The Waterloo Gallery, from not being arranged as a Gallery, is a disjointed failure. No Portrait has reference to the other; there is no composition as a whole; they are separate pictures.

The rapidity of railroad communication destroys the Poetry & mystery of distant places. You went to Windsor as an exploit for two days. Now, down you go in an hour, see it in another, & home in a third. It is attainable, & therefore to be despised.

The view over Eton is Splendid, & the whole Castle has a fine, gloomy barbarism, but the Public rooms dissappointed me. The ceilings by Verrio, the Gobelin Tapestry from Coypel, & the Paltry ceilings with gilt tridents are ludicrous. The finest Portrait is Wilkie's Willm. 4th in the Waterloo Room.

June 27. I am sorry to say what I believe to be True – that Sir Robert Peel has ruined more families, blasted more Fortunes, & broken more hearts than any Minister that ever ruled a great Nation.

First came the bullion question & return to cash. Was not all *our* embarrassment owing to incurring debts in paper & being called to pay them in gold, 27 shillings in the pound.

Now, in his Tariff, he endangers all property in the Kingdom except Landed property. Friends at Liverpool are for a time paralyzed! Employment ceases, money is scarce, people are starving, Artists & Artisans ruined.

Nothing is so dreadful as the inexorability of Time! The half of the Year was last week. Oh Time, Time – dreadful. If the falls of Niagara were near, I would go over them shouting to put an end to this horror of living *here!* Would it put an end? *Here* it might, but where might you *wake?*

This is sheer '*stomach strain*' from foul air & anxiety.

July 1. Worked in great anxiety. 3 bills due this month & no funds.

Wordsworth on Helvellyn, 1842

Called on William Woodburn, he gave me a touching account of Wilkie's last journey & Death! Poor fellow! Woodburn said he quacked himself to death; his only anxiety wherever he went was, 'if there was a medical Man in the Town; and if there were *none*, he brought medicines of his *own*.'

July 6. Called in to see my dear old Painting Room at 41, Great Marlborough St., where I painted my Dentatus, Macbeth, Solomon, & a part of Jerusalem.

The house was bought & undergoing repair – the rooms stripped & desolate; the Cupboard, the little room where I slept, & the Plaister room, with all their associations, crowded on me. I thought once of putting up a brass plate, 'Here Haydon painted his Solomon, 1813.' For the want of Engraving the Picture is now forgotten and the Surgeon who has bought the house would perhaps have papered it up. So much for the brass plate!

July 8. Out all day on business. Had the inexpressible pleasure of walking in the rain after a Sum of money I expected and was put off, & no less inexpressible delight of coming back in an omnibus, which cost me 6d.

July 9. The greatest curse that can befall a Father in England is to have a Son gifted with a passion & a genius for High Art. Thank God my children have witnessed the harrassing agonies under which I have ever painted, that the very name of Painting, gives them a hideous & disgusting taste in their mouths. I pray God on my knees, that [he] will, in his mercy, inflict them with every other passion, appetite, misery, wretchedness, disease, insanity, or gabbling Idiotism, rather than a longing for Painting – this scorned, miserable Art.

July 11. I finished the Saragossa as far as Figures go on Saturday [July 9]. Thus I have painted it in 4 months, & grateful I ought to be, & grateful I am.

Now for my Cartoon. Edward the Black [Prince] entering London with John – Conqueror & Captive – or the Curse – which? The one is suitable to the building, the other is interesting to the World.

July 12. The Exhibition is closed & with it the annual miseries, dissappointments, absurd criticisms, hopes, follies, & immortalities of the Month of May! In going round the last day to take a fair view of the hopes of the Country, I can conscientiously say I could take out 6 & fit them by training to do honour to its fame!

Though Phillips is an able Painter of a head, he has a heavy hand, & has no notion of the Construction of the figure – Grant, Faulkner too, are not matched in any School in Europe.

A Lady of Faulkner, sitting with hands acoss on her lap, is exquisite in character, modesty & maternal air. Grant's Lady is also purer than any of

Lawrence's, something between Reynolds & Gainsborough, but it wants definition of female shape below. But the Lord deliver me from the milk & water action of Lord Cardigan's Horse. The Horse is feeble in bone, blood, sinew, vigour, & drawing. It has never been bred in a stable but in a boudoir!

The dogs of Landseer are exquisite, but why does he not paint a Lion, not a drawing room Lion like Van Omburg's but a down right, savage monarch of the Woods? It is extraordinary that Landseer has no notion of the totality of a Picture. His backgrounds are always disjointed, & his colour always wrong.

Calcott is feeble, Stanfield a Scene Painter in little, Shee's works look as if a Cook had beat them up as she does an Egg, & after the Yolk & White had settled, they had ran into a human resemblance.

But enough of this ebullition. The Exhibition is always to be taken as evidence of the taste of the Employers & not what the English Artists can best do.

August 9. Put in the head of Eve. Obliged to go out as I put in the Eyes to arrange about a 50 bill. Come home in the heat, & finished the head, my model, a sweet girl, wondering what I was doing, I think, in the midst of the grossest misery. My Landlord called & gave me £3 – I paid my rates in the evening, the rest left for necessities.

August 20. Completed Adam & Eve. Now for Satan on Monday, with only 1/6 in my pocket. Huzza!

August 21. Sunday. At Church, & heard an excellent Sermon on the Union of Soul & body – but how the one is independent of the other, I should like to know. How can the Soul be independent of the body? The Soul acts by the body – the construction of the body regulates the Soul.

August 22. My want of money & want of means of raising money is dreadful. I have now got Satan's head to do – in the midst. In the middle of the night, I saw his large, fiery, cruel rimmed eye & kept staring in the dark where nothing was for an hour.

Made a study for the head of Satan.

August 24. Worked very hard & got the Devil's Figure in. Wrote Dukes of Devonshire & Richmond about my necessities.

August 29. No answer from the Dukes of Devonshire or Richmond. I suspect the Aristocracy rather wish to check the advance of the Middle Class.

August 31. I borrowed £4 last night of my Landlord to pay a Servant; £10 today of my butter man, Webb, an old pupil recommended me by Sir George Beaumont 25 years ago, but who wisely, after drawing hands, set up a butter shop.

'Webb,' said I, 'when you were a poor youth I gave my time to you for nothing.' 'You did.' 'I want £10.' 'You shall have it, Mr Haydon. I shall ever feel grateful.'

I Paid £7 out of the 10, & borrowed 10 of the Man I paid £7 to, to meet my Son's bill on board Impregnable, due at Coutts' tomorrow. Came home, took out our Saviour, & tried him walking in the Garden. He would not do, so put him in again sitting & reposing. Better than ever. Satan looked powerfully.

September 3. I wrote Eastlake, complaining of his saying he hoped 'a Portion at least' would be devoted to Fresco. I said if in the 2nd year a portion only was recommended, in the 7th it would be a very small portion indeed.

September 4. Lucas called today & told me that Prince George of Cambridge said to him, 'That Shakespeare is a very clever fellow – but it's a sort of *knack*!'

September 10. Worked hard, & so completely lost, the Clock struck to my astonishment 3 hours later than I expected.

September 12. Monday. Out all day – for Money.

September 18. What right has any people to complain of an Aristocracy, which admits into its ranks the lowest subject in the realm, whom God blesses with talents, character, honesty, & decorum. The English Aristocracy is perpetually renovated by accession from the middle and lower Classes.

Democracy was never meant to be the predominant principle of Government; it is unnatural; by analogy it is not born out. What in Astronomy or Natural history is not based on the Aristocratic principle of leaders & subordinates? Democracy is a principle that cannot be excluded but ought never to be the leading principle of any Constitution where national liberty as opposed to licentious Freedom is the object in the Constitution. B. R. Haydon.

It is an Evil that any given number of human beings should be fed, pampered, & made believe it is the duty of the people to feed & pamper them. If all men were Christians, no Government would be required. B. R. H.

September 19. At the Musaeum in the morning, & studied Reptiles. Sketched several, & came home & put in my own snake. I find tracing the spine is the secret of drawing snakes.

October 6. Awoke with a beautiful conception of Charles taking leave of his Children – all their faces red with weeping, except the Duke of York on Charles' knee looking with wonder & childish anger at Cromwell, who stands like a *rock*! This will do – thank God. I saw Cromwell distinctly.

Wrote hard but did not paint. Worked & thought & sketched & composed.

October 11. Collins called today, and in course of conversations, said, '*I really think you ought to join us!*' I said nothing.

My dear old Friend Collins, & fellow student, is anxious for me to join the Academy, but how can I? It is too late. After having brought up my family through every species of misery to distinction & honour, am I now to shew that after all, *their* honours were necessary? Oh no, no – the compromise of principle would be dreadful. Let me die as I have lived. B. R. Haydon.

And O God, give me strength of mind to resist Temptation, for I see it's coming. Amen.

November 9. Worked, not powerfully. Went out on money matters. Succeeded. Came home & having seen a bad Picture with good rocks, made great improvement. Fell in with an undoubted Rembrandt for £4, but I could not afford it, & was obliged to forgo it to some lucky dealer.

November 16. I awoke at 4 saying, 'On the principle laid down, sound imitation on the principles of the great masters exists at this moment no where but in England. This power has descended alone to the British & yet they are so silly they will not acquire the power, which every Noodle abroad has at his fingers' ends, a power of defining anatomically the human figure, which would place them at once at the head of Artists of the World.'

November 16*. Worked hard, & felt all the delight of having duty done. The day was so dark I could not see the upper part of my Picture, so I turned it upside down, & painted the part wanted capitally. Thank God for today – I feel wings growing.

November 29. God bless me through this, another day of wretched anxiety. ½ day at work, but out from sheer money miseries. In an agony I rushed up to Wagstaff the Engraver & he advanced me instantly £10, which I paid into Coutts for my Son at Sea, & came home.

December 17. Ordered another Cartoon Canvas. Thought deeply on a fine historic subject – I hope it may be Richard Coeur de Lion.

December 25. Christmas Day. In the middle of the night I awoke rather depressed from the multiplicity of anxieties. I put my hand in the Testament I always sleep with, & opened a passage in the dark, folded down the leaf, and in daylight found this blessed consolation: 'And our hope of you is steadfast knowing that as ye are partakers of the *suffering*, so shall ye be also of the *consolation*.'

*Diary gives two entries for this date.

December 31. On reviewing the past year, it is wonderful to think how I have been assisted by my Creator. January, I wrote my lecture on Fresco. February, I began to prepare to do something, having had 3 commissions deferred amounting to 700 gs. I plunged at the Saragossa & got it done. I then in July began a Cartoon in appalling necessities, & by his Blessing I got through that. I flew at Curtius & finished that, & this day began to sketch the arrangement of a second Cartoon, so that I have worked well.

SIX

1843–1846

1843

January 6. Got all my Cartoon in, grumbling all the Time like the Jews in the Desert. Influenza, indigestion, want of money, and if that does not make a Man grumble, what will? The little sketch last night I altered, so that the whole thing looks grand & national. Huzza. Pawned one pair of Spectacles for 3/. Oh dear.

January 7. Much pleased with my Composition. These little evening Sketches, made in the bosom of my family, are of the greatest use next day. Who would have thought that out of so much grumbling & indigestion, influenza & fog, such beautiful composition would have come.

January 12. Lord Colborne took a second share in Saragossa, & my dear Talfourd sent me effective help, so I return thanks to God I have escaped ruin at present.

March 24. Dined at Lupton's with Carew & Clint, & had a very pleasant night. Carew told us a capital story of the Duke. In the middle of the Battle of Waterloo he saw a Man in plain clothes riding about on a Cob in the thickest fire. During a temporary absence the Duke beckoned him, & he rode over. He asked him who he was, & what business he had there. He replied he was an Englishman accidentally at Brussels, that he had never seen a fight, & wanted to see one. The Duke told him he was in instant danger of his life, & he said 'not more than his Grace,' & they parted. But every now & then he saw the Cob Man riding about in the smoke, and at last having no body to send to a regiment, he hollowed for this little fellow, & told him to go up [to] that regiment & order them to charge – giving him some authority the Col. would recognise. Away he galloped, & in a few minutes the Duke saw his orders obeyed. The Duke asked for his card, & found he lived in Birmingham, & was a button manufacturer!

March 27. [Attached to the diary is a newspaper cutting of an announcement by Eastlake that the cartoons to be entered in the competition [for the House of Lords frescoes] must be received at Westminster Hall during the first week in June 1843.]

It would be prudent to get a Fresco ready by the Time the Cartoons are out. But I have devoted so many months without remuneration, I almost think it dangerous to do more in that way.

15 March. Got in another Cartoon – revised. But still I feel fretted I am not now on a grand work, but must be. 21 days have been occupied in trifles – preparing lime, revising & improving, beginning a new Cartoon, but not a great work, as my next Fresco.

April 15. It is interesting to analyze one's feelings during, before, & after the Sacrament. The Dean of Carlisle said it was a mystery, but not more than propagation! The mystery is the sacrifice – not the act, in remembrance of it. The mystery is why blood is necessary & always has been to reconcile God to Man – but the bread & Wine are only types of the mystery, and the way they act on the mind is natural, because believing them to be the mode of approaching the Savior, the preparation to fit yourself produces those consequences on the Intellect & heart, which the holy Spirit blesses & accepts.

April 18. In the City & deferred a payment, but suffered excrutiating anxiety for want of money.

April 20. Went out in great misery to raise 6.10., the balance on a Judge's order – Dr Darling, my old Friend, helped me. Just as I was going to set my palette I was served with the copy of a writ! – for another debt. I came home & corrected my figure, raised the arm, & prepared for my model tomorrow.

April 22. Now Reader, whoever thou art – young & thoughtless, or old & reflecting – was I not right to trust in God? Was it Vanity? Was it presumption? Today – *this very day* – I have sold my Curtius, when only yesterday I had no hope, & my heart beat, & my head whirled, & my hand shook at my distress. I had taken the butter knife off the Table to raise 13/.

April 22. Poor Duke of Sussex died yesterday, & today the Queen gives birth to a Baby – such is Life & Death.

The Duke was an amiable Man, & when he sat to me & I had made him Comfortable & let him smoke, he left his Pipe behind him. I sent the next day to Lord John Churchill to say so, & the Duke ordered him to write & say he presented it to me. I keep it in remembrance of the fact.

April 29. Hard at work, & completed the arrangement & composition of Alexander. Greatly interrupted by eternal Visitors. As I was setting my palette I felt disgust at the Savage ferocity of the Lion, & felt if I could make it either touching or beautiful it would be better. I tried it dying.

May 3. Out the whole day on money. Came home weary, hot, pennyless; lunched & fell asleep. Awoke by the Servants fighting in the Kitchen. Went to my painting-room & looked at Alexander & remembered a beautiful day lost! Brunskill my model obliged to go, as I could not attend to him. Called on a Lawyer & begged for mercy for £27, till Saturday – refused. At dinner Bishop came & sent in a note. I came out & was served with a writ!

May 5. Worked at a Comic picture called 'the First Child'. As I painted the red, snuffling Infant, I caught sight of Alexander killing the Lion & thought I should have died with laughing!

May 12. Wrote the Duke of Sutherland & told him my condition. He took another Share, which was a help. Came home, & setting my palette in a fury, got in the leg & thigh of Alexander.

May 18. A Young Pupil came today & paid me £100, part premium of 200.
Made a capital Sketch of Nelson at Copenhagen!

May 19. Made a study of a head of Nelson for the Distressed Seamen Society – & finished my Sketch. I have honoured the Duke & Napoleon – & now for Nelson – I should like to do that before I die!
I did not sleep so well with my £100 as when I had not a hal[f]penny! I lay abed in the morning! – & did not set my palette till *after* breakfast!

June 1. O God, I thank thee that this day I have safely placed my Cartoons in Westminster Hall. Prosper them. It is a great day on my mind & Soul. I bless thee I have lived to this hour. Spare my life, O Lord, untill I have shewn thy strength unto this generation.
I found Eastlake, my Pupil, walking about. He was most happy to see me. 'Do you remember,' said he, 'Coming with me into Westminster Hall, & drawing a gigantic limb on the wall with the end of the umbrella, saying "This is the place for art!"' I did not. He said I actually did it, 30 years ago, & he remembers my jumping up to reach highly.

June 13. Out in the morning to the Anti-Slavery Convention. The Committee had hung my Picture at the head of the great room at Freemasons, and it looked remarkably well.
The different state of feeling to the first great meeting 3 years ago was extraordinary. There was a deadness today in the whole thing – though Sturge said 9 nations since the last meeting had abolished Slavery in their dominions.

June 17. Out on cursed business, for now begin my anxieties for future payments! – in God I trust.
I said to Eastlake the whole thing will end in the Queen appointing

some Court Painter. 'Never were you more mistaken,' said Eastlake! What will he say now? 'Sir W. Ross, R. A., laid before Her Majesty & Prince Albert his Sketches from Comus, and her Majesty commanded Sir W. Ross to begin Fresco tomorrow!' – without Cartoon! – from Sketches. In all probability Ross, who is a first rate miniature painter, will paint sweetly small Figures in Fresco, & bye & bye you will have 'her Majesty commanded Sir W. Ross to begin the Frescoes of the House of Lords immediately.'

June 26. Called on Lord Grey, who is in danger. For accessible amiability, as Minister or Friend, no Man surpassed him. His vanity amounted to dotage, but his firmness, perseverance, & Victory in a noble Cause were an example!

He had no taste for High Art, yet he was a kind Friend to Artists, very amiable – a Radical by nature, perpetually checkmated the pride of his Aristocratical tendencies. He was an indulgent Father, but not a moral husband, & nothing flattered him so much as insinuations of his being a gay deceiver – even at 75.

June 27. Worked a little, but very anxious, as the Cartoon prizes are not yet settled, and I am much embarrassed, after paying away so much.

[A letter from Eastlake, dated June 27, is attached to the diary. He informed Haydon that his 'drawings are not included among those that have been rewarded' in the Cartoon competition.]

June 30. I went to bed in a decent state of anxiety. It has given a great shock to my family, and revived all the old horrors of Execution & arrest & debt. I called on William Hamilton, & he adopted, with exquisite tact, the tone of Society. He told me Sir Robert felt annoyed at my restless activity about the Art – that I interfered in every thing I had no business to do. I said, I had; that the School of Design had gone to ruin, as I predicted, & that they had been obliged to adopt the Figure, which they would never have adopted but for my repeated interference.

July 1. A Day of great misery. I said to my dear love, 'I am not included!' Her expression was a study! She said, 'We shall be ruined.' I locked up my lectures, papers, & Journals, & burnt loads of private letters, & prepared for executions. Lords Alford and Northampton & William Hamilton took additional shares in Saragossa. £7 was raised on my daughter's & Mary's dresses.

On Monday I went down, & was astonished at the power displayed. There are Cartoons equal to any School. My own looked grand, but like the effusion of a Master, soft & natural but not hard & defined, too much shadow for Fresco – fit for oil; but there were disproportions. I gained great knowledge. But the great mistake & it has been a tremendous one, is the selection of a Pupil of De La Roche's for the prize. I understand Albert said, 'it were worth Tousands' – & they were afraid. The shocking drawing is absurd! There is not a limb, or body in proportion or form, and on my introduction to the Artist, and on enquiry, I found Anatomy was not the *first part* of Study in his school.

July 13. Worked a little. Began Nelson Sealing the Letter at Copenhagen & improved Alexander. God be thanked!

August 2. Took a Room for a Lecture. God grant it success.

August 4. Wrote my lecture.

August 5. Finished it, but much harrassed in money. Went out in all the horrors of an Execution, which I got delayed till Tuesday.

August 8. Thank God, my lecture was the most brilliant Success! How mysteriously am I influenced, O God! Accept my deepest gratitude, Amen! Many members were there & cheered me much. It was the Completest success in a lecture I ever had.

August 9. I am now sitting in my room longing for some great work – some vast space, & waiting for a sitter with a stupid head & silly expression.

August 10. Noodled a whole day at Portraits!

August 14. Monday. Another day to go through. I am waiting for sitters I *detest*, and could vomit over. As poor Ingres said, 'Je vomirais pour trois jours,' I say, 'Pour toujours.' All this is wicked, & has been produced by indigestion & my dear Mary's health – so I have two sorts of indigestion to obscure my intellect. In such humours Men shoot themselves – but not me.

September 8. Went to see my Son Frederic on board the Penelope, who is going to Africa, I fear. We spent the day in a nook at Greenhithe worthy of Boccacio. God bless him & protect him & bring him safe back.

September 9. Perhaps I presumed too much on the goodness of my Creator, appealed to him too much & too freely.

September 16. I think I have suffered so much, my Imagination is diseased about ruin. I get possessed for days. Came home & changed the whole back ground of Alexander & the Lion, & improved it immensely – enormously.

September 20. Spent the whole day with a living Lion, & came home with a contempt for the human species. Before the day was over we got intimate. He shewed me his hideous teeth, & affectionately leaned his head aside as I patted him, suffered me to touch his paw & smooth his mane. The Lioness was in heat, & as playful as a Kitten, and on my stooping down to get my port crayon, gave me an affectionate pat like a sledge hammer, on my head which luckily had my hat on. The Lion & Lioness were kept separate. I made most useful Studies, & came home rich in knowledge & ready to begin.

September 27. There is a class in High Life called 'Diners out' who nestle in the neighbourhood of Piccadilly, St James St., & May fair, who congregate in the Park between 5 & 7, upon Livery Horses (on account) or Horses of their Friends, when they can get them, who make way to a table by intriguing with the Wife, or wait in anxious expectation at the Effect of a joke as My Lord passes in his ride, in hopes of an invitation.

If they are handsome & successful the Taylor dresses them as a speculation, the Horse Dealer furnishes them as a show off, the Coachmaker has no objection to let 'em try some new springed Cab, and away they sally at the hour of meeting before dinner. Any one of common sense in human air & expression can tell as the Park breaks up, who have been *invited* and who have *not!* Doleful is the air of a Dandy of this description as he turns his Horse's head for an exclusive Walk back from whence he came to his solitary bouilli & no wine – or to keep himself elegant a biscuit & lemonade till the rout commences.

These young men are literally the pests of London life – obliged to find the joke for the evening at any Cost, they soon discover the unpopular Men, in Art or Literature, and are quite sure of a welcome reception for any ridicule of all that is noble in Wordsworth or questionable in Haydon's works.

October 1. Prayed sincerely in the Fields today in a delicious walk to Willesden. God bless me through this month.

'Independence cannot be made honorable except Pauperism is made disgraceful – employment can be made an object of desire only by making relief an object of aversion.' Brougham, Ed. Rev., July, 1843. This sophistry is the basis of the New Poor Law & a mistake.

October 17. Lectured at Greenwich on the Elgin Marbles. The people exceedingly enthusiastic. The people of this great Country are more fit to receive grand Art than the Aristocracy are to grant it.

October 21. Anniversary of Trafalgar! huzza! huzza! huzza! Out all day on money!

November 3. Supped out at a kind Friend's. Several Artists – one from Munich, who told me my attack on the German School in the Spectator last year had been translated at Vienna & made a great noise at Munich – it was thought impudent, but it did good; they could not defend *line*, which they labored hard to excuse.

November 22. What a Man Sir Robert Peel is – hankering after liberality, without moral courage to do it effectual good – longing to encrease the influence of Authority and yet aware of the necessity of checking it – courting popularity, yet cringing to rank, he passes life in a perpetual torture of opposite appetites.

December 1. Out on money matters & paid half, & paid right & left, till I reduced my exchequer, but still I cleared off. Came home & worked ¼ of a day. All of a sudden fatigue so overpowered me, with my incessant activity of body & mind, for the last 10 days – I gave in and was gone in a sort of brain drowsiness. I went to bed, slept two hours outright, & arose at dinner, clear & active. Good Heavens, what anxiety & activity I go through! I lectured last night for two hours; the applause was so great that the dust rose in Clouds & nearly suffocated me.

December 7. Out in the City. Ill from eating too many walnuts. Came home & sulked in pain. Did nothing.

Went to the Cattle show at the Bazaar & saw the finest black Cart Horse I ever saw. Studied him for Bucephalus, & made the man hold out his leg in the action; it was superb. He measured 3 feet from bottom of Biceps to top of the Withers.

December 10. Sunday. Went to St George's & heard an excellent sermon on a 'broken spirit.' Many passages on pride, &c., pricked me well.

December 12. Worked. Sir Joshua used to say there was nothing more injurious than the pursuit of health. What are the consequences of following books on health? You find you have been doing wrong all your Life, you must break up all the habits of 50 years, & live the remaining 20 in vain longings which must not be gratified, according *to the new system*, and in all probability you die at the end of 10 because you have been undoing all that brought you to 50.

December 13. Worked hard, & finished another Napoleon – 'Haydon's patent for rapid manufacture of Napoleons musing.' This is the 8th.

December 22. Moved Alexander to the British Gallery and hung it up preparatory to Glazing. Studied its deficiencies an hour.

December 25. Christmas day! – to me always a day of poetry & pious musing!

I hate the vulgar revelry which usually accompanies it – the fat beef, the gross turkeys, the stuffed sausage, as evidences of human joy at the Salvation of Christ – are to me utterly disgusting! – But my boys will consider me a brute if I don't eat till I can't see, to prove my joy at their presence.

December 30. Finished Alexander at the Gallery today by toning down the sky, & the whole looked strong & rich; I carried my lunch with me, & did what no mortal ever did before in that room, broiled it on the coals, & with a pint of the coldest pump water, lunched heartier than the Queen. It was the South room, where all that were illustrious & great have walked. Such is human destiny! – or room destiny! Alexander the Great was before me – a mutton chop on the coals. It was cooked to a *tee*; I eat it like a Red Indian!

December 31. Went to Church & knelt & thanked God for bringing me to the end of another year – & such a year! I prayed sincerely & felt awfully – & tomorrow to work!

1844

January 10. It is extraordinary what a guard I am obliged to keep on myself. The moment the excitement of a great Work is over, if I do not go at another, I am sure to burst out – in writing. My brain seems to require constant pressure to be easy, & my body incessant Activity. In a great public work alone I shall ever find rest, which will never be afforded me.

Moved the Napoleon to the Gallery; it looked well.

January 23. I was much fatigued in mind & body, so I called on a Pupil & we went to Greenwich for 6d. each in [the] Train. I wanted to look at the Hall. What useless unintellectual stuff it is.

January 25. My birth day – 58! – Good Heavens – 40 years ago I surveyed my Acquirements & life & planned a course of study – the course of study I have pursued – but in French, Italian, Latin, & Greek I think I do not know an atom more than I did at 18.

Worked. I was warming some oil when it caught fire & roared up the Chimney – a good omen on my birth day. I shall yet make a blaze in the World! more than ever.

March 7. Nearly finished the Duke & Copenhagen. I have painted 19 Napoleons! – 13 musing at St Helena, & 6 other musings, and 3 Dukes & Copenhagens. By Heavens! how many more!

April 18 Occupied & harrassed in a just distribution of my gains. Obliged to lean on the *good* natured to get rid of the *ill-natured*. Not just, but too often done.

April 24. I called on Barry, the most amiable of God's creatures, & had a long & interesting conversation. He explained to me his views, listened to my objections, & admitted the Frescoes were not large enough. This is a great point to have brought him to.

Barry said, 'What I admired your Cartoons for was they were *filled*. I told every body so. However angry you may be with Eastlake, by hints I *know* he thinks you ill treated.

'The fact is,' said Barry, 'you say what you think so completely, & carry it to such an extent, that they are afraid of you.'

April 25. Went to the Houses, & examined the frescoes' spaces. Fresco decoration should look as if it was as much a part of the building as the columns or the stone. Was more convinced than ever that unless Frescoes fill up the Spaces, the decoration will look like a Turkey carpet against the wall.

April 30. Lectured at the Royal Institution, & finished the Introductory lectures – 3. It is a great triumph indeed to have made people of fashion go through the process of an Artist, & I hope it will have its effect.

May 1. I this day again (after lecturing till I am exhausted, 22 lectures in 16 days, & beginning again the instant I came to Town) have reset my palette. It pains me ever to leave it. O God, bless my recommencement, progression, & conclusion till the end of the year, & whilst I live. Amen. Painted ½ a day.

May 3. Drew ½ a day. Oh! – did not paint. I have not yet fixed on a Subject. Nothing moves me but the Heroic or the Sacred.

May 8. The conduct of the upper Classes in regard to first promulgating a law & then passing an act to violate the Law they had solemnly pledged themselves to maintain is disgraceful. A law was passed that no Foreigner should compete for the Houses, but who had resided 10 years.

A wretched German, because he has pleased Mr Vernon Harcourt, promised him naturalization, so that he might compete in spite of the law. A Bill is smuggled through the House of Lords, & then so hurried by Harcourt through the Commons that it was passed 3 stages the last day of the Session before Easter.

Never in my life did I see any thing so highly indecorous.

May 19. As I sit looking at my Picture, I cannot help remembering the Friends who are gone that used to call in on a Sunday, & talk & criticise & cheer up – Lord Mulgrave, Sir George, Wilkie, Jackson, Genl. & Augustus Phipps. Then all was hope & novelty & anticipation, and after 40 years of most anxious study, here I am again at it in just as much necessity, or more, as when I began my first Picture, 1806 – 38 years ago.

May 23. Raffled Saragossa today. There were 30 Subscribers; Duke had 6 shares. Eucles, Xenophon, & now Saragossa, were all raffled.

May 29. Finally settled Uriel & Satan. I copied an Angel from Raphael's Bible but it was too gentle for an arch-angel, not sublime enough, tender but not solemn. I did [it] to compare.

May 31. Put Uriel right.

June 3. Carew [called] & told a capital story of Nelson, which he had from Ball, son of Sir Alexander. Nelson had a horrid tooth ake & never could bring his courage to the point of having it out. Even when the Doctor came, Nelson swore he had no pain. It began again the moment he left him. 'A sail,' was cried from the top. Nelson sprang from bed, took his glass, and ordered to get clear for action. He never had any more tooth [ache] for months.

June 10. I dined with a Pupil at Richmond, at the Star and Garter. I met Bailey the Sculptor who told me his rencontre with the Duke. The Duke had written Storr & Mortimer he would see Bailey on Wednesday; they told him nothing of it till *Wednesday afternoon!* Off he set Thursday.

The Duke came down as soon as Bailey was announced, & on entering flew at him in a fury. Bailey told me he actually said, 'God damn & blast your eyes & God damn & blast all Artists for tormenting me in this blasted manner. My Career, Sir, was over at 47, God damn & blast ye; why can't ye be content with what ye have all done without harrassing me in this damn & blasted manner?'

Bailey took his bag up to the Steward, & retired to the Inn to dine. The Steward said, 'Sir, the Duke expects you at dinner, & to sleep here.' 'Tell the Duke,' said Bailey, 'I'll be damned if I'll dine at the table of any man who used me as he has done.'

June 23. Sunday. Wrote all day. Sent my dear family to Dover. & all day Monday – 11 hours.

July 1. Worked hard, & earned 10 gs.

July 6. Went to Dover & swam & shouted & dived. My dear Daughter looked worse. We were affected & both cried & so did my dear Mary. I have had no recreation for 3 years, & swimming always braces me, but then comes this calamity – Life.

July 15. Rubbed in Uriel, but harrassed so much my brain becomes turgid with apprehensions.

I have been tormenting myself with fears I had not painted all the year! I find I finished Napoleon musing in January, several sketches, rubbed in the Duke & Napoleon, & painted up to March 11. I then began lecturing, which broke in [on] my habits of study, & since then I have done little [more] than rub in Uriel, parry pecuniary payments, suffer on acct. of my family & dear & only daughter – up to this day. But still I feel longing for a great work.

July 21. The Frescoes are by no means what they ought [to be]. Instead of carrying the beauties of oil into Fresco, they seem delighted to carry the horrors of Fresco into oil.

All the flesh of their Frescoes looks as if dipped in the stain of a tan-pit, so utterly are they without cool tones. If they can put blue into the Sky, surely they could put a due mixture of it into the flesh. There are also no reflections, and the effect is hot & offensive & dirty; black, sooty – as if painted with boiled fish eyes.

July 26. By the blessing of God, I this day, by an advance from a pupil of £100 have been saved from ruin.

August 15. Worked & finished the head-tackling of the Duke's horse, in George IV & the Duke visiting Waterloo. But worked laxly. Corrected a proof of my Lectures, but by no means in the high tone I was yesterday. Weather, indigestion, a glass of wine beyond my three, oversleeping, not working hard – all these causes help to depress the physique & then the mental – yet what a Blessing is life.

August 24. Disraeli is very much improved since I met him at Caroline Norton's, 1832, in velvet trowsers & ruffles, and where he did the Dandy just returned from travel, to perfection.

In the City all day, but I had worked hard this week. Advanced George IVth, did a Napoleon & a head.

September 3. I should be happy, if it pleased God, to die in my Painting room, after a successful completion of some grand head. In reality I have no other real delight, but it would be happier if my mind did not overrun in writing & deductions.

After painting, I always look back at the time I have lost in writing – but still I go on writing.

September 7. Out & superintended the restretching the Solomon, began 1812, finished 1813, 32 years ago. I really am astonished at the Picture, and I do not wonder at the enthusiasm of the people at seeing such a work come out from a young man of 26 – in the midst of the hooting of the World.

September 12. Out all morning on money & got it – £25 for a Portrait. It occupied all day, so there goes another day – it is shocking, but what is one to do?

October 2. Worked till 3. Painted & improved the drapery of Uriel. The art is becoming a beastly vulgarity. The solitary grandeur of Historical painting is gone. There was something grand, something poetical, something mysterious, in pacing your quiet Painting room after midnight, with a great work lifted up on a gigantic easel. There was something truly poetical to be devoting yourself to what the Vulgar dared not touch.

October 10. My wedding day – 23 years! 'I wish you may live 23 years more,' said Frank my Son to us.

Worked hard & very tired.

October 14. Idiotic & cloudy – Idle.

October 18. Out on money matters – ¼ a day at work.

Rossi's family in great distress – 1 daughter mad, one Son private in lancers, the other a ticket Clerk on the Rail-way! The other daughter called with a petition for subscription. Duke of Northumberland gave £5 – my proportion was 2/6 – all I could spare.

November 15. Poor old Lord Saye & Sele dead! No man took more trouble to keep himself alive. I have come to the conclusion that a Man may make himself more or less comfortable by excessive care, but he does not prolong his existence one hour – in short, that the average of Life is pretty nearly alike.

November 30. Worked, & it was hard Work to Work, from eternal calls. I heard yesterday, from Kendall, the Duke's valet, he had a hat ready for me, so down I went, & tipping a Sovereign, carried off a Genuine hat, the glorious hat which had encircled the laurelled head of Wellington. I trusted it to nobody; I took it in the hat box, called a Cab, & gloried in it. I sat to work instantly, & before Kendall called had finished the hat in the Picture. Kendall brought a pair of his boots; I told him I must have a whole suit, cravat & all, & I am promised.

Colin Mackenzie called & we had a great deal of fun. He put on the hat – I must lock it up or it will be ruined.

December 9. Sorry am I to say, money matters obliged me to walk furiously into the City – & furiously back – so that I only altered a pair of Eyes & put in a new Duke & his Horse. ½ a day.

December 25. Xmas day. Eastlake called – a good sign. Eastlake & David Wilkie never call unless it is a safe thing so to do.

December 28. Hard at work.

Duke of Devonshire called, & to help me to pay the expences before my Dear Frank took his degree, gave me two orders to paint two Sketches for two pannels for a window at Chatsworth. I said, 'Napoleon musing at St Helena, & the Duke at Waterloo.' He replied, 'Capital Idea,' & so at it I go. He paid me half by a cheque for £20.14.11. How kind! & I despatched it by P.O. to Cambridge, for Frank's college bill. How grateful to God I am!

December 30. Began & finished a Napoleon in 2½ hours, the quickest I ever did & the 25th.

December 31. Thus ends 1844. This year, at the beginning, I received a blow by the Directors not taking Alexander & the Lion. I was obliged to dash it before the Public at once; it did not sell, so the dreadful struggle, through this Picture after being disappointed in the prize for the Cartoons, not bringing me reward was another blow. Dennys, a Cotton Printer, ordered Uriel for 200 gs., 100 of which was paid to Jesus College, so that with two Sons, 1 at sea & the other [at] Cambridge, I contrived to bear up. If I can only now finish Uriel, Aristides, & the 5 other great Works, my original designs, I will resign my Spirit into his hands from whom I received it.

1845

January 4. I have cleared dear Frank of all but his Xmas bill, £30.17.11. God grant I may accomplish that, or his degree will not be granted. In him I trust.

January 6. Mackenzie gave me an order for a small repetition of George IV & the Duke & so dear Frank is safe. God accept my gratitude. Amen.

February 4. At the House of Lords, & much affected at the sight! – the Queen hideously altered! – evidently *peculiarly* nervous. She hurried every thing, was hardly 10 minutes in the House, came out so soon Officers, Heralds, & attendants were obliged to scamper. One of the Mace Men nearly knocked Lyndurst in the head, & he lame as he was, scrambled to his [feet] to be in Time. In the Robing room she had hardly unrobed, & the doors shut, when they opened again, and out they all *fought* their way, she & Albert following. When I remember her first girlish air, 1837, & looked at her now – red nose, fat, irritable, nervous! – I was melancholy.

February 24. Sidney Smith is dead! Where be thy jests & jibes now? 36 years ago Wilkie & I used to go & hear him at London Street chapel – he was 73. He always said when he saw us come in he was on his *good behaviour!*

He was a Man of great Genius! but he was too careless of his wit, where Religion ought to have restrained him. I have heard him say irresistible things which ought not to have been irresistible on such a subject. Well, he is gone, & he will be missed.

April 3. Dennys, my Employer, is boring me to send Uriel to the Academy. Why should I hurry a work on – for a Spring Season? I love my own silent, studious, midnight ways. I hate the glare, the Vulgarity, & the herd. The solitary majesty of High Art is gone now! There was a time when its dangerous glories frightened the coward & alarmed the conceited! Now the paltry flutter of farthing candles dim its steady fire & obscure its splendour.

April 4. O God bless my daily labour. Amen. Worked hard.

Higginson lunched with me (a fine fellow), who sailed with Napoleon in the Bellerophon. He said his influence on the men was fascinating. He used to borrow sixpence of the men, pinch the ears of the Officers, & bewitch them in so extraordinary [a way], without the least familiarity, it was unaccountable.

[The following extract from *The Times*, reviews the Royal Academy exhibition. Haydon labeled it, 'Times, Tuesday, May 6.']

There is one picture which makes us depart from our design of adhering to the great room exclusively on this occasion; that is, Haydon's large painting of 'Uriel and Satan' (605), which must arrest even those who are hastening to depart from the Exhibition as a most remarkable work. A striking contrast to the gaudy colouring on which the eye has been feasted, it appears with subdued tone, reminding one of a fresco. The figure of the angel is drawn with a boldness which some might call exaggerated, but with the simplicity and anatomical effect of sculpture, every muscle looking hard and unyielding as iron. The face is noble and ideal, and a fine effect is produced by the golden colour of the hair. This huge commanding figure is backed by limitless space, represented by a very dark positive blue, and the whole conveys the impression of simple vastness. There is a certain crudity about the picture, but the impress of genius is unmistakeable.

Here's a miracle after 22 years of abuse, because I offended Barnes, the Editor, who married a Whore, & which neither T. Moore, nor Ruff, nor I would take our wives to see. How little do the public know the secret motives of the writers in the press.

May 13. Passed the day in excrutiating anxiety about my son Frank, who for neglecting Chapel has been *sent down* – when getting a good Income & 3 pupils – how provoking! I hope he will have sons of his own!

May 15. Hallam called today. He told me with great gusto Wordsworth at the Levee was passing by, when Lord Delawar said 'Kneel, kneel.' Wordsworth, totally ignorant of Court ways & Court etiquette, plumped down on both knees! – & when he was down, he was too feeble to get up again. Lord De la Warr & Lord Liverpool were obliged to help him up. The Queen was much touched.

May 31. Worked hard, but harrassed with calls from Students, Painters, Creditors, Tradesmen, Ladies, & Poles. I got into a rage, & the poor Pole had the whole. I rushed down brush in hand. 'Qui est vous?' 'Je suis, Monsieur, un pauvre Polonnais, de la Garde Imperiale.' 'Bah. Napoleon n'avait jamais un Polonnais dans le Garde. Vous vous trompez, Monsieur!' 'Je ne me trompe pas, Monsieur. Je suis pauvre.' 'Et moi aussi. Je suis un Peintre D'Histoire Anglais.' '& un très celèbre, Monsieur,' said he, handing me a subscription list. 'Voila un shilling, et c'est plus que vous me meritez.' He looked frightened & bowing went.

I rushed up to work & swore the next who came I'd put the brush in his face.

June 20. Having got thoroughly through my leading group of Aristides, & my rooms never having been thoroughly routed for 2 years, hired a woman & worked like a galley slave. Moved all my fine Plaisters into my painting room & had it thoroughly washed & cleaned, moved all my things back, & tomorrow do the same to my Painting room, & then to work on Monday.

This is the way an Artist should keep his health. The violent exercise did me enormous good – the journeyman & the Genius should always be conjoined.

June 25. I declare solemnly that after cleaning my Studio, it never seems fit to work in. What machines we are. Digestion is the great cause of every virtue & every vice & I am very much inclined to agree with my Son Frank – perhaps the Devil is but a personified fistula.

July 21. Poor dear Lord Grey! – gone at last. How many times he graced my Painting-room.

His talents were not first rate, but his virtue in public matters was unimpeachable. If he from tenderness of heart put relations in public places, it was not because he was reckless of public good, but because he thought himself justified in choosing a relative if as able as any other – nor do I think him wrong on that principle.

August 9. The Queen dissolved Parliament today. I could not go as usual, but gave my tickets to my Son Frederick, R.N. The most extraordinary thing happened which perhaps never happened before in such a Scene – in carrying the Crown of England fell off the Cushion, & he says split in two. Several of the smaller diamonds could not be found. How carelessly it must have been carried! I take it frightfully – I hate such things.

September 19. This day I took a Pupil, a very interesting Youth. His Mother, a woman of great energy, his guardian, came with him. Good heavens! the Premium was a blessing to me after fagging through Aristides, & the boy seemed delighted.

September 23. The King of Hanover has bought Napoleon Musing, a repetition of the one belonging to Sir Robert Peel.

Thus I have received by the blessing of God £410 in 5 days, after painting the whole of Aristides (except £60) on borrowed money. Good God, how grateful I ought to be.

October 13. On the 7th I left Town by Express train to visit Mrs Gwatkin at Ply[mou]th, to examine Sir Joshua's private memoranda concerning the Academy quarrel. Mrs Gwatkin was Miss Palmer, & niece to Sir Joshua.

After calling on many old Friends of my Youth, I waited on the last relick left us of the Johnsonian Burkeian period – she is in her 89th year – & at 12 I called, went up & found on a sofa, leaning on pillows, a venerable aged Lady, holding a ear trumpet like Sir Joshua, shewing in her face great remains of regular beauty, and evidently the model of Sir Joshua in his Christian Virtues, which she afterwards confirmed. After a few minutes chat, we entered on the purport of my visit, which was to examine Sir Joshua's private papers relating to the Academy dispute which produced his resignation.

Mrs Gwatkin rose to give orders; her figure was fine & elastic, upright as a dart, with nothing of decrepitude.

Mr Gwatkin, her grandson, brought down a bundle of arranged papers, & on the very first bundle was 'Private papers relative to my resignation of the Presidency.'

The first was a letter to Sir W. Chambers, refusing to resume the Chair. The latter part bearing on my subject, I extracted. Mr Gwatkin, getting interested at my anxiety, offered his services, & giving him part of the papers we worked away.

The dear old Lady was soon in a bustle, for she did not seem to know the value of what she possessed, and said she had a trunk full, and ordered it down. Then there was no key, and then her eldest daughter, about 50, was dispatched, and her niece, a little spirited thing, hunted, and the key was found. In about two hours I finished. I then joined her, and we had a delightful chat. She said the most delightful man was Goldsmith. She saw him & Garrick keep an immense party laughing till they *shrieked!* Garrick sat on Goldsmith's knee; a tablecloth was pinned under Garrick's chin & brought behind Goldsmith, hiding both their figures. Garrick then spoke, in his finest style, Hamlet's speech to his Father's ghost. Goldsmith put out his hands on each side of the cloth & made burlesque action – tapping his heart & putting his hand to Garrick's head & nose, all at the wrong time.

She said Sir Joshua now & then during Parliament, had large parties. She remembered that first party with Fanny Burney, 1779. She said she & her sister plagued her in the garden at Streatham to know who was the Author of Evelina, never suspecting *her*. As they rode home, Sir Joshua said, 'Now you have dined with the Author – guess which of the party?' They could not guess – when Sir Joshua said, 'Miss Burney.'

Lunch was now announced, & we had all got so intimate that they made me promise to stay the day. At lunch down came young Mrs Gwatkin and a fine dear little boy, the *fourth* generation. It was quite a Patriarchal Party. I dined, & retired at 10 to my Inn. As I took her venerable hand, I *kissed it*, which brought a tear into her Eye.

October 17. Though going out of Town is of much benefit, it turns too much the current of your thoughts, & it has cost me an effort to get on the High road. I set my palette & mused. The day passed. Copying out being easy, I plunged at it, & now all will be soon right.

November 8. I have always said of Peel he had a tender heart. Now, my dear son Frank, shrinking from the display of the Pulpit, after 860. 10. expense for a College Education, in anguish of mind I wrote Sir Robert – and told my anguish.

[This letter is attached to the diary.]

7th Nov. 1845.

Sir,

I am directed by Sir R. Peel to inform you that there is a vacancy for a clerk in the Record Office, salary £80 a year, with the usual prospects of promotion, to which he will be happy to appoint your son, if it meets your wishes.

Sir R. Peel was induced to select this Clerkship for him, as from your description of him as a young man of retiring and literary habits, he thinks it will suit him.

If your son will present himself at the Record Office, Rolls Yard, Chancery Lane, he will be examined as to his qualifications.

Your obedt. Servant,
John Young.

He presented himself and was passed, & has given great satisfaction.

November 27. Hard at Work – at Nero. The object is to shew, in the most powerful way I can, the *Evil* of a Sovereign without *popular check*.

December 2. Awoke in very great anxiety, yet Trusting. My City Friends, pressed by the Times & panic, want payment. I went out, my heart bursting to go on with Nero, but obliged to go. I sallied forth, and my presence did everything.

December 12. Worked hard. Col. Leake thought the fire looked too near Nero, so I made it more distant by intervening more temples, which improved it amazingly.

The waltz is surely grossly indelicate. I could not bear it; as Johnson said [to Garrick], 'Davy, Davy, the white bosoms & silk stockings of your actresses excite my amorous propensities.'

December 30. Good heavens! Gurwood [private secretary to the Duke of Wellington] has cut his throat! The Man who had headed the forlorn hope at Ciudad Rodrigo! the rigid Soldier, the iron-nerved Hero! had not morale to resist the relaxation of nerve brought on by his overanxiety about the Duke's Dispatches.

Where is the responsibility of a Man with mind so easily affected by body? Romilly, Castlereagh, & Gurwood!

1846

January 8. Anxious about the next three months. My Fate hangs on doing as I ought and seizing moments with energy. O God bless me with energy & vigour to seize the moment & make the most of it. Amen. Amen. Amen.

January 12. O God, bless the beginning, progression, & conclusion of my taking rooms for Exhibition of my Pictures this day. Amen.
Took my rooms, so the die is cast!

January 17. Concluded the week well, & Nero is advanced nearly to completion. Thank God with all my heart.

January 22. Worked hard, and I think except Trifles finished Nero. Now for *Anarchy* – *three* cheers for Anarchy.

January 24. O God bless me through this day. Amen. Sent my opening advertisement. Success!

January 25. My birth day – 60 years old!

January 27. I went out in misery & there is nothing like the forlorness of feeling of knowing you have not a pound to meet the bill of a rascal, who is hoping you may fail that he may make property of the Costs. Coutts & Co. had written to say it was against their rules to help me – still, personally, I had hopes. I went today. I saw Mr Majoribanks; I said, 'Sir, do help me.' He is humane. 'You know it is against all rule. I regret to see a man of your eminence so hard run. Shall it [be] the last time?' I gave him my honor. I signed a promissory note for 2 months, & he placed the amount to my account. Away I marched.

February 4. In the greatest anxiety about money matters. Accommodation in the city out of the question. My Friends with faces longer than my arm, croaking & foreboding.
I have lost three glorious days, painted hardly at all, & have not succeeded in getting £5, with £62 to pay. I must up with my new canvas, because if not with a new large Picture to *lean* on, I feel as if deserted by the World.

February 5. O, O, O. I sat all day & looked into the fire! I must get up my third canvas, or I shall go cracked! I have ordered it up on Saturday, & then I'll be at it.

February 7. Thus ends the week; by borrowing £10 of Talfourd, £10 of Twentyman, 5. 10. of my hatter, I contrived to satisfy claims for £62, but next week I must be at it again. Though I have Wordsworth's and the Duke's head engraving I can sell neither, & though I have not had a farthing on my Lectures yet, I am now revising a 2nd volume.

February 9. Laid up [with] an inflamed lid; always get ill in the interval of great works. Did nothing. Considered deeply my next subject. They advised me to paint the last Charette at the Revolution. I prefer *now* the quiet beauty of Alfred.

February 10. My dear Mother's birthday.

February 17. God bless me through this day.
Settled every thing before leaving Town for dear Auld Reekie. God bless my arrival there, success, & safe return. God protect my dear family till I come back, & my pictures and property.

In case of accidents, I hope my dear Friends Darling, 6 Russell Square, & Mr Serjeant Talfourd will act as Executors.

I made my will as my grand father did, 1745 – when leaving Kingsbridge a fortnight on the road – 100 years since this will be as absurd.

February 23. Lectured on Fuzeli, and was heroically received by a Brilliant audience. Ah, Auld Reekie, I smile then again to my heart's joy!

February 25. Lectured on Wilkie. They listened as if entranced; not a breath, or a whisper, or a hum.

March 11. Went to a Soiree of Jeffrey's.
Macready was there, looking as if he had just escaped from the tortures of the damned, & that his features had not yet recovered the calmness of humanity. There was not in that man's eye, nose, or mouth one spark of Genius. Actors must feel as if in an iron mask in Society.

March 14. Started from Newcastle, & arrived in London by train at 8. Thank God for the safety of my family & self. Amen.

March 18 and 19. Occupied preparing for my exhibition. I wish it was over. Wrote my Catalogue.

March 26. Directed 224 Envelopes for Private day, with the tickets, & signed in the corner. Kept the men at work all day – Pictures framed; all alive, as I relish. God bless the whole career.

March 28. Finished & got all Covered in & ready for toning & ordering next week – Thank God. How I have worked this week – 400 private tickets signed & sealed, my daughter sealing, I signing & naming. Bless the next week. Amen.

April 4. O God bless this day with complete success. Amen.
It rained the whole day! Nobody came. 26 years ago, the rain would not have prevented them! But now it is not so! However I do not despair.

April 6. Receipts Aristeides, £1. 1s. 6d., 1846. Receipts 1820, £19. 16s., Jerusalem. In God I trust. Amen.

April 7. Rain! 1. 8. 6.

April 8. Fine. Receipts worse, 1. 6. 6.

April 16. My situation is now of more extreme peril than even when I began Solomon 33 years ago! – I awoke this morning at 4, as usual, and my mind immediately filled with the next in my series – Alfred & the Jury!

April 17. Worked hard, & got on with Alfred gloriously; made a small Sketch, in a few minutes, of light, colour, & shadow, & then rubbed in the Whole Picture another Stage.

It had a splendid Effect. God be thanked. How mysterious is the Whisper which in such anxieties impels to paint, conceive, & invent. How mysterious!

May 5. Came home in excrutiating anxiety, & found a notice from a broker for a Quarter's rent from Newton, my old landlord for 22 years! For a moment my brain was confused! I had paid him half, & therefore there was only 10. left.

I went into the painting room in great misery of mind. That so old a Friend should have chosen such a moment to do so gross a thing is painful. After a hour's dullness, my mind suddenly fired up, with a new background for Alfred. I dashed at it, & at dinner it was enormously improved.

May 6. I went out yesterday, called on the Lawyer, an amiable man! He promised to try to get me time. I came home – my exhibition bringing nothing – & would any man believe, as I waited in the Lawyer's Chambers, the whole background of Alfred flashed into my head? I dwelt on it, foresaw its effects, & came home in anxiety & anticipation. I went on with my palette, in a giddy fidget. & looking at my great work, I flew at my Picture, & dashing about like an inspired Devil by 3 had arranged & put in the alteration.

May 18. I closed my exhibition this day, & have lost 111. 8. 10. No man can accuse me of shewing less energy, less spirit, less genius than I did 26 years ago. I have not decayed, but the people have been corrupted.

May 20. Continually attending to Exhibitions is dreadful and if you do not, you get robbed. These things an Artist should have nothing to do with; details of business injure my mind and when I paint I feel as if Nectar was floating in the Interstices of the brain. God be praised, I have painted today.

June 1. Edwin Landseer has received this year nearly 7000 – sale & copy right – & here am I his old Instructor, obliged to withdraw my Pictures with the loss of £111. 8s. 10d.

Went to Christie's to see a Collection for sale – saw a Holy family by

Rubens. Colour exquisite, but nothing will give that brilliancy but Chrome in the lights – judiciously used. Made a drawing for Alfred & sat the drapery.

June 16. I sat from 2 till 5 staring at my Picture like an Idiot, my brain pressed down by anxiety and anxious looks of my dear Mary & children. I dined after having raised money on all our Silver.

I had written Sir R. Peel, Duke of Beaufort, Lord Brougham, saying I had a heavy sum to pay. Who answered first? Tormented by D'Israeli, harrassed by public business, up came the following letter:

Sir,

I am sorry to hear of your Continued Embarrassments.

From a limited fund which is at my disposal I send as a Contribution towards your Relief from those embarrassments the sum of fifty pounds.

I am, Sir
Your obedient Servt.
Robert Peel

June 18. O God bless me through the Evils of this day. Amen. Great anxiety. My Landlord Newton called. Good hearted Newton! I said, 'Don't put in an execution.' 'Nothing of the sort,' he replied, half hurt.

No reply from Brougham, Beaufort, Barry, or Hope! – & this Peel is the man who has *no heart*.

June 20. O God bless us all through the evils of this day. Amen.

June 21. Sunday. Slept horribly. Prayed in sorrow and got up in agitation.

June 22. God forgive – me – Amen.

Finis

of

B. R. Haydon

'Stretch me no longer on this tough World' – *Lear*.

End

Epilogue by Willard Bissell Pope

Frederic Haydon believed that the immediate cause for his father's suicide was his intense disappointment at the failure of a friend (designated only as L——) to fulfil a promise to lend him £1000. When Haydon learned of this miscarriage, on or about June 13, he drank heavily and the next day was mentally upset. Extremely hot weather and intense insomnia greatly aggravated his condition, but he stubbornly refused to consult his physician, though his mental distress continued intermittently throughout the week, and by Sunday, June 21, his mind was fixed upon suicide. On the next day he arose early, went to Rivière, a gunmaker in Oxford Street, and bought a small pistol, with which, in a few hours, he shot himself.

On returning from the gunmaker's, Haydon locked himself into his painting room, and wrote his will, invalid because it was signed without witnesses.

After composing his will, Haydon wrote letters to his wife and three children. The note to his wife is as follows:

London, Painting-room, June 22, 1846.
God bless thee, dearest love. Pardon this last pang, many thou hast suffered from me; God bless thee in dear widowhood. I hope Sir Robert Peel will consider I have earned a pension for thee. A thousand kisses.
Thy husband & love to the last,
B. R. Haydon

Mrs. Haydon.
Give dear Mary £10 & dear Frank £10; the rest for your dear self of the balance from Sir Robert's £50.

The brief notes to Mary, Frank, and Frederic are similar. He bestowed his paternal blessing on each of his children and hoped fervently that they would be an honour to their country and a comfort to their mother.

While he was engaged upon this writing, Haydon was disturbed by his wife and daughter, who innocently attempted to enter the painting-room. He spoke sharply to them, and they left the door. Soon afterward he appeared; he expressed deep regret for his outburst, and kissed them both warmly. He then returned to his painting-room, which he carefully arranged. Opposite his unfinished picture of 'Alfred,' he placed on an easel a small portrait of his wife. On a nearby table he put the last volume of his diary, opened at the final entry; and a prayer book, opened at the account in the twenty-fourth chapter of Matthew of the second coming and the appearance of false Christs and prophets which will precede it. He placed his farewell letters and his watch beside these books, and then wrote a few paragraphs, headed 'Last thoughts of B. R. Haydon, ½ past 10.'

Then he shot himself. Mrs Haydon and Mary noticed the report, at a quarter before eleven, but they were accustomed to hear soldiers firing in a nearby parade ground and paid no attention to this report.

Haydon had suffered extreme trials during his sixty years, but Fate reserved the cruellest blow for his last day: the shot did not kill him. He had evidently bought a pistol of too small calibre, and the bullet, instead of piercing the brain, was partially deflected by the skull. But, though seriously wounded, Haydon retained consciousness and his invincible determination. He seized one of his razors, which he had brought into the painting-room that morning, and gashed his throat with a fearful cut.

No mortal could have survived this wound, and Haydon fell dead before his 'Alfred,' splattering the great canvas with his life's blood.

At about noon, his daughter entered the painting-room, the door of which Haydon had unlocked, when all was ready for his death; she found her father's body and spread the alarm.

Haydon was buried in the Old Paddington churchyard, behind Mrs Siddons' grave, and beside his five dead children. This epitaph marks his grave: 'Sacred to the memory of Benjamin Robert Haydon. Born January 25th 1786. Died June 22 1846. He devoted 42 years to the improvement of the taste of the English people in high art and died broken hearted from pecuniary distress.'

Haydon's suicide attracted wide attention, and most of the leading newspapers and periodicals published extensive obituary notices. Almost unanimously, the press awarded him encomia such as he had never read and gave full publicity to his beloved ideas on art.

Public sympathy ran high, and on June 30, 'a meeting of gentlemen took place at the chambers of Mr Serjeant Talfourd, in Serjeants'-inn, to devise some means of providing for the widow and daughter of the late Mr Haydon.' The subscription, organized under the chairmanship of Lord Morpeth, flourished, and within two months the sum had reached £2000, which included a contribution of £50 from Haydon's arch enemy, the Royal Academy. In addition, the widow was granted an annual civil list pension of £50, which she drew until her death in 1854.

Like Chatterton, Haydon won a certain personal victory in his suicide. He believed, and many of his contemporaries agreed with him, that a heroic death atoned for his past transgressions; looking back with a perspective of more than a century, we cannot altogether subscribe to this belief, but we can and must acclaim Haydon as a brave and persevering man, who endeavoured to make amends for his wrecked career by unflinchingly offering up his only possession, his life.

Paintings Begun by Haydon

When available, the following facts are supplied: the dates of beginning and completion, the dimension in inches, the original purchaser, the price, the place of first exhibition, and the present location. Readily available reproductions are also noted. Information has been obtained from the diary, supplemented by Edmund Blunden's 'An Alphabetical List of Haydon's Pictures', in his World's Classics edition of Haydon's *Autobiography* (1927, pp. 401–407) and by Algernon Graves's two works, *The Royal Academy of Arts*, Volume IV (1906) and *The British Institution* (1908). I am also indebted to Frederick J. Cummings, Esq. For abbreviated names and titles; to this list are added: 'Boase, T. S. R. Boase, *English Art*, 1800–1870, Oxford, 1959'; 'Elwin. *The Autobiography and Journals of Benjamin Robert Haydon*, edited by Malcolm Elwin, 1950'; 'Paston. George Paston (pseudonym for Emily Morse Symonds), *B. R. Haydon and his Friends*, 1905'; 'Penrose. *The Autobiography and Memoirs of Benjamin Robert Haydon*, edited by Alexander P. D. Penrose, New York, 1929'; and 'Sewter. A. C. Sewter, "A Revaluation of Haydon," *Art Quarterly*, Autumn 1942, 5:323–337.'

1. **Joseph and Mary Resting on the Road to Egypt.** October 1, 1806 – March 31, 1807. 61 × 84. Originally purchased by Thomas Hope for £105. First exhibited at the Royal Academy, 1807.

2. **The Assassination of Dentatus.** January 1, 1808 September 20, 1808 – March 31, 1809. 93 × 75. Originally purchased by Lord Mulgrave for £220. 10s. Received premium of £105 from the British Institution on May 17, 1810. First exhibited at the Royal Academy, 1809. Now owned by Lord Normanby, Mulgrave Castle, Whitby. Reproduced in Elwin, p. 94; George; Paston, p. 34; and Penrose, p. 76.

3. **Macbeth** (1). Before May 23, 1809, December 17, 1809 – December 31, 1811. 119 × 144. Originally purchased by Sir George Beaumont for £210. First exhibited at the British Institution, 1812.

4. **Romeo Leaving Juliet at the Break of Day.** 1810. 58 × 49. Originally purchased for £52. 10s. First exhibited at the Royal Academy, 1810 but withdrawn from the exhibition; exhibited at the British Institution, 1811.

5. **The Judgment of Solomon.** April 4, 1812 – April 1814. 154 × 130. Originally purchased by Sir William Elford and J. W. Tingcombe for £735. First exhibited at the Water-colour Society, Spring Gardens, 1814. Now owned by Jack Gold Esq., Richmond, Surrey. Reproduced by Frederick Cummings in

'Poussin, Haydon, and *The Judgement of Solomon*,' *Burlington Magazine* (April 1962), p. 147.

6. Christ's Entry into Jerusalem. May 7, 1814 – March 1820. 228 × 192. Originally purchased by Edward Binns in 1823 for £350. First exhibited at the Egyptian Hall, March 25, 1820. Now at Mount Saint Mary's Seminary, Norwood, Ohio. Reproduced by Marcia Allentuck in *Art Bulletin* (March 1962), p. 53; in *Autobiography*, II,524; Elwin, p. 318; George; Amy Lowell, *John Keats* (Boston, 1925), I,192, 194; Olney, p. 283; Penrose, p. 242; and Sewter, p. 334.

7. Christ's Agony in the Garden. April 4, 1820 – February 26, 1821. 120 × 84. Originally purchased by Sir George Philips for £525. Now in the Victoria and Albert Museum. Reproduced in Penrose, p. 252.

8. The Raising of Lazarus. Before July 5, 1820 – before February 1823. 168 × 249. Originally purchased by Edward Binns for £350. First exhibited at the Egyptian Hall, March 3, 1823. Now in the Tate Gallery. Reproduced in Elwin, p. 351; George; Olney, p. 285; Penrose, p. 278; and Sewter, p. 325.

9. The Crucifixion (1). Begun March 7, 1823.

10. Portrait of a Gentleman. September 8 – September 25, 1823. First exhibited at the Royal Academy, 1826.

11. Silenus, Intoxicated and Moral, Reproving Bacchus and Ariadne. September 10, 1823 – April 1824. Originally purchased for £150 – *'half price!'* (II,500). First exhibited at the Society of British Artists, 1824.

12. Puck Bringing the Ass's Head for Bottom. October 1 – December 3, 1823. 52 × 46. Originally purchased by Thomas Kearsey for £20. First exhibited at the British Institution, 1824.

13. Mercury and Argus. December 9, 1823, April 9, 1826, July 27, 1830 – September 3, 1830. 35 × 41. Originally purchased by William Newton for £21. First exhibited at the British Institution, 1831.

14. Satan Alighting. Begun December 10, 1823.

15. Cimon Bearing off Iphigenia. Begun December 10, 1823.

16. Mayor Robert Hawkes. May 7 – July 1824. Originally purchased by the Corporation of the City of Norwich. First exhibited at the Society of British Artists, 1825. Now in St Andrew's Hall, Norwich. Reproduced in George.

17. A Family Piece. May 7 – after May 29, 1824. Originally purchased by Thomas Kearsey.

18. Pharoah Dismissing Moses. May 28, 1824, February 17, 1825 – December 31, 1825. 102 × 88. Originally purchased by John Hunter for £525. First exhibited at the British Institution, 1826. Now in Paisley Abbey. Reproduced by Yvonne ffrench in 'Some Unrecorded Haydon Drawings,' *Apollo* (November 1958), p. 151.

19. Juliet at the Balcony. January 3 – March 8, 1825. Originally purchased by Thomas Kearsey. First exhibited at the Society of British Artists, 1825.

20. Mary Haydon. January 17 – after January 18, 1825. 'Half-length'.

21. Dr George Darling (1). First exhibited at the Society of British Artists. May 1825. Reproduced in Olney, p. 291.

22. **The Convalescent.** First exhibited at the Society of British Artists, May 1825.

23. **Mary Russell Mitford.** First exhibited at the Society of British Artists, May 1825. Reproduced in Paston, p. 142, and in W. J. Roberts, *Mary Russell Mitford*, 1913, p. 260.

24. **John Hunter.** First exhibited at the Society of British Artists, May 1825.

25. **The Orange Boy.** May 20, 1825 – before March 21, 1826. Originally purchased by Sir John Leicester.

26. **Venus Appearing to Anchises.** February 27 – March 1826. 29½ × 39. Originally purchased by Sir John Leicester for £210. First exhibited at the Royal Academy, 1826. Now owned by S. A. Oliver, Esq., Egham, Surrey.

27. **Alexander Taming Bucephalus.** April 12, 1826 – March 10, 1827. 60 × 76. Originally purchased by Lord Egremont for £525. First exhibited at the Royal Academy, 1827. Now at Petworth House. Reproduced in Elwin, p. 382.

28. **Dr George Darling** (2). Begun before September 17, 1826.

29. **The Judgment of Paris.** Begun December 5, 1826.

30. **The Death of Eucles.** December 8, 1826, November 24, 1828 – February 13, 1830. Won by Newman Smith in a raffle which netted £525. First exhibited at the Western Exchange, May 1830. Reproduced in Penrose, p. 340.

31. **The Mock Election.** April 15 – beginning of December 1827. 56 × 72. Originally purchased by King George IV for £525. First exhibited at the Egyptian Hall, January 1828. Now at Buckingham Palace. Reproduced in Elwin, p. 415; George; Penrose, p. 340; and Sewter, p. 333.

32. **Thomas Noon Talfourd.** September 18 – November 4, 1827. John Roffe's engraving reproduced in Olney, p. 297.

33. **Mrs Thomas Noon Talfourd.** (1). Begun after November 4, 1827.

34. **Chairing the Member.** March 1 – August 30, 1828. 60 × 75½. Originally purchased by Mr Francis of Exeter for £300. First exhibited at the Western Bazaar, October 6, 1828. Now in the Tate Gallery. Reproduced in Boase, Plate 63, and Elwin, p. 446.

35. **Ariadne.** Begun April 1, 1828. Originally purchased by Charles Kelsall.

36. **Romeo and Juliet** (1). 'April 12, 1828. Rubbed in a small picture of Romeo & Juliet'.

37. **Sir Walter Scott.** Begun May 5, 1828.

38. **Samson and Delilah** (1). January 14, 1829, February 7, 1830, January 30, 1836, July 4, 1836 – February 18, 1837, September 21, 1838. Originally purchased by William Newton.

39. **Samson and the Philistines.** The dates of beginning and completion of this picture cannot be differentiated from the dates of number 38, as Haydon usually referred to both merely as 'Samson.' First exhibited at the Society of British Artists, March 1840.

40. **Punch, or May Day.** April 14, 1829, July 22, 1829 – November 12, 1829, February 20, 1830. 59¾ × 73½. 'Mortgaged to Dr Darling for £100'

(Blunden, p. 406). First exhibited at the Western Exchange, March 1830. Now in the Tate Gallery. Reproduced in *Autobiography*, II,476; Elwin, p. 479; George; Olney, p. 288; Penrose, p. 380; Sewter, p. 334; and *The Times Literary Supplement* (September 23, 1949), p. 609.

41. **Xenophon and the Ten Thousand** (1). July 1, 1829, March 20, 1830 – October 22, 1831. 138 × 114. Won by the Duke of Bedford in a raffle which netted £840. First exhibited at the Egyptian Hall, March 24, 1832.

42. **Marius at Carthage.** Begun November 16, 1829.

43. **Lady Macbeth**, or **He is about it.** November 22 – December 9, 1829. 'Little'.

44. **Napoleon Looking at a Sunset.** November 28 – December 11, 1829. Originally purchased by Thomas Kearsey. First exhibited at the Western Exchange, May 1830.

45. **Uriel Revealing himself to Satan** (1). November 29, 1829 – January 12, 1830. 'A small Picture'.

46. **Achilles Solacing his Anger with the Lyre.** August 24, 1830 – before January 3, 1831. Originally purchased by J. Clarke (Blunden, p. 401). First exhibited at the Egyptian Hall, March 24, 1832.

47. **Dr George Darling** (3). August 25 – after September 4, 1830.

48. **Xenophon and the Ten Thousand** (2). September 9, 1830 – October 4, 1831. 'On the *saleable* size – of *Eucles*'.

49. **Venus and Anchises Quarrelling.** Begun October 26, 1830. Originally purchased by Lord Stafford.

50. **Napoleon Musing at St Helena** (1). December 8, December 16, 1830 – June 21, 1831. 108 × 96. Originally purchased by Sir Robert Peel for £136. 10s. Now owned by Maurice Solow, Esq., Mamaroneck, New York. Reproduced in Olney, p. 286; Paston, p. 185; and Penrose, p. 402.

51. **Napoleon Contemplating his Future Grave.** April 19, 1831, May 3, 1832 – May 5, 1832.

52. **Napoleon in Egypt by Night, Meditating his Return to Europe.** Begun April 20, 1831.

53. **Napoleon Musing at St Helena** (2). Begun May 5, 1831 – 'half finished' June 21, 1831.

54. **The First Child** (1). October 3 – October 4, 1831. Originally purchased by Thomas Kearsey. First exhibited at the Egyptian Hall, March 24, 1832.

55. **Waiting for *The Times*** (1). October 11 – November 4, 1831. 25 × 30½. Originally purchased by Thomas Kearsey. First exhibited at the Egyptian Hall, March 24, 1832. Now owned by *The Times*. Reproduced in the *New York Times Magazine* (January 2, 1938), p. 6, and in Olney, p. 289.

56. **Waiting for *The Times*** (2). November 6 – November 28, 1831. 10 × 13½. Originally purchased by Lord Stafford for £50. Now owned by Dr T. F. Hewer, Bristol. As Olney notes (p. 193), which is the original and which the replica of 'Waiting for *The Times*' cannot be determined.

Paintings Begun by Haydon

57. The Dying Boy. (Alfred Haydon). November 25, 1831 – January 23, 1832. Originally purchased by Edward Smith for £26. 5s. First exhibited at the Egyptian Hall, March 24, 1832.

58. The Blessings of Matrimony. Begun December 16, 1831.

59. David and Goliath. Begun December 23, 1831.

60. Falstaff and Doll Tearsheet. Begun December 23, 1831. First exhibited at the Egyptian Hall, March 24, 1832.

61. Hope. January 27 – February 12, 1832. Originally purchased by Edward Smith.

62. The Sabbath Evening of a Christian. (1). Begun and finished before March 24, 1832, when it was exhibited at the Egyptian Hall.

63. The First Start in Life. Begun and finished before March 24, 1832, when it was exhibited at the Egyptian Hall. 30 × 25. Now owned by Mrs Charlotte Frank, London.

64. A Margate Steamer after a Gale. Begun April 26, 1832.

65. The Spanish Nun (1). May 1, 1832 – before March 18, 1833.

66. Reading the Scriptures (2). 'May 16 and 17, 1832. Worked hard, a second Reading the Scriptures.' This picture is probably a replica of no. 62, 'The Sabbath Evening of a Christian.'

67. The Crucifixion (2). 'May 22, 1832. Rubbed in a Small Crucifixion.'

68. Reading the Scriptures (3). May 30 – June 1, 1832.

69. Reading the Scriptures (4). Begun June 5, 1832.

70. The Meeting of the Unions on Newhall Hill, Birmingham. Begun June 10, 1832. 28 × 36. Drawing and sketches for this unfinished picture are in the Birmingham City Museum and Art Gallery. Reproduced by P. J. Barlow in 'Benjamin Robert Haydon and the Radicals,' *Burlington Magazine* (September 1957), pp. 309–310; George; Olney, p. 290; and Sewter, p. 329.

71. Reading the Scriptures (5). Finished July 6, 1832. Originally purchased by Thomas Kearsey.

72. The Reform Banquet. July 11, 1832 – March 22, 1834. 144 × 96. Originally purchased by Lord Grey for £525. First exhibited in the Great Room, 26 St James's Street, March 22, 1834. Now at Howick, Alnwick, Northumberland. Reproduced in Elwin, p. 510; George; and Penrose, p. 420.

73. Lord Grey Musing, or A Statesman at his Fireside (1). Begun November 27, 1832. 29½ × 25. Now in the Laing Art Gallery and Museum, Newcastle upon Tyne. Reproduced in George; Penrose, p. 433; and Sewter, p. 330.

74. Falstaff (1). Begun February 16, 1833. Originally purchased by William Newton.

75. The Spanish Nun (2). Finished March 18, 1833.

76. Adam and Eve (1). Before June 24 – October 4, 1833.

77. Lord Grey or A Statesman Musing after a Day's Fag (2). April 9, 1834 – March 18, 1835. 'My little Picture'.

78. **Cassandra Predicting the Murder of Agamemnon.** April 23 – December 31, 1834. 72 × 55 (see IV,206). Originally purchased by the Duke of Sutherland for £420. First exhibited at the Society of British Artists, March 1835.

79. **The Spanish Nun** (3). Finished April 26, 1834. Originally purchased by the Duke of Sutherland.

80. **Lord Saye and Sele.** April 28 – June 23, 1834. 28 × 35. Originally purchased by Lord Saye and Sele. Now owned by Lord Saye and Sele, Broughton Castle, Banbury.

81. **Falstaff and Prince Hal.** Finished August 9, 1834. First exhibited at the Society of British Artists, March 1836.

82. **Achilles Discovered by Ulysses at the Court of King Lycomedes.** January 2, April 1 – August 22, 1835. 72 × 56. Originally purchased by William Newton for £420. First exhibited at the Society of British Artists, March 1836.

83. **Milton and his Daughters** (1). Begun January 6, 1835.

84. **Eloisa and Abelard.** Begun January 6, 1835.

85. **Milton at his Organ.** Begun January 7, 1835.

86. **Mary at her Glass.** Begun January 7, 1835.

87. **Samson and Delilah** (2). Begun January 17, 1835.

88. **An Imperial Guard Musing at Waterloo.** (The picture was begun on January 31, 1835, as 'Wellington Musing at Waterloo.') February 12 – February 13, 1835. Originally purchased by Rudolph Ackermann for £31. 10s.

89. **The Burning of the Houses of Parliament.** Begun February 19, 1835.

90. **Lord Grey Musing** (3). February 26 – March 18, 1835.

91. **Napoleon Musing at St Helena** (3). March 3 – March 7, 1835. Originally purchased by the Duke of Sutherland.

92. **Orestes Hesitating to Murder Clytemnestra.** Begun March 9, 1835.

93. **The Scotch Girl and her Lover** (Mrs Leicester Stanhope and the Hon. William Francis Cowper. The picture is also known as 'The Highland Lovers' and 'The Charade Picture'). March 19, December 10, 1835, March 27 – April 30, 1840. Originally purchased by 'Miller of Liverpool'.

94. **John Bull at Breakfast – We are a Ruined Nation** (1). Begun April 25, 1835. Originally purchased by the Duke of Sutherland. First exhibited at the Society of British Artists, March 1836.

95. **John Bull at Breakfast** (2). August 15 – August 18, 1835.

96. **Christ's Raising the Widow's Son** (1). August 26 – December 23, 1835. 72 × 56. Originally purchased by William Newton for £420. First exhibited at the Society of British Artists, March 1836.

97. **Macbeth** (2). Begun December 19, 1835.

98. **The Adoration of the Magi.** Begun January 5, 1836.

99. **Samson and Delilah** (3). January 30, July 4, 1836 – February 18, 1837, September 21, 1838. Originally purchased by William Newton.

100. The Black Prince Thanking Lord James Audley for his Gallantry in the Battle of Poictiers (1). Begun March 5, 1836. 78 × 114. Originally commissioned by Lord Audley but purchased by William Newton for £525. First exhibited at the Edinburgh Society of Artists, December 1837. Now in the City Museum and Art Gallery, Plymouth. Reproduced in Elwin, p. 543.

101. Lord Willoughby de Eresby. Begun June 10, 1836.

102. The Maid of Saragossa. June 21, 1836, February 21, 1837, March 9 – July 15, 1842. 80 × 122. Won by James Webb in a raffle which netted £525. First exhibited at the Royal Academy, 1843. Now in the City Museum and Art Gallery, Plymouth.

103. Falstaff (2). August 25, 1836 – before September 15, 1837. Originally purchased by Henry T. Hope.

104. Curtius Leaping into the Gulf (1). August 31, 1836, October 17 – December 15, 1842. 126 × 90. First exhibited at the British Institution, 1843. Now in the Royal Albert Memorial Museum, Exeter. Reproduced in Elwin, p. 607; Olney, p. 284; and Paston, p. 251.

105. A Knockdown in a Street. Begun August 31, 1836.

106. Macbeth (3). Begun December 5, 1836. 'Small'.

107. Christ Blessing Little Children. September 12, September 23, October 8, 1837 – August 21, 1838. 130 × 110. Originally purchased by the Liverpool Asylum for the Blind for £420. Now at Upholland College, Wigan, Lancashire. Reproduced in Penrose, p. 492.

108. Lord Burghersh. Begun June 20, 1838.

109. Wellington Musing on the Field of Waterloo, or A Hero and the Horse which Carried him in his Greatest Battle, Imagined to be on the Field again Twenty Years After (1). December 19, 1838 – November 30, 1839. 103½ × 127½. Originally purchased by M. D. Lowndes. First exhibited at the British Institution, 1842. Now in St George's Hall, Liverpool. Reproduced in *The Times* (June 17, 1960).

110. Milton and his Daughters (2). January 14 – February 14, 1839. Originally purchased by John Clow. First exhibited at the Society of British Artists, 1840.

111. The Reverend Walter Farquhar Hook. Begun June 1, 1839.

112. The Duke of Wellington. Painted in October 1839. 29¼ × 24¼. Originally purchased by the Duke of Sutherland for £26. 5s. Now at Apsley House. Reproduced by Philip Guedalla in *The Duke* (1931), p. 444, and in *Time* (December 7, 1931), p. 71.

113. Napoleon Musing at St Helena (4). January 27 – March 25, 1840. Originally purchased by Samuel Rogers for £31. 10s.

114. Mary Queen of Scots, when an Infant, Stripped by Order of Mary of Guise, her Mother, to Convince Sadler, the English Ambassador, that she was not a Decrepit Child, which had been Insinuated at Court (1). April 10, May 25, 1840, June 22 – July 1841. 56 × 72. First exhibited at the Royal

Academy, 1842. Now in the Leeds Art Gallery. Reproduced in Elwin, p. 574, and Penrose, p. 528.

115. Romeo and Juliet (2). April 20 – May 26, 1840. Originally purchased by 'Wharton at Hull' for more than £45.

116. The Black Prince Thanking Lord James Audley for his Gallantry in the Battle of Poictiers (2). June 9, 1840, May 17, September 25, 1841 – March 8, 1842. Originally purchased by William Newton for £525. First exhibited at the Royal Academy, 1842.

117. The Anti-Slavery Convention. June 24, 1840 – April 30, 1841. 117 × 151. First exhibited at the Egyptian Hall, 1841. Now in the National Portrait Gallery. Reproduced in *Autobiography*, II,684, and Penrose, p. 420.

118. Napoleon Musing at St Helena (5). Begun November 13, 1840. Originally purchased by Sir John Hanmer for £31. 10s.

119. Daniel O'Connell. Begun February 9, 1841.

120. Agave. Begun July 26, 1841. Originally purchased by Sir John Hanmer for £31. 10s.

121. George IV and Wellington Visiting Waterloo (1). Begun January 20, 1842, and again January 8, 1844. 76 × 88. Originally purchased by Francis Bennoch and Richard Twentyman. First exhibited at the British Institution, 1845. Now at the Royal Hospital, Chelsea. Reproduced in Olney, p. 287.

122. Alexander's Combat with the Lion. January 24, December 15, 1842 – December 30, 1843. First exhibited at the Pantheon, 1844.

123. Curtius Leaping into the Gulf (2). Begun January 27, 1842.

124. Mary Queen of Scots, when an Infant (2). February 2 – February 9, 1842.

125. The Black Prince Entering London in Triumph. May 10, December 24, 1842 – March 15, 1843. First exhibited at the Cartoon Exhibition, Westminster Hall, June 1843.

126. Napoleon Musing at St Helena (6). June 9 – June 13, 1842. Originally purchased by Sir Henry Russell for £21.

127. Wordsworth on Helvellyn. Begun June 14, 1842. 49 × 39. Now in the National Portrait Gallery. Reproduced in *Autobiography* II,732; Frances Blanshard, *Portraits of Wordsworth* (Ithaca, 1959), plate 23; George; *Life* (March 4, 1957), p. 77; Olney, p. 293; Penrose, p. 563; Sewter, p. 330; and Frances Winwar, *Farewell the Banner* (New York, 1938), p. 328.

128. Adam and Eve (2). July 18 – September 28, 1842. First exhibited at the Cartoon Exhibition, Westminster Hall, June 1843.

129. Curtius Leaping into the Gulf (3). October 17 – December 15, 1842.

130. Wellington Musing on the Field of Waterloo (2). Finished February 17, 1843. 23½ × 29½. Now owned by the Countess of Dudley, London.

131. The Virgin and Child. Begun March 25, 1843.

132. The First Child (2). Begun May 4, 1843.

Paintings Begun by Haydon

133. Nelson Sealing the Letter at Copenhagen. Begun June 15 and again July 13, 1843.

134. Sir George Cockburn. Begun August 29, 1843.

135. William Wordsworth. November 10 – November 22, 1843. 36 × 28. Originally purchased by Francis Bennoch. Now at Dove Cottage, Grasmere. Reproduced in Frances Blanshard, *Portraits of Wordsworth* (Ithaca, 1959), plate 25b, and Paston, p. 117.

136. Napoleon Musing at St Helena (7). Begun November 27, 1843. 'Size of Life'. Probably originally purchased by Frances Bennoch.

137. Napoleon Musing at St Helena (8). Begun and finished on November 28, 1843. 'Painted a little Napoleon in four hours'. Probably originally purchased by Richard Twentyman.

138. Napoleon Musing at St Helena (9). Begun December 6, 1843. 'Nearly finished another Napoleon in 4 hours'. Probably originally purchased by 'Hardy, ... [a] city friend'.

139. Napoleon Musing at St Helena (10). December 12 – December 13, 1843. If Haydon was correct in writing, 'This is the 8th', two had not been finished.

140. Curtius Leaping into the Gulf (4). December 15 – December 19, 1843.

141. Napoleon Musing at St Helena (11). December 19 – December 22, 1843.

142. Napoleon Musing at St Helena (12). December 22 – December 23, 1843. Originally purchased by Edward N. Dennys.

143. C'est Lui. Finished before the British Institution's exhibition of 1843, where it was first exhibited.

144. Napoleon Musing at St Helena (13). January 1 – January 6, 1844. 126 × 105. Originally purchased by King Ernest Augustus of Hanover for £200. First exhibited at the British Institution, 1844. Now at Marienburg Castle, Hanover.

145. Macbeth (4). Begun January 12, 1844.

146. Romeo and Juliet (3). Begun January 30, 1844.

147. Curtius Leaping into the Gulf (5). January 30 – January 31, 1844.

148. Napoleon in his Bedroom the Night before his Abdication, 1814 (1). Finished February 15, 1844.

149. Napoleon Musing at Fontainebleau Garden. Begun February 20, 1844.

150. Napoleon in his Bedroom the Night before his Abdication, 1814 (2). Begun February 23, 1844.

151. Napoleon Musing on the King of Rome, Sleeping. February 27 – February 28, 1844.

152. Napoleon Meditating at Marengo. March 2 – March 4, 1844.

153. Napoleon in Egypt, Musing on the Pyramids at Sunrise (1). March 2 – March 5, 1844.

154. **Wellington Musing on the Field of Waterloo** (3). March 6 – March 8, 1844.

155. **Napoleon in Egypt, Musing on the Pyramids at Sunrise** (2). Finished March 11, 1844.

156. **Napoleon Musing at St Helena** (14). Finished March 12, 1844.

157. **Napoleon Musing at St Helena** (15). Finished March 13, 1844.

158. **Wellington Musing on the Field of Waterloo** (4). Finished March 14, 1844.

159. **Francis Bennoch.** Begun March 15 and again November 11, 1844.

160. **Napoleon Musing at St Helena** (16). Finished March 21, 1844.

161. **Napoleon Musing at St Helena** (17). Finished March 22, 1844.

162. **Napoleon Musing at St Helena** (18). May 1 – May 2, 1844.

163. **Uriel Revealing himself to Satan** (2). May 10, 1844 – March 31, 1845. Originally purchased by Edward N. Dennys for £210. First exhibited at the Royal Academy, 1845.

164. **The Progress of Society.** Finished June 15, 1844. Originally purchased by 'worthy little Morgan'.

165. **Napoleon Musing at St Helena** (19). Begun and finished August 21, 1844.

166. **Napoleon Musing at St Helena** (20). Begun and finished August 24, 1844.

167. **Napoleon Musing at St Helena** (21). Begun and finished September 18, 1844

168. **Curtius Leaping into the Gulf** (6). October 21 – October 26, 1844.

169. **Richard Twentyman.** November 4 – after December 3, 1844.

170. **Algernon Frederick Greville.** November 28 – December 5, 1844.

171. **The Banishment of Aristides** (1). December 26, 1844, April 17 – September 26, 1845. 144 × 108. Originally purchased by Richard Twentyman. First exhibited at the Egyptian Hall, April 4, 1846. Now in the Exhibition Building, Melbourne.

172. **Napoleon Musing at St Helena** (22). Begun and finished December 30, 1844.

173. **Napoleon Musing at St Helena** (23). Finished December 31, 1844. Originally purchased by the Duke of Devonshire for £25. Now at Chatsworth House, Bakewell.

174. **Wellington Musing on the Field of Waterloo** (5). January 1 – January 2, 1845. Originally purchased by the Duke of Devonshire for £25. Now at Chatsworth House, Bakewell.

175. **Christ Raising the Widow's Son** (2). Begun April 3, 1845.

176. **Uriel Revealing himself to Satan** (3). Begun April 13, 1845.

177. **George IV and Wellington Visiting Waterloo** (2). June 2 – June 5, 1845. Originally purchased by Colin Mackenzie.

Paintings Begun by Haydon 245

178. Nero Playing on the Lyre. September 10, September 29 – December 31, 1845, January 24, 1846. 144 × 108. Originally purchased by Richard Twentyman. First exhibited at the Egyptian Hall, April 4, 1846. Now in the Exhibition Building, Melbourne. Reproduced in Boase, plate 63.

179. Byron Musing on a Distant View of Harrow. Begun September 15, 1845.

180. The Banishment of Aristides (2). November 1 – November 22, 1845. Originally purchased by George Tawke Kemp.

181. Mrs Thomas Noon Talfourd (2). Finished November 6, 1845.

182. Anarchy, or Banditti. Begun January 27 and again February 10, 1846.

183. Revolution, or The Last Charette. Begun January 28, 1846.

184. Alfred and the First British Jury. Begun January 30 and again February 12, 1846.

185. Christ before Pilate. Begun April 13, 1846. Originally purchased by William Fairbairn (*Correspondence*, I,235).

Pictures which cannot be dated and which are not mentioned in the diary

186. Death the Gate of Life. 37½ × 33. Sold to Gray at Christie's sale of April 24, 1924, for £2. 2s (Blunden, p. 403)

187. Dozing. 16 × 15. First exhibited at the British Institution, 1827.

188. Quizzing. 16 × 15. First exhibited at the British Institution, 1827.

189. A Greek Lady of Zante. First exhibited at the Society of British Artists, 1824.

190. Mrs Robert Hawkes. First exhibited at the Society of British Artists. 1825.

191. Benjamin Robert Haydon (1). 9 × 6½. Now in the National Portrait Gallery. Reproduced in *Autobiography*, II,780; Elwin, p. 638; George; Olney, p. 292; and Paston, p. 230.

192. Benjamin Robert Haydon (2). 'From an engraving by Thomson after Haydon.' Reproduced in Sidney Colvin, *John Keats* (New York, 1925), p. 62; and Olney, p. 295.

193. Benjamin Robert Haydon (3). Black chalk, signed and dated, '1816 B R H,' 9⅝ × 6. Now in the Victoria and Albert Museum. Reproduced in Sewter, p. 326.

194. Leigh Hunt. 23⅜ × 19¼. Now in the National Portrait Gallery. Reproduced in George; Olney, p. 292; Paston, p. 85; Penrose, p. 108; and Sewter, p. 329.

195. Three Portraits of a Lady. First exhibited at the Society of British Artists, 1825.

196. Scenes from Shakespeare. 25 × 30. Sold to Lullington at Sotheby's sale of March 24, 1911, for £4 (Blunden, p. 406).

197. Sleep. First exhibited at the Society of British Artists, 1824.

198. Charles Heathcote Tatham.. First exhibited at the Society of British Artists, 1824.

199. Mrs George Darling. Reproduced in Olney, p. 291.

200. Thomas Alcock. 18 × 14. Now at the Royal College of Surgeons.

201. The Head of an Arab Horse. 29 × 24½. Originally purchased by Lord Willoughby de Eresby. Exhibited at the British Institution, 1843. Reproduced in *Country Life*, June 8, 1961, Supplement 35.

202. Self Portrait as the Spirit of the Vine. 10½ × 9½. Now in the Royal Albert Memorial Museum, Exeter.

203. Man in Armour on Horseback. 36¼ × 28. Now in the City Museum and Art Gallery, Plymouth.

204. William Roughsedge. 28½ × 24½. Sold to Christie's, April 12, 1929.

Events in the Life of Haydon

1786

January 25   Born at Plymouth

1793–1799

Attends Bidlake's school

1799

Attends boarding school in Plympton

1800

Studies accounting in Exeter

1801

Apprenticed to his father

1803

Seriously ill and temporarily blind

1804

Indentures to his father broken

May 15   Arrives in London to study at the Royal Academy

1808

January 1   His mother dies
January   First sees Elgin Marbles
July 23   Begins his diary and goes to Dover
August 9   Returns to London

1809

June 22   Goes to Devonshire with Wilkie
August 3   Returns to London
August   Visits Sir George Beaumont at Coleorton; their misunderstanding about the size of 'Macbeth' begins

Events in the Life of Haydon

1810
Begins borrowing money when his father withdraws his financial support

1812
August 14	Goes to Devonshire
September	Returns to London

1813
June 25	His father dies

1814
May 26	Goes to France with Wilkie
July 17	Returns to London
September	Goes to Kent
September 26	Elected a Freeman of Plymouth
October 8	Returns to London

1815
June 18	Battle of Waterloo
September 20	Goes to Brighton
October 30	Returns to London

1816
Introduced to his future wife

1817
July	Goes to Blenheim, Oxford, Bridgwater, and Yarmouth
September 27	Moves from 41 Great Marlborough Street to 22 Lisson Grove North
December 28	Gives his 'immortal dinner'

1818
September	Goes to Bridgwater

1820
November 18	Goes to York and Edinburgh
December 8	Goes to Glasgow, Keswick, Ambleside, Liverpool, and Chester

1821
July 19	Attends coronation of George IV
October 10	Marries Mrs Mary Cawrse Hyman
November	Goes to Edinburgh

Events in the Life of Haydon

1822

December 12	His son Frank Scott is born

1823

May 22	Imprisoned for debt
July 26	Released from prison

1824

January 5	Signs lease for 58 Connaught Terrace, Edgware Road
March 17	His daughter Mary Mordwinoff is born

1825

December 5	His son Alfred is born

1826

September 18	Goes to Brighton
September 26	Returns to London
November 4	Goes to Brighton
November 12	Visits Lord Egremont at Petworth House
November 20	Returns to London

1827

January 25	Goes to Brighton
January 29	Returns to London
June	Imprisoned for debt
July	Released from prison
September 14	His son Frederick Wordsworth is born

1828

February	His address changed from 58 Connaught Terrace, Edgware Road to 4 Burwood Place, Connaught Terrace
April 21	George IV purchases 'The Mock Election'
July 15	Goes to Oxford and Stratford-on-Avon
July 21	Returns to London
September	Goes to Plymouth and Cadhay
September 22	Returns to London

1829

March 6	His daughter Fanny is born
September 12	Goes to Plymouth
September 25	Returns to London

1830

April 5	Raffles 'The Death of Eucles'

250   Events in the Life of Haydon

May 19	Imprisoned for debt
June 26	George IV dies and is succeeded by William IV
July 20	Released from prison
August 19	His son Harry is born

1831

August 21	Goes to Ramsgate and Margate
August 28	Returns to London
November 18	His daughter Fanny dies

1832

June 4	The Reform Bill passed
June 9	Goes to Birmingham
June 21	Returns to London
July 11	Attends the Reform Banquet
August 11	Goes to Broadstairs
August 23	Returns to London

1833

May 17	His son Alfred dies
June 27	His daughter Georgiana born

1834

April 14	His son Harry dies
October 16	The Houses of Parliament destroyed by fire

1835

June 7	His daughter Georgiana dies
August 22	His son Newton is born
September 9	Delivers his first lecture

1836

May 16	His son Newton dies
June 28	Examined by the Select Committee on Arts and Principles of Design
September 12	Imprisoned for debt
November 18	Released from prison

1837

March 11	Goes to Edinburgh to lecture
April 22	Attends public dinner held in his honour
April 24	Goes to Glasgow, Liverpool, Manchester, and Leicester to lecture
May 11	Returns to London
May 20	Goes to Manchester to lecture
June 20	William IV dies and is succeeded by Victoria

Events in the Life of Haydon 251

June 24	Returns to London
July 1	Goes with his family to Broadstairs
July 29	Returns to London
October 5	Goes to Liverpool
October 11	Returns to London

1838

January	Publishes *Painting and the Fine Arts*, in collaboration with Hazlitt
January	Goes to Manchester to lecture
February 5	Goes to Leeds to lecture
February 21	Returns to London
April 30	Learns of the death of his stepson Simon Hyman in India on October 9, 1837
October 19	Goes to Liverpool, Manchester, and Leeds to lecture
December 16	Returns to London

1839

February 17	Goes to Bath to lecture
March 4	Returns to London
March 31	Goes to Newcastle, Hull and Warrington to lecture
May 6	Returns to London
July 7	Begins to write his *Autobiography*
August 7	Goes with his wife to Ostend, Brussels, Waterloo, and Antwerp
August 15	Returns to London
October 11	Goes to Walmer Castle to paint Wellington
October 15	Returns to London
December 10	Goes to Leeds to lecture

1840

January 23	Returns to London
February 23	Returns to London after lecturing in Bath
February 26	Goes to Oxford to lecture
March 14	Returns to London
June 12	Attends the Anti-Slavery Convention
November 21	Goes to Birmingham, Liverpool, Manchester, and Sheffield to lecture

1841

January 16	Returns to London
April 6	Goes to Ipswich to visit Clarkson
April 8	Returns to London
May 10	Goes with his wife to Dover

252   Events in the Life of Haydon

May 13	Returns to London
August 18	Is instructed in fresco painting
October 3	Goes to Sheffield to lecture
October 18	Returns to London
December 3	Goes to Liverpool, Birmingham, and Leeds to lecture
December 23	Returns to London

1842

April 25	Learns of the competition for fresco cartoons to be executed for the new Houses of Parliament

1843

June 27	Learns of his failure in the cartoon competition

1844

March 23	Goes to Liverpool and Manchester to lecture
April 15	Returns to London
July 15	Goes to Dover
July 20	Returns to London
July 23	Learns that he will not be employed to decorate the House of Lords
October 23	His *Lectures on Painting and Design*, Volume I, published

1845

January 14	Goes to Cambridge and Bristol
January 22	Returns to London
October 7	Goes to Plymouth to see Mrs Gwatkin
October 14	Returns to London

1846

February 18	Goes to Newcastle and Edinburgh to lecture
March 14	Returns to London
April 4	Opens his final exhibition
May 18	Closes his final exhibition, losing more than £111
May 21	Writes preface for his *Lectures on Painting and Design*, Volume II
June 22	Commits suicide

List of Illustrations and Acknowledgements

All illustrations by Benjamin Haydon except where otherwise stated

Study for *Macbeth*, by permission of the Royal Albert Memorial Museum, Exeter	10
Study from *St Peter Martyr* by Titian, Louvre, 1814, by permission of the Royal Albert Memorial Museum, Exeter	27
Study for Christ for *Christ's Entry into Jerusalem*, by permission of the Royal Albert Memorial Museum, Exeter	33
Mask of John Keats; Mask of William Wordsworth, 1815, by permission of the National Portrait Gallery, London	36
Benjamin Robert Haydon by Sir David Wilkie, 1815, by permission of the National Portrait Gallery, London	38
Benjamin Robert Haydon by John Keats; John Keats by Benjamin Robert Haydon, 1816, by permission of the National Portrait Gallery, London	45
Mary Haydon (the artist's wife), by permission of the Royal Albert Memorial Museum, Exeter	79
Study of murderer James Leary, 1813; study of a woman's head (Miss Durville), 1816; studies of a crippled boy; two studies of a baby's head; two studies of a child's head; portrait study of a lady; studies of physiognomy; studies of eyes, 1816; two sketches *From Myself*; study of a child's head, by permission of the Royal Albert Memorial Museum, Exeter	112–13
Lord Grey Musing or *A Statesman at his Fireside*, from the collection at the Laing Art Gallery, Newcastle-upon-Tyne. Reproduced by permission of Tyne and Wear Museums Service	139
Three details from *The Reform Banquet*, 1832, from the collection at the Paul Mellon Centre, London, by permission of Lord Howick	153–4

List of Illustrations and Acknowledgements

Portrait of Benjamin Robert Haydon by Georgiana M. Zornlin, 1828, reproduced by permission of the National Portrait Gallery, London   161

Napoleon, 1829; *The Duke of Wellington*, 1839; by permission of the Trustees of the Chatsworth Settlement   188–9

Wordsworth on Helvellyn, 1842; by permission of the National Portrait Gallery, London   205

I am grateful for the gracious permission of Her Majesty the Queen for the use of the reproduction of *The Mock Election* on the cover of this book. I would also like to thank the owners of the various other pictures to be found in the list of illustrations, in particular, Lord Howick and the Trustees of the Chatworth Settlement, and above all, Miss Jane Baker of the Royal Albert Museum, Exeter, for her help in locating the drawings reproduced from its collection.

Index

NB Titles of paintings are in *italic*

Aboukir, Battle of, 14
Achilles Solacing his Anger with the Lyre, 164, 165, 167
Acton, Sir Harold, vii
Adam and Eve, 207
Adelaide, Queen, 133, 156
Albert, Prince, 203, 214, 223
Alexander Taming Bucephalus, ix, 105, 106, 109–110, 116
Alexander's Combat with the Lion, 203, 212, 213, 215–16, 217–18, 222–3
Alfred and the First British Jury, 230, 231, 233
Althorp, Lord, xi, 140, 142, 143
Angerstein, John Julius, 92, 95
Anglesey, Lord, 78, 172
Anti-Slavery Convention, The, 213
Arbuthnot, Mr, 190, 191
Asquith, H.H., xii
Assassination of Dentatus, 2–4, 6, 55, 104, 110, 171, 206
Attwood, Thomas, 137, 141
Auckland, Lord, 143
Audley, Lord, 168, 171, 174
Autobiography (Haydon), vi, 48

B.R. Haydon and his friends (Paston), vi, xi, xii
Bagot, Sir Charles, 199
Bailey (sculptor), 220
Baily, Miss, 96–7
Banishment of Aristides, The, 223, 225
Baring, Sir T., 110
Barnes, Thomas, 224
Barnes, William, 88
Barrett, Elizabeth (later Browning), viii, x
Barry, Sir Charles, 11, 218–19, 200, 231
Bath, 8

Beaufort, Duke of, 231
Beaumont, Lady, 59, 125
Beaumont, Sir George, vi, 6, 9, 10–11, 37, 41, 59, 77, 101, 107, 125, 176, 203, 207, 219
    death, 110
Bedford, Duke of, 121, 155, 167, 168, 169, 171
Bedford, Lady Ann Carr, Countess of, 109
Beechey, Sir W., 93
Beerbohm, Max, vii
Belloc, Hilaire, ix
Belzoni, Giovanni, 91
Bewick (pupil), 53, 55, 57, 80, 194
Black Prince Entering London in Triumph, 206
Blessington, Lady, 154, 155, 166
Booth, Mr, 190
Broadstairs, 138–9
Brougham, Henry, 1st Baron, 88, 91, 95, 96, 150, 160, 216, 231
Brougham, Lady, 144
Bruno, Count, 191
Burke, Edmund, 35
Burney, Fanny, 226
Buxton, Sir Thomas Fowell, 1st Bart., 196
Byron, George Gordon, 6th Baron, 58, 69, 71, 96–7, 142, 156, 172
Byron, Lady, 142

Calcott, Sir Augustus, 176, 207
Campbell, Thomas, 49, 91, 95
Canalett, Bernardo Belletto, 201
Canning, George, 127
Canova, Antonio, vii, 39
Carew, 211, 220
Carlisle, Dean of, 212

Cassandra Predicting the Murder of Agamemnon, 154, 155, 156, 157, 159, 160, 163
Castlereagh, Robert Stewart, Viscount, 60, 75, 75–6, 115
Catalini, Angelica, 156
Cavendish, Lord, 146
Cawrse, Mary, *see* Haydon, Mary
Chairing the Member, 116, 124
Chambers, Sir W., 226
Chantrey, Sir Francis Legatt, 95
Charles I, King, 208
Chatterton, Thomas, 233
Cheddar Rocks and Cavern, 7–8
Chichester, Bishop of, 198–9
Christ Blessing Little Children, 176, 181
Christ Raising the Widow's Son, 165, 167
Christ's Agony in the Garden, 68
Christ's Entry into Jerusalem, x, 23, 32, 43, 44, 46, 50, 52–3, 59, 60–2, 63, 67, 87, 91, 96, 109, 125, 206
Churchill, Lord John, 212
Churchill, Lord Spencer, 150
Clarke, Dr, 34
Clarke, Sir Charles, 163
Cleveland, Duke of, 145, 146
Cobbett, William, 172
Cochrane, Lord, 5
Codrington, Sir Ed., 88
Coke, Mr, 147, 148
Colborne, Lord, 211
Collins, William, 209
Cooper, Sir Astley, 190
Corregio, Antonio Allegri da, 74, 99, 143
Coutts, T., 50–2, 73
Cromwell, Oliver, 208
Crucifixion, The, 86, 108, 174
Curtis, Sir Roger, 6–7
Curtius Leaping into the Gulf, 210, 212
Cuvier, Georges, 91

D'Orsay, Alfred, Count, 154
Darling, Dr George, 127, 169, 212
  portrait of, 108
De La Roche, Hippolyte (Paul), 215,
De La Warr, Lord, 224
Death of Eucles, The 110, 111, 116, 117, 118, 121, 159, 219
Devonshire, Duke of, 110, 165, 207, 222
Diana and Actaeon (Titian), 91–2
Dieppe, 24

Disraeli, Benjamin, 146, 221, 231
Dover, 1
Drury Lane theatre, 4
Dudley, Lord, 146–7
Duncannon, Lady, 148
Duncombe, Tom, 148
Durham, Lord, x, 194, 197, *see also* Lambton
Dying Boy, The, 136

Eastlake, Charles, 150, 200, 208, 211–12, 213–14, 219, 222
Ebrington, Lord, 141, 145, 146
Eden, Miss, 147
Edinburgh, 67
Egremont, Lord, ix, 105, 106, 108, 109, 110, 111, 116, 176
Egypt, 28
Elgin, Thomas Bruce, 7th Earl of, 5, 8, 18, 34
Elgin Marbles, 5, 8, 19, 33–4, 47, 49, 95, 134–5, 216
Ellice, Mr, 149
Ellis, Agar, 117
Elwin, Malcolm, x
Eucles, *see Death of Eucles, The*

Fairbairn (engineer), 178
Falstaff, 173, 176
Ferguson, Cutler, 164
Ferguson, Sir Ronald, 147
Fielding, Henry, 19
Fitzroy, Lord, 186
Foote, Maria (later Lady Harrington), 39
Foreman, M. Buxton, xi
Fox, Charles James, 35, 147, 148
France
  BH's views on British policy, 195–6
  BH visits 24–9
fresco painting, 201, 202, 219, 220–21
Fuzeli, Henry, 3, 11–12, 20, 22, 40, 57, 111
  death, 100–101
  lecture on, 229

Gainsborough, Sir Thomas, vii, 207, 167
Garrick, David, 226, 227
George, Eric, xi
George III, King, 140
George IV, King (formerly Prince Regent), 18, 94, 97, 114, 117, 121, 123–5, 136–7, 179

coronation 77–8, 132
death, 126
George IV and Wellington Visiting Waterloo, 221
George of Cambridge, Prince, 208
Gloucester, Duke of, 8
Goderich, Lord, 141–2
Goethe, W., 134
Goldsmith, Oliver, 226
Gordon, Sir W., 151
Gower, Lady, 137
Gower, Lord, 137
Graham, Sir James, 141, 142–3
Grant, Sir Francis, 206–7
Gravesend, visit to, 181–2
Grey, Charles, 2nd Earl, x, 133, 138, 140, 142, 144, 145, 146, 147, 149, 150, 151, 154–5, 155–6, 157, 160, 162, 164, 192, 214
death, 225
Grey, Lady, 147, 156, 157
Grey, Lord, x
Grisi, G., 156
Grosvenor, Lord, 76, 101
Guizot, F., 128
Gurwood (private secretary to the Duke of Wellington), 227
Gwatkin, Mrs (Miss Palmer), 225–6

Hallam, Henry, 224
Hamilton, William, 39, 186, 200, 214
Hamlet (Shakespeare), 27, 29
Hammer, Sir John, 203
Hammond, Sir Thomas, 136, 179
Hanmer, Sir John, 197
Harcourt, Vernon, 219
Haydon, Alfred (son), 131, 134, 140, 147–8
Haydon, Fanny (daughter), 133–4, 148
Haydon, Frank (son), 85–6, 99, 109, 111, 114, 115, 126, 127, 131, 132, 169, 184, 185, 203, 221, 222, 223, 224, 225, 227
Haydon, Frederick (son), 111, 131, 156, 215, 225, 232
Haydon, Georgy (son), 163–4
Haydon, Harry (son), 131, 154, 155, 164, 169
Haydon, Mary (daughter), 95, 131, 147, 214, 220, 233–4
Haydon, Mary (wife, née Cawrse), 47–8, 64–5, 72, 77, 78–81, 84, 86, 89, 94, 98, 99, 102, 106, 107, 108, 109, 119, 120, 121, 122, 125, 126, 127, 131, 144, 156, 157, 158, 160, 162, 164, 165, 167, 169, 181, 183, 185, 187, 192, 193, 214, 215, 220, 231
births of children, 85, 87, 95, 111, 128, 149, 165
and BH's suicide, 233–4
death of son Harry, 154, 155
illness, 194, 197, 198, 199, 202
visits BH in prison, 87, 88, 171–2
Hayter, Sir George, 175, 176, 201
Hazlitt, William, vi, viii, x, 19, 46, 49, 50, 82–3, 88, 89–90, 90, 97–8, 102, 116, 140, 203
death, 128
Headfort, Lord, 143
Higginson, 224
Hobhouse, Sir John, 142
Hogarth, William, 167
Holbein, Hans, 116
Holland, Lord, 49, 148
Homer, 16
Hook, Dr W.F., 185
Hope, Thomas, 56
Hoppner, Lascelles, 101
Hoppner, Mrs, 167
Howard, Lord, 78, 170, 171
Howick, Lady, 147
Hume, David, 59
Hume, Joseph, 144
Hunt, James Henry Leigh, *see* Leigh Hunt
Hunt, John, 82, 88
Huxley, Aldous, vii, viii
Hyman, Orlando (stepson), 81, 99, 128, 132
Hyman, Simon, 48

Ingres, J., 215

Jeffrey, Francis, Lord, 229
Johnson, Samuel, 20, 71, 103, 117, 199, 227
Judgment of Solomon, The, 17, 22–3, 32, 40, 44, 57, 88, 94, 107, 201, 206, 221, 230

Kean, Edmund, 29, 50, 68
Kearsey, 96, 99, 114, 120
Keats, John, vi, x, x–xi, 44, 48–9, 52, 55, 72, 91, 140, 203
death 70–1

Keats, Tom, 70–1
Keen (actor), 149–50
Kemble, John, 49–50, 68
Knowles, James Sheridan, 91

La Fayette, Marquis de, 195
Lake District, 67
Lamb, Charles, x, 52, 68, 91, 116, 203
Lamb, George, 149
Lambton, Mr, 95, 96, 97, 100, *see also* Durham
Landseer, Charles, 57, 80
Landseer, Edwin, 80, 207, 230
Landseer, Thomas, 57
Lannes, Jean, 25
Lansdowne, Henry Petty-Fitzmaurice, 3rd Marquis of, xv, 110, 140–1, 184
Lante, Duchess of, 194
Lanzi, Luigi, 90
Latilla, 201
Lawrence, Sir Thomas, 107, 120, 136, 141, 201, 207
Lazarus, *see Raising of Lazarus, The*
Leake, Col, 227
Leigh Hunt, James Henry, x, 18, 44–6, 47, 48, 69, 70, 75, 76, 88, 140, 151
Leopold, Prince, 94
Liverpool, Robert Banks Jenkinson, Earl of, 224
Lockyer, Captain, 119
London, Bishop of, 200
Londonderry, Lord, 104, 110, 130, 132
Long, Sir Charles, 91, 104
Lord Grey Musing, 160
Louis XIV, King of France, 127
Louis Philippe, King of France, 128
Louvre, the, 24–5, 27
Lowndes, William Thomas, 176, 183
Lushington, Dr, 196–7
Lyndhurst, John Singleton Copley, Baron, 223
Lyndhurst, Lady, 146

Macbeth (painting), 10, 11, 13–14, 31, 91, 107–8, 167, 173, 206
Macbeth (Shakespeare), 2–3, 5
Mackenzie, Colin, 222, 223
Mackenzie, Stewart, 150
Maid of Saragossa, The, 173, 175, 176, 180, 206, 210, 211, 214, 219
Majoribanks, Mr, 228

Maria Louisa, Empress, 25–6
Martin, John, 136, 170
Mary, Queen of Scots, 201
McDonnell (Catholic radical), 202
Meeting of the Unions on Newhall Hill, Birmingham, 138
Melbourne, William Lamb, 2nd Viscount, ix, x, xi, 140, 146, 149, 158, 159–60, 162, 164, 165, 166, 170, 179, 180, 192, 196, 204
Mellon, Miss (later Mrs Coutts), 50
Mercury and Argus, 127, 128
Michelangelo, 2, 3, 5, 21, 50, 130, 194
Milton, John, 16, 141
Mitford, Mary, viii, xi
Mock Election, The, ix, 114, 123–4
Moore, Sir John, 4
Moore, Thomas, 49, 95, 96, 102, 103, 172, 224
Morpeth, Lord, 146, 164, 165, 233
Mott, Lucretia, 194
Mulgrave, Lord, vi, 6, 31, 88, 141, 171, 176, 219
Murat, J., 25
Murillo, B.E., 28, 99, 175, 182

Napoleon, vi, 4, 13, 14–15, 24, 25–7, 29, 37, 60, 115, 126, 195, 224
  death of, 76–7
  portraits of, 129, 130, 131, 197, 217, 218, 220, 222, 223
Nelson, Horatio, 16, 220
  portraits of, 213, 215
Nelson Monument, 181, 182, 184, 185, 186
Nelson Sealing the Letter at Copenhagen, 213, 215
Nero Playing on the Lyre, 227, 228
Newton, Sir Isaac, 43, 52, 182
Newton (landlord), 127, 129, 145, 167, 171, 193, 207, 230, 231
Newton (miniature painter), 176
Nicholas, Grand Duke of Russia, 47
Normanby, Lord, 141, *see also* Mulgrave
North, Frederick, 8th Lord, 140
Northcote, James, vii, 39–40, 102
Northumberland, Duke of, 222
Norton, Caroline, 147, 157, 221

O'Connell, Daniel, 151, 154, 198
Ouseley, Sir Gore, 169
Oxford, visit to, 192–3

Index

Paget, Lord William, 172
Palmerston, Henry John Temple, 3rd Viscount, 140, 150, 180, 192, 195
Paris, 24–6
Parkes, Joseph, ix
'Paston, George' (Emily Morse Symonds), vi, xi–xii
Payne Knight, Richard, 31, 33–4
Peel, Sir Robert, x, 122, 124, 125, 129, 130, 131, 171, 176, 199, 201, 204, 214, 216–17, 225, 227, 231
Penrose, Alexander, xii
Pharoah Dismissing Moses, 102, 108
Philips, Mr (Member of Parliament), 35
Phipps, General, 6
Picton, Sir Thomas, 187
Pitt, William, the Younger, 35
Plunket, Lord, 147
Plymouth, 7
Pope, Willard Bissell, xi
Portsmouth, 6
Poyntz, Mr, 149
Procter, B., 91
Puck Bringing the Ass's Head for Bottom, 96, 99
Punch, or May Day, ix, 117, 119, 121, 124–5

Racine, Jean, 40
Raising of Lazarus, The, 68, 75, 84, 85, 86, 87, 91, 107, 114, 159, 175
Ramsgate, 131
Raphael, 21, 22, 72, 80, 131, 199, 219
Raphael Tapestries, 98–9
Reform Banquet, The, x, 157–8
Reform Bill (1832), 137
Rembrandt, 27, 33, 209
Reynolds, Sir Joshua, 11, 20, 73–4, 99, 102, 110, 120, 132, 167, 170, 175, 179, 207, 217, 225–6
Richardson, Samuel, 19
Richmond, Duke of, 130, 141, 145, 146, 207
Rigo (French artist), 14
Rogers, Samuel, 199, 203
Romeo and Juliet, 193
Romeo and Juliet (Shakespeare), 5
Ross, Sir W., 214
Rossi, 83, 106, 222
Rousseau, Jean-Jacques, xii
Royal Academy, 104–5, 111, 141, 170, 174, 233

Rubens, Peter Paul, 5, 19, 21, 28, 59, 105, 106, 116, 179, 187, 231
Ruskins, John, vii
Russell, Lord John, x, 141
Ruthven, Mary, 90
Ruthven, Duke of, 122

Sallust, 135
Samson and Delilah, 116, 174, 202
Sandby, Paul, 170
Saragossa, *see Maid of Saragossa, The*
Saye and Sele, Lord, 222
Scott, John, 69–70
Scott, Sir Walter, viii, x, 9, 62, 67, 68–9, 72, 88, 91, 107, 114, 203
Scott, Sir William, 62
Sebright, Sir John, 149
Seguier, William, 3–4, 15, 110, 114, 121, 123–5
Seymour, Lady, 148, 155
Shakespeare, William, 1, 16, 40, 200, 208
Shee, Martin Archer, 120–21, 170, 171, 199, 207
Shelley, Percy Bysshe, viii, 44, 47, 82, 140, 198
Sheridan, Mrs, 148
Sheridan, Richard Brinsley, 102–3, 149
Sheridan, Tom, 170
Shuttleworth, Dr (Vice Chancellor of Oxford), 192
Siddons, Sarah, 2, 62, 68, 130, 134, 233
Silenus, Intoxicated and Moral, Reproving Bacchus and Ariadne, 89, 91, 92, 93, 95, 98, 99, 108
Smith, Ed, 136
Smith, Sidney, 3, 147, 223
Snyders, Frans, 66
Soane, Sir John, 71
Solomon, *see Judgment of Solomon, The*
Soult, Nicolas Jean de Dieu, Marshall, 180
Southey, Robert, 67
Stael, Madame de, 190
Stafford, Lady, 128
Stafford, Lord, 91, 125, 128
Stanfield, Clarkson, 207
Stanhope, Mrs Leicester, 157, 163
Storace, Steven, 102
Strutt, Joseph, ix
Sturge, Joseph, 213
Suetonius
    Life of Caesar, 135

260   Index

Sussex, Duke of, 21, 71–2, 82, 147, 148, 212
Sutherland, Duchess of, 174, 194
Sutherland, Duke of, 156, 157, 158, 163, 182–3, 213

Taglioni, Maria, 156
Talfourd, Mr Serjeant, 228, 233
Talfourd, Sir Thomas Noon, 116, 132, 203
Talleyrand, Charles Maurice de, 27–8, 95, 195
Tatham, Mr (architect), 85, 89
Tavistock, Lord, 148
Taylor, Watson, 124
Teniers, David, 27, 74
Tintoretto, 28, 143
Titian, 3, 19, 28, 50, 74, 82, 90, 101, 179, 187, 203
  Diana and Actaeon, 91–2
Tom Jones (Fielding), 19
Turner, Joseph, 118, 136
Twentyman, Richard, 228

Uriel Revealing Himself to Satan, 207, 208, 219–20, 221, 223, 224

Vandyke, Sir Anthony, 33, 72, 89, 90, 107, 116, 179, 182
Vasari, G., 90
Velasquez, Diego de Silva y, 28
Veronese, Paul, 28
Verrio, Antonio, 204
Versailles, visit to, 26–7
Victoria, Queen, ix, 174, 175, 176, 184, 185, 191, 198, 203, 212, 213–14, 223, 224, 225
  coronation, 180
Vitoria, Battle of, 20–21
Voltaire, F., x, 43, 46, 52, 90

Warburton, Mr, 150–1
Waterloo, Battle of, 35–7, 211
Watteau, Jean Antoine, 43
Watts, G.F., ix, x

Webb (former pupil), 207–8
Wellington, Arthur Wellesley, Duke of, ix, xi, 23, 37, 75, 78, 116–17, 122, 128–9, 130, 133, 149, 160, 165, 195, 198
  character, 192–3
  portraits of, 162–3, 183, 184, 186, 187–92, 218, 220, 221, 222, 228
  at Waterloo, 211
West, Benjamin, 6, 170
Westmacott, Richard, 105, 186
Wheeler, Sir Robert, 147
Wilkie, David, x, 2, 3, 12, 15, 24, 28, 44, 47, 54, 59, 62, 68, 75, 76, 88, 91, 94, 95, 96, 101, 117, 136, 173, 184, 186, 201, 219
  appointed Sergeant painter, 120
  death, 199, 206
  Haydon's criticisms of, 57
  journey to Devonshire with, 6–8
  portrait of King George IV, 94, 97
  portrait of Queen Victoria, 176
  portrait of William IV, 204
William IV, King, 133, 156, 164
Willoughby D'Eresby, Lord, 170
Wilson, Richard, 167
Winckleman, J., 4
Windsor Castle, 204
Winstanley, Mr, 180
Woodburn, William, 206
Wordsworth, Frederick, xi
Wordsworth, William, vi, vii, x, xi, 35, 47, 49, 50, 54, 67, 91, 95, 98, 130, 196, 203–4, 224
  Haydon compares with Scott, 69
  portrait, 228

Xenophon and the Ten Thousand, 118, 121, 122, 127, 128, 129, 131, 132, 133, 159, 164, 169, 219

Yarmouth, Lord, 46–7
Young (actor), 49–50

Zornlin, Georgiana, vii